Praise for *Flagging the Therapy*

'Dr Barry's first book was truly unique. In *Flagging the Therapy*, he develops his highly accessible approach to mental health with a particular emphasis on how different treatments for depression, anxiety and other psychological problems work. Another superb contribution from one of Ireland's most insightful doctors.'
Dr Muiris Houston, medical correspondent, the *Irish Times*

'Writing in his inimitable style, Dr Barry describes the various pathways in the brain that underpin the myriad symptoms of depression, anxiety, post-traumatic stress disorder and so on. By reading the book, which is liberally studded with case descriptions, patients will be able to identify closely with many of these reports. Therapists too will find this book very useful as it not only describes pharmacological interventions but also details the various talking interventions and alternative therapies. Once again, Dr Barry has achieved his goal of removing the barriers that deter people from seeking professional help due to embarrassment or lack of knowledge. He is to be lauded for this.'
Prof. Patricia Casey, Department of Psychiatry, University College Dublin

'This is a truly ground-breaking, innovative and profoundly enlightening work. Dr Harry Barry leads the reader on a holistic journey through the mind and its emotional responses in a way that is both explorative and explanatory. Brilliantly written, it is essential reading for anyone who wants to develop a comprehensive knowledge of effective approaches to positive mental health in our society.'
Maria Carmody, President, National Counselling Institute of Ireland (NCII)

'In this intelligent and enlightening study, Dr Barry has managed to combine everyday stories with an easily understood discussion on the neurobiological basis of mental ill-health. His non-judgemental attitude to the various therapies which are at our disposal for recovery and his holistic approach to mental and spiritual well-being are revolutionary. *Flagging the Therapy* is not just a book for sufferers of mental illness; it is mandatory reading for all those who have the slightest interest in good health and human happiness.'
Carol Hunt, *Sunday Independent*

'Dr Barry has done medicine and mental health a great service by writing an authoritative yet accessible exposition on cutting-edge thinking relating to recovery from states of anxiety and depression. This is a remarkable achievement but, more importantly, the book is a reliable field guide for patients and practitioners alike. The Salmon of Knowledge has revisited the Boyne! I strongly recommend that you read this book.'
Dr Justin Brophy, President, The College of Psychiatry of Ireland

'*Flagging the Therapy* offers a great understanding to all on how to better one's life. It will help thousands with anxiety and depression to understand that they are not alone, and how and why they feel the way they do; most of all, it offers them hope. I could not put this book down.'
Lisa Fitzpatrick, media/stylist consultant

'In *Flagging the Therapy: Pathways Out of Depression and Anxiety*, Dr Harry Barry has once more gifted us with his encyclopaedic knowledge of depression and anxiety as it presents to the general practitioner. Extending his unique model of analysing human distress, which he provided in his previous book, *Flagging The Problem: A New Approach to Mental Health*, Dr Barry now presents a bio-psychosocial approach that covers everything from medication to meditation, herbal therapies to homeopathy, and the range of drug-therapy pathways, alternative-therapy pathways and talking-therapy pathways, to mention but a few. Most importantly, Dr Barry demonstrates his care, compassion, creativity and commitment, and the importance of the work of general practitioners, who are at the forefront of promoting health and dealing with ill-health and societal problems.'
Marie Murray, health columnist with the *Irish Times*, Director of Student Counselling Services in University College Dublin, and Director of Psychology at St Vincent's Hospital Fairview

'This book provides a highly readable account of the biology of stress, with appropriate advice for those seeking to rid themselves of the symptoms of anxiety and depression. For those troubled by mood disorder, the book is an invaluable source of information.'
Prof. Ted Dinan, Department of Psychiatry, University College Cork

'*Flagging the Therapy* is a wonderfully insightful book that helps people understand themselves, their anxiety and depression, and gives them the chance to embrace life again.'
Cathy Kelly, author and UNICEF ambassador

'Dr Barry is a general practitioner with an extensive range of experience working in communities where mental-health difficulties abound. Drawing on a wealth of first-hand clinical experience, this very readable book captures how physical and psychological therapies complement one another in helping people to overcome anxiety and depression. He charts a truly holistic path to mental health, where both the head and the heart are viewed as indispensable to achieving healing.'
Tony Bates, founding director of Headstrong: The National Centre for Youth Mental Health

'Dr Barry has written a fascinating and information-packed tour of mental-health therapies. He takes us through the science of emotional problems and describes this complex topic using easy-to-understand concepts and language. The tone brims over with his enthusiasm, wisdom, and everyday experiences as a treating clinician. Throughout, the emphasis is on the holistic approach, and he couples the research evidence with his personal views when assessing the effectiveness of the bewildering range of medication and talking-therapy choices facing anybody with anxiety or depression today. *Flagging the Therapy* will help making the right treatment choices easier.'
Prof. Patrick McKeon, Aware

FLAGGING
THE THERAPY

First published in 2009 by

Liberties Press

Guinness Enterprise Centre | Taylor's Lane | Dublin 8 | Ireland

www.LibertiesPress.com

General and sales enquiries: +353 (1) 415 1224 | peter@libertiespress.com

Editorial: +353 (1) 415 1287 | sean@libertiespress.com

Trade enquiries to CMD Distribution

55A Spruce Avenue | Stillorgan Industrial Park | Blackrock | County Dublin

Tel: +353 (1) 294 2560 | Fax: +353 (1) 294 2564

Distributed in the United States by

Dufour Editions

PO Box 7 | Chester Springs | Pennsylvania | 19425

and in Australia by

James Bennett Pty Limited | InBooks

3 Narabang Way | Belrose NSW 2085

Liberties Press is a member of Clé,

the Irish Book Publishers' Association.

Copyright © Harry Barry, 2009

The author has asserted his moral rights.

ISBN: 978–1–905483–65–5

2 4 6 8 10 9 7 5 3 1

A CIP record for this title is available from the British Library.

Typeset in Garamond by Sin É Design

Printed in Ireland by Colour Books | 105 Baldoyle Industrial Estate | Dublin 13

DR HARRY BARRY

FLAGGING
THE THERAPY

PATHWAYS OUT OF DEPRESSION AND ANXIETY

The author would like to acknowledge the particular assistance provided by leading CBT psychotherapist and ICGP CBT project director Enda Murphy in writing this book. His advice, support and technical expertise were invaluable.

Contents

Acknowledgements

There are so many people that have played a part in making this book possible. I would like to start by thanking my editor, Seán O'Keeffe (and his background staff) of Liberties Press, for seeing its potential and agreeing once again to create order out of my ramblings. I also thank Peter O'Connell of Liberties for his wise advice at crucial stages of writing the text and his help with media and marketing.

I have already mentioned my friend and colleague Enda Murphy and his invaluable assistance. I have to thank his lovely wife Mei for putting up with the pair of us through nights of soul searching and hard work.

My thanks go to Cathy Kelly, author and UNICEF ambassador, for her continuing support and for taking the time from a hectic schedule to review the book. I also welcome the support and interest of fellow Raggy Doll Club 'honorary member' and media organiser Lisa Fitzpatrick, and of well-known *Sunday Independent* journalist Carol Hunt, whose articles are so filled with humour and humanity. These women represent the best of modern Ireland and it is a privilege to be associated with them.

I also would like to thank Dr Muiris Houston for taking the time to review the text, and for his friendship and support. His reports in the excellent *Irish Times* Health Plus supplement under editor Barry O'Keeffe are widely respected by us all.

I would like once again to thank Prof. Ted Dinan, UCC, for his support and useful articles; also Prof. Patricia Casey, whose opinion I greatly value. I would like to thank reviewer Dr Justin Brophy, President, Irish College of Psychiatry – a fellow 'neuroplastic' advocate; and Prof. Pat McKeon of St Pat's and founder member of Aware, for sharing his extensive knowledge of bipolar disorder.

I am indebted to Prof. Paul Salkovskis of King's College London, an internationally renowned expert in the psychology of anxiety, for taking the time to review my humble text. As always, to my dear friend Dr Tony Bates for his support; and for taking time over dinner and a glass of red wine to share his wisdom in the area of mindfulness. His work with young people with the organisation Headstrong deserves our full support; it is a blueprint for what youth mental-health services should be all about. As always, I am indebted to psychologist Marie Murray for her constant support and encouragement. UCD are indeed fortunate to have such a warm, caring person looking after the well-being of their students.

I must also mention Caroline McGuigan of the No Panic organisation (which helps so many with anxiety disorders), for her support. My thanks go to Maria Carmody, of the National Counselling Institute of Ireland (NCII) for reviewing the book. Having spent some time sharing my knowledge with her students, I can vouch for the calibre of counsellors being produced.

To all at Aware, particularly CEO Geraldine Clare, Sandra and all the executive and regional staff, David, our most able chairman, the hard-working members of the board, and many members around the country – this book is for you all.

To my loyal and devoted staff at 5 Leland Place – Fiona, Carmel, Susan, Anne and my practice nurse, Brenda – for all their help and support throughout the period of writing this book. I am indeed fortunate to have such a wonderful team at my back. A special thank-you to Lee, and also to Darina, as always, for her help and support.

To my mother Dilly Barry (Thurles), who has battled illness with bravery and courage; and my brothers Gerald and Kevin and in-laws Patricia, Una and Nora for their support and encouragement. To my mother-in-law, Ciss Lahart (Eyrecourt), who also has shown great courage in coping with illness, for her help and support down through the years; and to all our friends and relatives who have backed this project.

There are a number of people who sadly will not be here to see this published. The first is my brother David. We miss you. The second is our great family friend, Sister Kieran Saunders, MMM, who is mentioned in the main text. We miss you so much, Kieran, and pray that you will remain our 'spiritual guide' throughout this mysterious journey through the pathways of life and beyond. We also remember my father Harry and father-in-law Nicholas, who are sadly not with us to share this moment.

I have to give special credit to my son Daniel, who has been my right-hand man throughout the writing of this book. His background in psychological research has been invaluable, and his superb diagrams adorn and enhance this book. Without his help, it would have been almost impossible to put it all together. I am indeed very proud of him. As I am of my son Joseph, whose sunny disposition, observations and support have kept me going; and my daughter Lara, who constantly fretted that her dad was overdoing it (as indeed he was) and whose love and caring nourishes us all. A special welcome to Hans, who has lit up her life!

I reserve my biggest thank you for my wife Brenda, whose love, friendship, support, encouragement, and particularly patience have made this book possible. Writing is a lonely experience not only for the author but also for loved ones who have to endure their 'absences' when writing. Your love has sustained me through it all.

This book is about connections and in particular pathways. All of us will have key moments when our lives are transformed by particular occurrences, and future pathways can be shaped by such. Mine was the moment when, more years ago than I care to remember, in the Great Hall of Earlsfort Terrace (now the National Concert Hall), I 'lost my heart to a Galway girl'. *'Mo ghrá, mo chroí'*.

Connections

A person's wealth lies not in their possessions, homes, cars or bank balances. Neither does it lie in their title or position in life, whatever that may be. A person's wealth lies in their connections; the bonds that tie us together. All of us are special and unique, and these connections are represented by the love between parents and children, husbands and wives, partners, brothers and sisters, close friends and all the other key relationships in our lives. These are similar to the connections between neurons in our brain. Both need a positive and nourishing environment in which to flourish, but shrivel in the presence of emotional famine. Stress, bereavement and separation, working, commuting and rearing our children in the cauldron of modern Ireland, and unemployment, disappointment and illness, can all have a devastating effect on these connections at various stages of our lives.

Those reading this book are a microcosm of Ireland of the past, present and future. Many are fortunate in experiencing positive, nurturing relationships with rich connections. Others, less fortunate, bear the pain and hurt of separation. Some will have suffered the searing loss of those closest to them, and accompanying this is the seeming loss of those vital connections. Others have suffered the pain of illnesses like depression, finding themselves in dark, lonely places where all connections to those they love seem absent. Some may have been damaged by interactions with the world of addiction, particularly alcohol abuse. Others have been damaged by the harsh brutality of life, with its seemingly uncaring ways.

Apart from the connections with those we love and care for in this world, there are the connections between us and those who have left to explore the next, where we pray they are in good company and at peace. Much is hidden from us, and all is shrouded in mystery. Sometimes those of us left behind struggle in the tempest of life to keep alive those connections.

Just as connections between neurons in our brains need nourishment, so do those between us and our fellow human beings. It is love that provides the greatest nourishment for these bonds. It is my wish that despite any damage, past or present, to these vital connections, all of us will always try to keep our hearts open to love: firstly, by shaking off any heavy emotional baggage we may be carrying, often for much of our lives; secondly, once free of this burden, by learning to accept and love ourselves for the special people we truly are; lastly, by sharing this love with each other. There lies the path to strong, vibrant connections, peace and true wealth.

As I reflect on the love, support and encouragement given to me personally by so many people, including loved ones, friends, colleagues and readers, I realise I am indeed a wealthy man. For you, dear friends, are my connections.

Dr Harry Barry

A Note to Readers

My first book, *Flagging the Problem: A New Approach to Mental Health*, introduced the reader to the mood system by using an innovative flag system to examine anxiety, depression, addiction and suicide. Many people requested that I follow it up by examining the various therapies used to tackle these conditions and how they work. And so, this book was born.

I have chosen to place particular emphasis on depression and anxiety, both of which are so prevalent in our society. The drivers of suicide are of course depression and alcohol. We will therefore be dealing indirectly with this problem.

There is little doubt that those who have read my first book have an advantage in terms of an overall understanding of our mood system; for those who have not, I would say that it is useful but not essential to have done so.

This book is for sufferers, their families, therapists, counsellors, GPs and practice nurses, self-help groups, help-line operators, and indeed anyone who has an interest in banishing for good the mystery and stigma underlying these illnesses.

Inevitably there will be some overlap between the two books, but I have tried to keep this to an absolute minimum. There are some exciting new concepts in this book, which only enrich those in the first. I have also tried once again to keep more complex neurobiological data for the technical section at the end of the book, for those who want to know more.

All names, occupations and other details used in this book are allegorical in nature.

Our Journey Begins

There are few places in Ireland, on a fine summer evening, more beautiful than the hills of Clogherhead. Perched above the rocks leading down to the waters of the Irish Sea, where seals cruise up and down looking for supper, the 'head' is crisscrossed with tracks and pathways.

Wandering down these pathways – the wind on your face, the scent of delicate flowers in your nostrils, sharing it with somebody you love – puts all else in life into perspective. It is an experience in both mindfulness and spirituality, and a lovely place to begin our journey into the pathways of the mind and brain.

I have learned much from my wanderings on the hill. There is the mystery of who created the paths: some are easy to traverse, while others are filled with difficulty and potential risk. Despite this variety, we instinctively follow certain pathways to the summit of the hill. Although generally travelling along sensible tracks, we still occasionally find ourselves on more potentially risky ones. Knowing the best pathway does not necessarily mean it would be the one we choose: as human beings, we are anything but rational. During summer, the tracks often become closed in by an overgrowth of ferns. On such occasions, we might end up making a new track, usually involving a significant initial effort. Once this new track has been begun, and is then used repeatedly on subsequent visits, a useful new pathway is formed.

Reflecting on the latter brings me back to a memory of a forest walk with my family. It was late in the evening and getting dark when, taking a wrong turn, we got lost. There were no signposts to guide us, and our anxiety levels rose, particularly when we discovered that we were circling around. As darkness fell, we struggled to find a route out of the wilderness into safety. I have often reflected on the fact that this is how many with depression and severe anxiety feel: 'If only I could find some pathway out of this darkness.' Thankfully, we did find our way home and ever since have become more attentive to signposts and choosing the right pathway.

For many people lost in the maze of the negative conditions mentioned at the beginning of the book, finding the correct path is not so easy. Lacking both signposts and guides, they too may find themselves travelling in circles. Many lose heart, becoming increasingly distressed and apathetic; others, more fortunate, find a route leading to peace and mental health.

The goal of this book is to explore these pathways. It is a journey into the mysteries of the mind and brain. We are like explorers shining a light into the secret caverns of both. Learning how individual pathways influence how we think, feel and behave can be a life-changing experience and a real shortcut to good mental health. Finding the right 'therapy pathway' is also the secret for those suffering from mental-health difficulties, not only to get well but to stay well. It is my hope that the journey we will take together through this book will help you to choose your path.

The Thought Pathways

Let us begin with our thoughts. Most of us never reflect on the cascading thoughts constantly flowing through our mind. There are two main thought streams:

THE MUSING PATHWAY is our background 'chatter' mode, where thoughts float into our conscious mind and a form of 'musing' occurs, with further thoughts related to the first quickly following on a 'cascade of thoughts'.

THE ATTENTION PATHWAY is more focused and directs attention to matters in hand, often switching off or dampening 'background noise' created by the first.

Consider the analogy of a driver moving slowly along the M50. Most of the time, his thought patterns follow THE MUSING PATHWAY, a stream of chattering background thoughts wandering through his mind: 'Good party last week, pity I had to leave early, would like to have met that girl who arrived as I was leaving.' The driver in front brakes hard, and he takes fast evasive action to avoid a collision. The background thoughts are silenced, THE ATTENTION PATHWAY takes over and the matter in hand is dealt with as he assesses the cause of the near-collision.

Our thoughts are best defined as 'the words, images, ideas, memories, beliefs and concepts that flow in and out of our conscious mind'.

- 'Just because a thought comes into our mind does not mean it is true' is one of the most important concepts in this book. Just because I 'think' it's going to snow doesn't mean it will become a reality. Many with anxiety and depression struggle with this distinction. In depression, the negative thought might be: 'I am worthless'; in panic attacks: 'I am going to die'. In both cases, the thoughts are obviously untrue, but they do not seem so to the sufferer.

- Thoughts rarely come individually but usually in a flow, one quickly following another; a cascade effect.

- Sometimes, particularly in the Musing Pathway, we can get seemingly random 'automatic thoughts' passing through our mind at lightning speed. As we will see when discussing 'mindfulness' (see page 66), becoming attuned to these thoughts is of great importance.

- Thoughts can be very visual – sometimes logical, sometimes emotional.

- Another major concept is that 'Thoughts influence emotions, which in turn influence behaviour'.

- They play a crucial role in the formation of our memories.

- There is a major emphasis on positive versus negative thoughts in mental health. The more profound concept of 'realistic thoughts' should perhaps be the real goal.

Thought pathways originate from both the conscious and unconscious mind. Musing Pathway thoughts frequently originate in our unconscious memory stores. Sometimes external or internal triggers initiate them; sometimes they just 'float' into our mind. Such thoughts may emerge from learned pathways originating from childhood, and significant events in our adult life – another important factor underlying anxiety and depression. Although thoughts streaming down these learned highways may be healthy, unfortunately this is not always so.

Attention Pathway thoughts exist more in the conscious mind. Sometimes this involves 'overruling' or 'quietening down' thoughts streaming up from the unconscious. It can direct attention towards external events or our internal environment.

Although both sets of pathways end up in our conscious mind (for us to be aware of them at all), the Musing Pathway remains in the background of our consciousness, the Attention Pathway preferring to take centre stage.

The Emotional Pathways

The rich tapestry of life is mediated through our emotional pathways. A world without emotion would be grey and empty. The gift of emotion sometimes comes at a price, for difficulties arising from these pathways lie at the heart of anxiety and depression. Emotions relate to 'how we feel' and last for relatively short durations, usually just minutes to hours. If lasting for longer periods, i.e. hours to days, we call them moods. Some experts join emotions and moods together, calling them 'feelings'. I have always preferred to keep the two things separate, as this reduces confusion when discussing depression in particular.

POSITIVE EMOTIONS include joy, happiness, pleasure, love, awe, trust, contentment and peacefulness.

NEGATIVE EMOTIONS include anger, fear, guilt, shame, hurt, jealousy, emotional pain, sadness and loss.

HEALTHY EMOTIONS include grief and loss, sadness, disappointment, annoyance, frustration and irritation, regret and remorse.

UNHEALTHY EMOTIONS include anxiety, depression, anger/rage, emotional pain, shame, guilt, jealousy, envy and hurt.

- Emotions are associated with physical symptoms. For example: fear with palpitations, dry mouth, difficulty taking deep breaths; depression with fatigue, poor concentration and sleep/appetite problems.

- Emotions can be negative but not unhealthy. For example: anger, guilt, sadness and loss are normal, healthy emotions when grieving over the death of a loved one.

- Emotions play a major role in our behaviour. For example: if we are sad, our response may be to cry or avoid other people; if we are angry, to become aggressive; if we are jealous, constantly checking our partner's phone.

- Decisions made in life are more influenced by emotions than logic.

- Modern therapists believe that suppressing emotions is unwise and recommend that we accept and embrace them.

- With emphasis on the role of negative emotions in illnesses like depression and anxiety, it is often forgotten how powerful positive emotions such as love, hope, joy, compassion, wonder, trust and forgiveness can be in our lives. We hear about the power of positive thinking but we need to hear more about the power of 'positive emotions'.

Many emotions ascribed to thoughts and events are sourced in unconscious emotional memory banks developed during upbringing and adult life. They may be triggered by internal or external events. An example of this might be where a girl who has been abused as a child, on noticing a particular face in a crowd, feels anxious and fearful but, because she has blocked out the conscious memory of the abuse, cannot understand the source of her fear. The reason is that her mind registers an unconscious link with her previous abuser's face.

Emotional and thought pathways are intimately interconnected, creating the beautiful web of our lives. Many assume that our emotions control our thoughts, and at first glance this seems to be true. But many seemingly completely emotional responses to situations have their base in the thoughts or beliefs lying dormant in our mind. It is the balance between these two pathways that will often determine the state of our mental health.

THE FEAR PATHWAY: Fear is a survival emotion allowing us to sense danger and act accordingly. Activation of this pathway is rapid, often beginning before our thought pathways swing into action. While it is useful, the fear pathway is also the source of unhealthy negative emotions like anxiety, panic attacks and phobias.

THE PLEASURE PATHWAY: This pathway has the task of rewarding us for essential survival duties, like eating and sex, and for exploring and learning new skills or information. It is underactive in depression in particular, but also in chronic stress and anxiety. It is overactive in addiction and in bipolar disorder.

THE SADNESS PATHWAY: Sadness is one of our most powerful human emotions, most often triggered by the loss of somebody close to us. This pathway is busy when we are reflecting on the beauty of the world, listening to beautiful music, sharing deep emotions with friends or loved ones, and so on. This pathway is the highway along which the prolonged bouts of intense inner sadness associated with depression travel.

THE ANGER PATHWAY: Anger, another powerful human emotion, originates in our evolutionary past. While it may on occasions be justified, indeed appropriate, it can also be an unhealthy and destructive emotion. This pathway is another busy highway, along which flows annoyance, frustration, rage, anger and the emotion of low tolerance for frustration, sometimes called 'disturbance anxiety' ('the world must change to suit me'). It is strongly activated by alcohol and other drugs, with the former being the main culprit. Many live their lives driving up and down this pathway, often destroying themselves and others in the process.

THE EMOTIONAL PAIN PATHWAY: We now appreciate what many with depression have known for years: the existence of an emotional pain pathway. While pain is normally considered as a physical symptom of distress sent out by the body when it is injured or ill, it can also be an emotion with its own mind pathway. This pathway is activated, often in conjunction with the sadness pathway, during times of loss, grief and depression, and in the minds of those who consider suicide.

The Behavioural Pathways
Behaviour, defined as 'what we do', is usually a response to events occurring in our internal or external environment.

THE LOGICAL BEHAVIOURAL PATHWAY is in use when we consciously assess a particular situation or thought. When we have worked out a plan of action, an appropriate behavioural response is activated. Usage of this pathway leads to a slower, more measured response to situations.

THE EMOTIONAL BEHAVIOURAL PATHWAY is a very busy one in our lives as we constantly make behavioural decisions based on emotions. Typical examples might involve aggressive behavioural responses to anger, avoidant behaviour in anxiety, withdrawal from human contact in depression, binge drinking or smoking to feed pleasure cravings, and so on.

There is a constant tug of war between these two pathways. Emotional behavioural pathways are usually activated before logical ones are. Even when the latter tries to exert 'control', it is often overruled. How often do we regret things we say or do, and on 'mature reflection' feel that we might have done things differently? In depression and anxiety, our emotional behavioural pathway is often highly activated, completely silencing our logical one.

- Behaviour can be healthy or unhealthy. Typical examples of the latter would be: in depression, not exercising, misusing alcohol or self-harming; in anxiety, avoidant or perfectionist behaviour, or misusing tranquillisers; in anger, violent behaviour.

- We can indirectly change behaviour by positively changing thoughts and emotions.

- We can change behaviour even if we are struggling to change thoughts or emotions. This can be a powerful tool in anxiety and depression. A good example of this is encouraging those with depression to exercise, which in turn helps to lift mood.

- Safety behaviour is a common mechanism used to prevent experiencing a distressing emotion, i.e. using tranquillisers or attending A&E in panic attacks.

- Avoidant behaviour is another similar response, i.e. avoiding public areas in phobias, or exercise in depression.

The Memory Pathways

All thoughts, emotions and behaviour end up stored in our memory reserves. Everything we do, say, feel and experience is both compared with previous memories and re-filed as new memories. This is what makes Alzheimer's disease such a distressing illness, as all those wonderful memories of love, relationships, friendships, and so on are wiped away as if they never were, resulting in

7

disorientation and alienation. Irrespective of the pathways involved, it is the destruction of the memory of such events that creates the problem. Memory pathways are vital for mental health.

1.   THE LOGICAL MEMORY PATHWAY allows us to store and
        consciously retrieve memories of events and thoughts.

2.   THE EMOTIONAL MEMORY PATHWAY assists us in storing
        and accessing unconscious emotional memories.

During life, we accumulate vast amounts of information within our memory banks: common sense tells us that we need to store such data in the background and only retrieve what we need at the present moment. Most memories become conscious when they are taken out of storage and are actively considered.

Generally though, emotional and behavioural pathways are in constant communication through both memory pathways. If memories are very distressing, they may influence final thoughts and actions. In depression, it is now widely accepted that each episode reinforces the negative thoughts and emotions of the previous attack. This is of particular importance in the case of previous suicidal thoughts and actions.

Memory pathways are the secret to reshaping all other pathways. If we can activate destructive memories and use logical thought pathways to challenge them, they can be re-filed as more positive ones for the future. This is essential in treating anxiety and depression.

Some negative memories drifting into our conscious mind may not be completely factually accurate. The emotional memory may be correct but the context may not. This was the basis of the 'recovered memories' (during hypnosis) phenomenon in the United States, which caused so much distress to women in particular. In such cases, the unconscious memory pathway dredged up emotions that were unpleasant but were not based on genuine abuse. Some, unfortunately, were persuaded through hypnosis that this abuse actually happened. The unconscious pathway may remember unpleasant emotions experienced in our past, but unless the conscious pathway has some accurate recollection of their context, we have to be careful in interpreting them.

The Empathy Pathway

This pathway lies at the heart of human interaction. Empathy is best defined as 'the ability to recognise, perceive and feel directly the emotions of another'. In the past ten years, we have begun to understand more about this most extraordinary of human capacities. How often, when we are with somebody close to us, do they begin to discuss something we were just reflecting on? It is as if they can read our minds. And they may, unconsciously, be doing just that. Through empathy mind pathways, they become attuned to our facial expressions and reactions, so much so that they can sense our thoughts, feelings and most likely behavioural response to given situations.

We use this pathway in normal social interactions every day. Sometimes these intuitive deductions keep us out of trouble; on other occasions, they may lead to the start of long-term friendships. When we are well, this pathway provides an entrance into other people's 'minds and souls'; when we are unwell, as in depression, it may lead us to erroneous conclusions about each other.

Later, we will examine the role of this pathway in healing. With some therapists, it is their ability to send out such signals, rather than the eloquence of their arguments, that unconsciously heals. This may also explain how some alternative therapies work, despite questionable scientific analysis of supposed mechanisms of action. Some people have the special gift of a highly defined empathy pathway. We often refer to them as being 'wise', for they possess an instinctive ability to see inside the hearts and minds of those crossing their path. Great healers, therapists, and those blessed with deep spirituality fall into this group.

The Spiritual Pathways

It seems natural to move from empathy to the spiritual pathways so naturally embedded in the deeper layers of our mind: it is part of what makes us human. Stretching back into prehistory, human beings have searched for meaning in life by trying to make 'connections' with a spiritual world they instinctively sense is there. In Ireland, this connection can be traced back to our Celtic ancestors and the great monastic traditions and Christian heritage of our island. For centuries, it was all that existed between us and the abyss. It now seems a distant memory – a long way from the busy lives we live. We don't need to

9

bother with such 'superstitions' and comfortably live without examining them. But can we do so, and if so, at what price to our mental and physical well-being?

Whether dealing with the great religious traditions of Christianity, Islam, Judaism, Hinduism or Buddhism, the mystic Celtic poetry of John O'Donohue, the ancient beliefs of Indian tribes, the bleak landscape of atheism, all of us are searching for meaning in our lives. Most religions are steeped in rituals that become built into our pathways as children. As adults, we can often become disillusioned with such rituals (although they can be reassuring in times of trouble, such as the loss of loved ones). The danger of course is that, in rejecting them, we lose sight of the pathways of spiritual longings deep within us.

In the Ireland of the twenty-first century, I sense that many young (and not so young) adults are 'lost' in this vacuum caused by the pace of modern life, the increasing dislocation of religious structures and rituals from 'real life', and the disappearance of communities looking after the vulnerable. Our own native spirituality is being gradually suffocated.

Our mind, in summary, is responsible for thoughts, emotions, behaviour, memories, social interactions and empathy, and the quest for a spiritual basis for existence.

2

The Brain Pathways

In *Flagging the Problem*, we discussed the mood system: the biological system controlling our mood, behaviour and responses to stress. To understand the neurobiology underlying mind pathways, we need to examine it further. Some will have no interest in the neurobiology of brain pathways and how they are formed, and may prefer to move on to the therapy pathways. Others may just want an overview. For them, I include a summary at the end of this section, to be read in conjunction with the relevant diagrams. For the rest, read on.

The Brain and Its General Layout

The brain is composed of two parts, or hemispheres, connected by a thick band of nerves which we will call the 'brain bridge' (*Corpus callosum*) (Figure 1). In some senses, we have 'two brains' – each side having a different approach to the world as we see it. Without the bridge between them, life could become very confusing indeed.

The left side controls the right side of the body and is the 'logical' part of our brain. It is practical, analytical, capable of planning, good at mathematics, factual, and capable of zoning in on things. It is also important in processing and comprehending language (both written and spoken) and generating positive thoughts and emotions. It seeks to provide a 'rational' explanation for our experiences (even if this explanation is incorrect), often in response to information emanating from the right side of the brain, thus keeping everything orderly.

The right side of the brain controls the left side of our body and is the 'creative' part of our brain. It enables us to store visual information and be spatially aware of where we are. It can comprehend the emotional significance of language and be imaginative or artistic. It also allows us to be to be intuitive, capable of examining the context of situations, and of processing negative thoughts and emotions. When we access memories, it provides us with a fuller, more comprehensive picture than the left brain. Crucially, attention/awareness is a function of our right brain, so it struggles to compete with the practical left brain in our everyday lives. When we are anxious and 'imagining the worst', this part of the brain is in overdrive.

The two sides of the brain are in continuous communication, particularly the two frontal lobes. This allows us to have the best of both worlds as we can fuse them together, forming a rich tapestry where creativity and practicality, the small print and the bigger canvas exist side by side.

There has been much research (and fun) into assessing differences between male and female brains: clearly we are 'hard-wired' differently. Sex hormones play an important role in this wiring process, mainly in the womb. The male brain is slightly bigger, with more neurons. Women have more connections between all parts of the brain. The bridge in women has much stronger connections from one hemisphere to the other —one study suggesting a figure of up to 30 percent. This explains why women are generally better 'multi-taskers' than men.

The speech area in men is almost completely situated in the left hemisphere; in women, it involves both. There are also more neurons in parts of the female brain associated with language processing and comprehension. So women are naturally talkative, men less so. This is important in times of emotional distress, particularly depression and suicide. Women tend to verbalise difficulties openly, often to each other, whereas men have this conversation within themselves – which is more fraught with risk. This may explain why we often struggle with the mental health of young adult males. Nature has already set the stage.

The main male emotional centres are in the right side of the brain. In females, they are more evenly distributed between both sides, explaining why women are inclined to be 'emotional' in situations where men would be more logical. As the right brain is the main source of negative emotions and thoughts and the left side of positive ones, men generally find emotional distress harder to deal with. Reduced connections between the two sides of the brain in males makes intervention by the left side more difficult.

The ancient brain (Figure 2) combines the 'limbic system' in the middle of the brain and the 'brain stem' attached to the spinal cord. The brain stem, inherited through evolution from reptiles like snakes and dinosaurs, is more primitive. In humans, this area controls the heart and lungs and is the site of mood and hormone control boxes. The limbic system was an advance on the above and evolved via mammal and human precursors. It looks after basic needs like sleep, appetite, sex, control of immune and stress systems, and monitoring of hormones.

This ancient brain, apart from dealing with the above 'vegetative' functions, helps us create and store emotional and logical memories. It is in charge of our whole emotional world, constantly scanning the environment for danger and threats, and preparing the body to face such events. It is also the source, when dysfunctional, of most psychological distress.

The modern brain (Figure 2), our 'cortex', is an extraordinary evolutionary addition separating us from evolutionary ancestors. It controls vision, hearing, speech and body movements, and is the attentive, planning, creative and logical part of the brain. It moves slowly but more thoughtfully, balancing out our more rash limbic brain. At the front of the modern brain lies the frontal mood department: the source of our ability to control impulses, emotions, mood and behaviour – the 'higher functions'.

Ancient and modern brains have different functions but are intimately connected. When the person is well, there is a harmonious relationship – a healthy balance between emotions and logic. When he or she is anxious or depressed, the ancient brain becomes more dominant, allowing destructive, negative emotions to take over.

The Frontal Mood Department

This department makes up 29 percent of the modern brain, with connections to every part, particularly the limbic system. The frontal mood department (prefrontal cortex) has four divisions (Figure 3) – the logic, emotional/behavioural-control, social-behaviour and attention boxes.

THE LOGIC BOX (DORSAL PRE-FRONTAL CORTEX) is the 'boss'. When logically analysing situations, planning strategies, focusing conscious attention on thoughts, emotions and behaviour, deciding on 'options', meditating, problem-solving or reasoning, this part of the brain is buzzing. The right logic box is associated with creativity/visual imagery, the left with the hard-nosed decision-making of everyday lives and concepts involving language and planning. Power failure in the left logic box is one of the most common findings in depression.

13

THE EMOTIONAL CONTROL BOX (VENTRAL PREFRONTAL CORTEX) monitors emotions: deciding when, if and how they should be 'modified', and the appropriate emotional behavioural responses. It is in constant communication with the stress box (see below), keeping it in check. When the person is healthy, this dialogue ensures that destructive negative emotions do not take over our lives. It also controls self-destructive impulses – important in preventing suicide.

THE SOCIAL BEHAVIOUR BOX (ORBITOFRONTAL CORTEX) is considered the most likely neural source of empathy. It assists us in deferring immediate gratification and suppressing emotions for long-term gain. It makes sense of our social world, making lightning-fast assessments of people we encounter, and deciding whether we face or withdraw from particular social situations. It may control our unique capacity to 'sense' where people we meet are, from an emotional point of view – the basis of empathy pathways. This box is also in constant communication with the stress box, dampening down emotional surges and impulses. There has been considerable interest in assessing its role in behaviour. When this box is malfunctioning, we lack motivation and behavioural control. Some regard it as the main link between our thinking (logic box), emotions (stress box) and automatic behavioural/physical responses (brain stem).

THE ATTENTION BOX (ANTERIOR CINGULATE CORTEX) links our logical and emotional worlds. Some regard it as the 'meeting point' between the information flowing up from our unconscious emotional limbic system and the conscious, logical, more rational areas of the prefrontal cortex. Known functions include information-processing, attention, focused problem-solving, error recognition, and the expression and modulation of emotion (emotional self-control).

When we are well, this box makes sense of our inner emotional world, ensuring a healthy 'analysis' of how an emotion is affecting us, and ensuring that our rational mind can assess whether such emotions are appropriate. The more activated our attention box is, the calmer and more 'sensible' emotional responses will be. The attention box may also be involved in the maturation of self-control as we progress from infancy/childhood to adulthood. There is increased functioning in individuals with greater social insight and maturity and higher levels of social awareness.

It is comprised of three parts (Figure 4):

- AREA 32 assists with awareness of our own emotional state and the mental states of others. It is in constant communication with Area 24 below – both key players in psychotherapy.

- AREA 24 forms the main bulk of the attention box and works closely with our logic box. It is involved in assessing and resolving emotional conflicts by helping us 'reason' them out.

- AREA 25 is still under scrutiny as to its exact role. We know from world experts like Prof. Helen Mayberg that it is highly activated when we are sad or depressed. It helps us become aware of and attentive to emotional pain and sadness.

The four divisions of the frontal mood department are in regular communication through a hierarchical chain of command (Figure 5).

The Limbic Mood Department

This department, in the heart of the ancient brain, has extensive connections with the frontal mood department, as well as the brain-stem mood and hormone-control boxes. There are four key divisions in this department: the stress, memory, and pleasure boxes, and the island (Figure 6).

THE STRESS BOX (AMYGDALA) controls responses to perceived threats both within the body and in the external environment. It is the main processor of the primary emotions of fear, hate, love and anger. It assists the brain in storing emotions related to unpleasant memories, which may or may not be consciously accessible. It plays a role in our assessment of facial expressions. By misreading other people's facial expressions, for example in depression, it can unleash a stream of negative emotional thoughts and behaviours. It is larger in men. The stress box is also in charge of our stress system.

THE MEMORY BOX (HIPPOCAMPUS) is where memory is manufactured, filtered and retrieved. It also puts these recalled memories into context. This box becomes extremely active when dreaming, as memories consolidate. Even when the stress box generates negative emotions like fear, it requires this box to store the contextual memory of the event in question. The memory box is larger in women. Every time we retrieve a memory from this box and use it, the memory is subtly altered. A good analogy is retrieving a computer file, opening, reading it, adding some relevant data to the file, saving it and returning it to its original storage area. The same process occurs when we access emotional memories with the help of the stress box.

THE PLEASURE BOX (NUCLEUS ACCUMBENS) is activated when participating in rewarding activities, e.g. food, alcohol, sex. It is part of the pleasure/reward circuit, which it shares with the island – see below.

THE ISLAND (INSULAR CORTEX) has leapt into prominence after years of being regarded as of little consequence. It was known to be important for our perception of pain, and the unusual emotion of disgust. But this tiny structure, deep in our limbic mood department, is now felt to be important in social emotions like pride, guilt, humiliation, lust, disgust and, in particular, empathy. It is also involved in the anticipation and feeling of pain and the ability to share in another person's pain.

The island receives information from the skin and internal organs. There is a crucial part at the front of this box in humans that reinterprets these sensations as social emotions – a bad odour is translated into the emotion of disgust, a caress into a feeling of loving warmth, and so on. The right side of our brain is more active in this transformation. The island is where we sense love and hate, resentment, embarrassment, trust and distrust, pride and humiliation, guilt, deception, and so on.

It has particularly strong connections with the social behaviour box, forming the basis of our empathy pathways. It also liaises closely with the stress box and is a major player in the world of the emotions. In depression, it is usually overactive.

Emotions are generated, controlled and finally reappraised within various sections of the frontal and limbic mood departments.

- GENERATION OF EMOTIONS: It is now believed that the stress box and island interpret physical data and symptoms arriving from every part of the body into the brain and process them, to generate emotions of fear, sadness, disgust, and so on. As a general rule, emotions generated from these two structures on the right side of the brain are negative, on the left side, positive.

- MONITORING/CONTROL OF EMOTIONS: The above information is rapidly sent to the social and emotional control boxes to see if the emotion generated is appropriate, and modulating it if necessary. These two boxes also suggest appropriate behavioural responses.

- REAPPRAISAL OF EMOTIONS: All of this information on emotions generated and control suggested is also being monitored by the logic box, the overall 'boss'. If there is a conflict of emotions, it, together with the attention box (particularly Areas 24 and 32), exerts a calming, measured effect. It may 'reappraise' the emotional situation, further modulating the emotions generated if appropriate. This is a slower process.

The more involved the attention box is in our emotional life, the calmer we will be. If the emotion generated is very powerful however (e.g. rage), this part of the brain may not get a look in. We all have experience of 'losing the rag' or 'seeing red'. In this situation, powerful emotions roaring in from our limbic brain overrule any reappraisal from our attention/logic boxes. This capacity of the logical brain to reappraise is crucial in our lives. Without it, we would constantly be in trouble when our emotional/social behavioural systems get things wrong. It also demonstrates the potential ability of our logical thoughts to help influence our emotions. The more we practise this reappraisal and store these changes in our memory box, the healthier we become emotionally.

The Mood Cables

Three mood cables connect the ancient and modern brains and their departments (Figure 7). They play a major role in our emotions, impulses, behaviour and vegetative duties, including appetite, sleep, concentration and sexual drive.

THE DOPAMINE MOOD CABLE: At the base of the brain is the dopamine control box. The dopamine cable travels from this box and continues through the limbic and frontal mood departments. It uses the neurotransmitter dopamine, which is produced and mediated by the dopamine control box. It is important in our reward pathways, as we learn more quickly when deriving pleasure from doing so. It is the main force behind the pleasure pathway in the brain. Underactivity of this cable is now thought to be the source of hyperactivity disorders in children and the lack of enjoyment of life in depression and chronic stress. Overactivity of this cable can lead to addiction and the elevated mood found in bipolar disorder.

THE SEROTONIN MOOD CABLE: Situated also at the base of the brain is the serotonin control box. The serotonin cable travels from this box and continues through the limbic and frontal mood departments. Its links with the memory and behaviour boxes are of particular importance. This cable uses the neurotransmitter serotonin to communicate, produced and mediated by the serotonin control box.

This is the primary mood cable which regulates sleep, concentration, memory, appetite, sexual drive, stress and destructive behaviour. It is also 50 percent less active in women, which may partially explain the increased incidence of anxiety and depression among women.

There is a great deal of interest in the idea that the serotonin system can be 'reset' at crucial stages in our development as children. If we grow up in a hostile environment, such as one marked by poverty, abuse and so on, our serotonin cable may be underactive when we come under stress as adults. The serotonin system is also felt to play a key role in how our brain actually develops.

There is evidence that certain genetic predispositions to malfunctions in this system make us more vulnerable to stress and future depression. Underactivity of this cable, for whatever reason, is associated with impulsivity, aggression, depression, borderline and antisocial personality disorders, and suicide.

THE NORADRENALIN MOOD CABLE: The source of this cable also lies in the brain stem, i.e. the noradrenalin control box. From here, it travels up through the limbic and frontal mood departments before dispersing throughout the brain. It has a strong connection with the stress box. The main chemical messenger used by this cable is noradrenalin, the production of which is mediated by the noradrenalin control box. It keeps us alert, vigilant and driven, and helps us sleep normally and manage stress.

The Adrenal Gland and Glucocortisol

The mood system is completed by the adrenal gland and the stress hormone glucocortisol (Figure 8), both major players in our stress system. There is a two-way conversation between the two big mood departments and the adrenal gland.

Glucocortisol is a critical hormone involved in making glucose available to all the cells in the body, neurons being no exception. It is a factor from birth to death in the formation and creation of the brain pathways. This is due to the fact that it is the chief agent involved in stress in our lives.

Our Stress System

The coordinator of the body's stress response is the stress box. When under attack from any internal or external stress, the frontal mood department activates the stress box. The stress box activates two areas in the brain: the hormone control box and the brain stem, both of which send information to the adrenal stress glands through the bloodstream and the spinal cord respectively. This, as we will see later, is also the basis of our fear pathway (Figure 10).

The brain stem, through the 'automatic nervous system' (see below), instructs the adrenal glands to release adrenalin and noradrenalin into the bloodstream. This instant response to stress can last from seconds to minutes. Heart rate increases, blood pressure rises, the mind is vigilant and alert, the mouth becomes dry, and the stomach starts to churn. This, as we will see later, is the mechanism underlying panic attacks.

The hormone control box (which is composed of two structures: the hypothalamus and the pituitary gland) controls all the major glands in the body and is in charge of our internal biological clocks and rhythms. It also receives instructions from the stress box and sends a message via the bloodstream to the adrenal stress glands, instructing them to release glucocortisol. This is a longer process and can last from minutes to hours. Both adrenalin and glucocortisol feed back to the brain. When the stress or threat has passed, they encourage the stress box to switch off.

Conditions like chronic stress, anxiety and depression lead to constant high levels of glucocortisol, which feed back to the brain and attack our mood cables, resulting in symptoms like fatigue, which are so prevalent in these conditions (for more on this subject, see *Flagging the Problem*).

Our Automatic Nervous System Pathways

This relates to a vital internal nervous-system pathway between the brain and the rest of the body. Its job is to keep us alive. It regulates all the body's internal organs and glands. It performs its functions quietly and subconsciously, even when we are asleep. It is composed of two opposing systems, which we will call the 'accelerating pathway' and the 'braking pathway'.

- THE ACCELERATING PATHWAY (SYMPATHETIC NERVOUS SYSTEM) has the function of arousing the body, particularly when it is under stress or threat. It causes the heart to beat faster and the mouth to go dry, inhibits digestion from the stomach and intestines, and makes the pupils dilate and the adrenal stress gland produce adrenalin and noradrenalin. It is our 'fight or flight' system.

- THE BRAKING PATHWAY (PARASYMPATHETIC NERVOUS SYSTEM) has the function of calming the body – particularly when it is not under stress. It does the opposite to the accelerating pathway. It causes the heart to beat more slowly, encourages digestion and causes the pupils to constrict, amongst other functions. It is best described as our 'rest and digest' pathway.

These two pathways are key players in acute stress and anxiety (panic attacks and phobias) and, to a lesser extent, in depression. Many alternative therapies, like meditation or massage, increase the braking pathway.

The Two Great Brain 'Mood Circuits'

Thanks to a large volume of modern research, which is being added to all the time, we can now identify two major mood circuits (Figure 9) linking the logical and emotional parts of our brain. They in turn are responsible for our thinking, emotional (including our physical responses to them), behavioural, empathy and spiritual pathways.

THE ATTENTION/LOGICAL CIRCUIT ('UPPER CIRCUIT') links the logic box, Areas 32 and 24, and the memory box. This circuit controls:

- conscious rational decision-making

- conscious ability to direct attention towards thoughts and events internally or externally

- future planning

- monitoring of our emotional/behavioural circuit

- 'reappraisal' of emotions and behaviour

THE EMOTIONAL/SOCIAL BEHAVIOURAL CIRCUIT ('LOWER CIRCUIT') links the social and emotional control boxes, Area 25, and the stress, memory and pleasure boxes. It has strong connections with the brain stem, including the mood-control boxes. This circuit controls:

- social interactions and behaviour
- background thoughts
- stress responses
- generation, monitoring and control of our emotions
- physical symptoms created in response to the emotions generated
- behavioural responses to the emotions generated
- creation and control of mood

Our lives run on 'automatic pilot'. The emotional/social behavioural circuit controls background thoughts, day-to-day social interactions, emotional and mood states, and subsequent behavioural responses. Many of our normal daily responses are instinctive and influenced by our current emotional state. Much of the information 'hidden' in our 'unconscious' mind, which has such an influence on all of the above, originates in this circuit. Some experts call it the 'lower circuit', as it is based in the evolutionary lower-order part of the brain. The Musing Pathway and the Emotional Behavioural Pathway, mentioned in the previous chapter, use the lower circuit in particular.

Balancing out this situation, the attention/logical circuit is the overseer and long-term planner. It also swings into play when emotional conflicts occur. It behaves like an airline pilot switching off the autopilot and taking over control when this is deemed to be appropriate. It becomes involved when a more 'logical' approach is called into play, particularly when our emotional/behavioural circuit is in need of assistance. It is often called the 'upper circuit' as it based in the evolutionary advanced upper parts of the cortex. The Attention Pathway uses mainly the upper brain circuit, as does the Logical Behaviour Pathway.

Sometimes we struggle to engage both circuits simultaneously, with activation of one dampening the other. Because there is a 'hierarchy' in the brain, with the logic circuit being more senior, we rely on it to achieve balance in our lives. This is crucial, as on some occasions we need to act emotionally, on others to be ruthlessly logical. When we are well, both systems work in harmony, but when we are anxious or depressed the emotional/behavioural circuit runs riot, with the attention/logic circuit being unable to intervene.

The goal of all mental-health therapy is to assist the two circuits in getting back into balance. Depression is sometimes described as a 'chemical illness', whereas in reality it is a 'systems failure', with these two circuits simply being out of sync. Similarly, in panic attacks the lower circuit completely swamps the upper one, overwhelming our logical mind. All psychotherapies have a behavioural component, usually involving identifying which emotional behaviours are most regularly used, and learning how to strengthen our logical behavioural pathway.

Stress is the great enemy to the smooth running of these two systems. It tends to 'hype' the emotional/behavioural circuit and switch off the logical one. The stress hormone glucocortisol, the main player in our stress system, is of particular importance in this regard.

THE EMOTIONAL PATHWAYS involve the main components of the lower brain circuit, particularly the stress box and the island, the mood-control cables and boxes, Area 25, and the emotional/social boxes. In most cases, the upper circuit can 'overrule' the lower one, but it has to work overtime to do so. The right side of the brain contributes to most of the negative emotions, like fear, sadness, and so on, whereas the left side contributes to positive ones like joy and happiness.

- THE FEAR PATHWAY (Figure 10) involves the stress box in particular, also the emotional and social control boxes, the noradrenalin / serotonin mood-control cables and boxes, the memory box, the hormone control box, the adrenal gland and glucocortisol. It powerfully activates the lower-brain circuit and, when this happens, inactivates the upper one. Fear can therefore 'paralyse us'. The physical consequences of fear involve the brain stem activating the adrenalin gland, which releases adrenalin and glucocortisol. To control this pathway, we must strengthen the upper logical circuit.

- THE PLEASURE PATHWAY (Figure 11) involves the pleasure box, island, emotional and social control boxes, and the dopamine/serotonin mood cables and boxes. Once again, the lower brain circuit is strongly activated, regularly inactivating the upper one. This is the key to addiction.

- THE SADNESS/EMOTIONAL PAIN PATHWAY (Figure 12) involves the stress box, island, the emotional control box and Area 25, and the serotonin mood cable and box. The stress box and island create feelings of sadness, the attention box, particularly Area 25, focuses our attention on the emotions: the emotional control box is where we 'sense' sadness and also tries to modulate it. To reappraise this pathway, we have to switch on the upper, logic circuit. This is what we do on a regular basis in situations like grief, or in relationship breakdowns.

■   THE ANGER PATHWAY (Figure 13) involves the stress box, the island, the social/emotional control boxes and the noradrenalin mood cable and box. It is a powerful stimulator of the lower circuit, often completely inactivating the upper one – the neural basis of 'losing the rag'. The upper, logic circuit has to work very hard to regain control.

THE EMPATHY PATHWAY involves lightning-fast interactions between the stress, attention, island and social control boxes. It uses the lower brain circuit and, through mirror neurons (see below), assists us in sensing 'where another person is emotionally'. This is the key pathway linking the doctor/therapist with the person suffering from anxiety/depression. If activated positively, it can be a powerful healing tool, if negatively; it can become their enemy – as in the case of young people who take their own lives. It is a powerful activator of the lower circuit. Reappraising this pathway requires a great deal of input from the upper circuit.

THE MEMORY PATHWAYS, as mentioned in the previous chapter, are amongst the most important in the brain:

■   THE SHORT-TERM MEMORY PATHWAY: The key structure is the logic box. We retain the memory here for ten minutes before transferring it to the memory box for evaluation, filing and storage. In depression and anxiety, this pathway is interrupted and our ability to retain this information is severely compromised. This pathway is particularly active when we are learning something new; this explains the mental fatigue we experience at such times.

■   THE LONG-TERM MEMORY PATHWAY: The central structure here is the memory box. All information from every part of the brain comes into this section, where it is filtered, categorised and transferred to different parts of the brain for storage. There is a busy set of highways between the stress, pleasure and frontal mood department boxes (particularly the logic box) and the island, linking our short-term, emotional and long-term memories. This highway is equally busy when we are asleep, as memories are consolidated.

- THE EMOTIONAL MEMORY PATHWAY: The main player here is the stress box. A constant stream of information flows to and from this box, providing an emotional component to our memories. It links with the emotional control box, the island and the memory box. In anxiety and depression, this pathway is overactive, causing chaos. When we dream, two-thirds of the emotional content is negative, with anxiety the commonest emotion.

- THE SPIRITUAL PATHWAY: This pathway involves the mood cables, the logic and attention boxes, the memory box and the stress/immune system. We will be discussing meditation later, but one of the key mechanisms underlying it, as identified by one of the leading world experts on neurobiology, Prof. Davidson, is the shifting of activity from the right brain to the left. In the technical section, we will examine this pathway in more detail.

THE MIRROR NEURON SYSTEM: One of the most important discoveries in understanding the modern human brain was made in 1992 by Italian researchers studying the brain of a particular monkey. They noticed that the monkey, when observing one of their team eating an ice-cream cone, showed evidence of brain activity as if it had been performing the same function, even though it was not. On further investigation, they identified special neurons in the human brain, which they called 'mirror neurons' – so called because they allow us to 'mirror', or reflect back, observed actions of others.

We have multiple mirror neuron systems in the human brain. They are activated, for example, on observing another person performing an action, or even when we anticipate that someone will perform such an action. This has profound implications for how we as human beings learn from each other.

Researchers are unravelling the multiple functions of this amazing system. When reading a book, for example, our mirror neurons keep imitating what we read. If the characters in the book perform different actions, mirror neurons fire as if doing the same. Similarly, on hearing certain sounds, mirror neurons in our language centres will build a picture of what they actually represent.

Mirror neurons are strongly activated in social interactions, particularly in our social behaviour box and empathy pathways. Empathy pathways' mirror neurons allow us to pick up emotions from each other, creating an internal picture of the other person's emotions and feelings, as if we are experiencing them ourselves. We do this by absorbing information from facial expressions, listening to the other person's speech, watching their actions and behaviour, and so on. All the while, our social control box and empathy mirror neurons activate as if it was us talking and acting.

We can strongly influence each other through this system. If we meet a person who is positive and upbeat, they seem to influence us, and we often find ourselves feeling better about ourselves. If someone is negative or angry and bitter, that also 'rubs off on us'. We may behave accordingly. In groups, the same system can be helpful or unhelpful. For example, if we are part of a group which is bullying a person, we may struggle not to 'join the fun'; if we are part of a group which is helping others, we may become involved in helping them too.

We are most influenced for the better by those who love and accept themselves and others without conditions. Through empathy/mirror systems, we become nourished and positive in their presence. This ability is present throughout our lives. Through this system, the baby can pick up their mother's distress in post-natal depression and respond accordingly. It is particularly important in the journey from child to adulthood. We always knew that the child learns by imitation, but now we also know how this is achieved. Some feel that this may be in part the mechanism by which we pass on emotional traits like anxiety to our children. The more their mirror neurons pick up these feelings, the more they build them into their future emotional lives; a similar situation exists with regard to depression and addiction. The classic example of this is depression, where the person begins to pick up only negative sensations and feelings from those around them; this can distress themselves and those close to them. It may be dysfunction in this crucial empathy mirror system pathways that allows this to happen.

Some people have a more highly developed mirror system than others in relation to empathy. Women seem more highly tuned in this area, due to their greater brain connectivity. The better we are at this internal 'mind reading', the more socially adept and comfortable we are, and vice versa. It is also one of the traits of the better therapists.

From a positive perspective, it is probably this system that allows us to be comfortable in the presence of a therapist we trust. It is a meeting of two mirror systems: a brain-to-brain passage of emotional information from one human being to another. We begin to build a new picture of ourselves through this mechanism. Just as dysfunction of the system can lead us into difficulties, the same mirror neurons can help us through this process back to mental health.

From a negative viewpoint, this may be the system that is most likely to be responsible for the 'emotional contagion' commonly seen in suicide. It allows a 'meeting of minds' in a negative sense, allowing the 'at risk' person to feel emotionally where the other person was before they took their own life or, in a group situation, to 'spread' similar negative emotions and associated impulsive behaviour. To those involved, it seems obvious through their mirror systems that this is the only way for both to end the pain.

THE SPINDLE CELL SYSTEM (Figure 14) relates to a small but vital collection of specialised neurons in the brain that are crucial in our social and emotional life. They exist in three main areas: the attention box, the island and the social control box. (In the case of the latter two, they are more abundant in the right brain.) They are heavily supplied by serotonin and dopamine cables and have multiple connections with many parts of our mood system. They are considerably bigger structurally than the rest of the neurons in the brain and transmit information at incredibly fast speeds. They are most unusual in having only one major dendrite (we will be discussing these later) present, as distinct from normal neurons. They begin to be formed from around four months of age onwards (although some experts wonder if they are present at birth but immature). The emergence of the spindle cells in four-month-old babies coincides with the infant's capacity to hold its head steady, smile spontaneously and track an object visually.

Spindle cells may participate in the neural circuitry responsible for functions related to focused attention and emotional expression, and are extremely susceptible to high levels of our stress hormone, glucocortisol. If we come under major stress as infants and young children, this system may be damaged. This may be the crucial link between our emotional past and subsequent illnesses like depression. Area 24 is especially rich in spindle neurons. Spindle neurons play a role in how we react emotionally to others (love, hate, like, dislike), in coordinating emotional, behaviour, social and empathy pathways, and in our ability to reappraise emotions (particularly negative ones). They assist us in 'reading' the emotional facial expressions of others, to adapt to new situations and to resolve emotional conflicts. They are part of what makes us human beings so distinct.

How Are Brain Pathways Formed?

Brain pathways are like railway tracks (Figure 15) laid side by side, which spread out like the strands of a spider's web rather than in straight lines. Each piece of track is comparable to individual neurons with tiny gaps (synapses) between them. Each neuron is connected to thousands of other neurons. Each section of the brain is in turn connected by these pathways, which form in the womb. From birth, nature and nurture combine to shape and reshape them – a process (with bursts of activity at different stages of child and adolescent development) that continues until the age of twenty-five to thirty. From then onwards, they are mature and more difficult to change but can, with appropriate interventions, be reshaped.

Our genes are the chief architects of brain pathway formation in the womb. Sex hormones exert a major influence on their development and whether our brains are hard-wired in a predominantly male or female pattern. Environmental factors like antenatal/birth difficulties can disrupt this process, causing long-term problems. From birth, empathy pathways swing into action, with anything affecting the mother in particular having an instant effect on the baby's developing brain. This is why recognising and treating post-natal depression is so important.

In the first two years, interactions between the infant/toddler and parents/family, together with the general environment encountered, will shape these pathways. Later, we will examine how genes and environment are intricately interwoven, the latter being increasingly significant in the way in which social empathy pathways develop from birth to adulthood.

While unconscious emotional memories are laid down from birth, conscious memory pathways only emerge from the age of three onwards. The memory box matures from the same age – explaining why, although strongly influenced emotionally and socially by events and interactions in those first few years of life, we have little conscious recollection of them. Between birth and twelve years, emotional/empathy/social/behaviour/thought pathways gradually develop. Then a massive explosion of sex hormones sets off a huge pruning and reorganisation of the teenage brain. It starts with the emotional thought/behaviour brain pathways between thirteen and eighteen, moving on to making the logical paths mature by twenty-five. The logic box is the last to mature.

Between birth and twenty-five, the biggest internal biological threat to the healthy growth of mood pathways is high levels of glucocortisol. This can stunt emotional/empathy circuits, predisposing us for the future to negative emotional consequences like anxiety and depression. Hostile family or environmental stresses can have powerful effects on the emergence of final adult brain pathways. Too high or too low a level of stress/glucocortisol at crucial developmental stages can damage future resilience in our teenagers and young adults.

Until recently, it was assumed that, when adult circuits were formed, they were set for life. If our pathways predisposed us to anxiety, depression, anger, hurt, and so on, we were 'doomed' to follow where they led, for better or worse. We now know that this is no longer the case: the same mechanisms that helped form these paths can, through differing therapies, reshape them. The secret to re-forming and reshaping tracks lies in the neuroplasticity of the brain. This describes the ability of individual neurons to increase or decrease the number of connections with other neurons and through this mechanism, strengthen or weaken various brain pathways.

It is worth examining this concept in more detail. The average neuron (Figure 16) is like a little factory, with a central body shape, lots of little spiky projections at one end and a single tail at the other. The central body contains both the genes and molecular machinery required to run the factory. The spikes, called 'dendrites', receive all the information being sent from other neurons. The tail is called the 'axon' and passes the relevant information on to the next cell. The real product of the factory is 'information'.

Each dendrite is receiving information from the axon of another neuron (Figure 17), and each neuron has thousands of dendrites, so information pours in. The plasticity of the brain is based on the number of dendrite connections each neuron chooses to have – if the numbers increase, pathways get stronger, if they decrease, the pathways get weaker.

The 'boss' of the 'factory' is the gene pool in the central nucleus of the cell. This sends out messengers to increase or decrease dendrite connections and is greatly influenced by outside environmental factors, so is adaptable to change. Within the brain itself, thought pathways strongly influence emotional and, in turn, behavioural paths, all of which are organised by increasing or decreasing the number of neuron dendrite connections within them. Outside the brain, other factors can have the same effect. Take, for example, the effect of interactions between a mother and her infant. Love and affection powerfully affect the empathy pathway of the child in a positive way, rejection and lack of affection in a negative manner. All this, processed through increases or decreases of dendrite connection in this pathway, shapes how the child will develop emotionally.

THE NATURE-VERSUS-NURTURE DEBATE AND THE ROLE OF EPIGENETICS: Are genes or environment more important in the development and maintenance of mood pathways? In practice, both seem to be equally important, and gene expression is hugely influenced by environment.

To understand the mechanisms involved, let's further examine our genes, which are contained within chromosomes passed on from parents/ancestors. We will confine ourselves to those genes that increase or decrease dendrite connections. Apart from developmental influences, outside social and environmental influences can change the internal chemistry of the cell close to where the relevant genes reside (Figure 18), encouraging them to switch on or off. This is nature's way of allowing us to evolve and adapt. So just having a particular gene does not mean that it will inevitably be switched on and become active. As these genes control the number of dendrite connections, it is a dynamic process as to whether neuron connections/pathways will prosper or not. The process by which gene expression can be modified in such a manner is called 'epigenetics' (which means 'beyond genes'). Epigenetics is the study of the small chemical molecules that are known to switch our genes on or off.

It's worth examining this process in detail (Figure 19). We all have twenty-three sets of chromosomes, composed of very long parallel strings of DNA. For the body to fit them into each cell, it has to wrap these strands tightly around 'histones', like thread around a spool. Genes embedded within these DNA strands influence, through busy little messengers called RNA, which proteins will be manufactured within the cell. These travel to a factory in the cell manufacturing the protein in question, BDNF (see below), which encourages dendrite production in the cell.

For genes to become 'active', the DNA strand wrapped around the DNA spool has to 'open up' to allow the messenger RNA to gain access to the vital information the gene contains. Some key chemical molecules we will call 'DNA unzippers' (e.g. acetyl groups) attach themselves to the DNA spools close to the relevant genes and encourage them to open and become active; others, called 'DNA zippers' (e.g. methyl groups), attach themselves to the DNA itself to 'close' and shut down gene activity. Nutrition, exercise, upbringing and stress throughout our lives greatly influence these chemicals.

Research into the positive effects of early childhood nurturing versus negative ones created by abuse and non-validation has shown the process to be mediated through DNA zippers as above. However, this process continues throughout our lives, removing preconceived notions that we human beings are set in stone. It offers hope to all those suffering from mental distress, and opens up a whole range of treatment options.

A fascinating model of complex illnesses like depression/type 2 diabetes is emerging. This suggests that, apart from inheriting our genes, we also inherit epigenetic proteins (DNA zippers and unzippers), which are sometimes only partially stable and which may pass down through generations or occur following conception. This potentially unstable epigenetic complex may remain silent until it is triggered by developmental and later environmental factors, in some cases not appearing for decades. Not everybody will reach a point where this potential instability triggers a bout of illness, but the risk still remains.

This also explains why identical twins may or may not both develop an illness like depression, despite having identical genes. Epigenetic proteins, of which a number may be potentially unstable, may be passed to one twin but not the other, making them more or less susceptible to expressing the genes causing the illness. For me, epigenetics is the 'missing link' between inherited genes and environment, and a crucial player in the development of our mind/brain pathways.

Genes control dendrite connections by encouraging the neuron to produce key internal cell messengers, the most important of which is called BDNF. Its job is to encourage dendrite production (Figure 20). Anything which increases or decreases BDNF levels within neurons will in turn increase or decrease their dendrite connections. This in turn controls activity in the relevant brain pathways.

If we take an overview of this process (Figure 21), we see that our genes are strongly influenced (through epigenes) by developmental, social and environmental factors. Genes in turn control BDNF levels. BDNF influences the number of dendrite connections. This leads to increased or decreased activity in brain pathways, underlying emotions, mood and behaviour. This is a dynamic, extremely adaptable system.

THE RESILIENCE GENE: We have been aware for decades that people cope differently with stress and that stress itself seems to be a constant precursor to bouts of anxiety and depression. Mystery surrounds the underlying mechanisms, but research is revealing some new explanations.

One of the genes involved in predisposing us to anxiety and depression is responsible for the manufacture and general levels of a key protein called the 'serotonin transporter' (the SERT molecule). This little protein has been under observation for the past decade as a potential culprit in anxiety/depression.

In the serotonin mood cable (Figure 22), serotonin is released by one neuron, crosses the synapse gap, activates the next neuron, and is then reabsorbed back into its cell of origin, courtesy of the SERT protein. The gene that controls the levels of this protein is passed on through generations. All of us have either short or long copies of this gene (Figure 23). It has been known for some time that those with two long copies are much more 'resilient' to stress than those with either one long and one short or, particularly, two short ones – who are much more likely to suffer from anxiety and, to a lesser extent, depression. We now know that those with small gene versions produce fewer SERT proteins. So as more serotonin builds up in synapses within the mood cable it serves, their serotonin system becomes 'over-hyped'. Although this has been known for some time, it did not explain why this triggered anxiety and depression in some people and not in others.

The key seems to lie in our stress box and, to a lesser extent, our attention, memory and social control boxes. It now seems as if those with two short versions of this gene in particular have a stress box in a constant state of hyper-vigilance, even when it is not being directly attacked by stress. Those with two long versions do not demonstrate this vulnerability. It seems as if the short version also affects our attention and memory boxes, reducing the normal ability of the cognitive brain to control this tendency. If we examine this through our two mood circuits, the lower one is in a constantly vigilant state and the upper one struggles to control it cognitively.

One fascinating experiment involving those with the shorter version, who had never been depressed to date, demonstrated evidence of structural volume reductions in the size of Area 24 and the stress box. These may already be in place before the illness itself arrives. Also, on following up over periods of time among groups with the short gene, there was a greater incidence of difficulties in coping with stress, anxiety, depression and suicidal potential, all triggered by successive or significant bouts of stress.

If we grow in an environment that, through epigenetics, encourages the stress box to be constantly overactive (i.e. if we are in a very anxious, perfectionist, deprived, abusive household): we will develop pathways which, by adulthood, predispose us to anxiety in particular. When pressures come (as they inevitably will), those with a short version will have a hypersensitive stress box that is easily sent into 'overdrive'. This in turn causes a huge outpouring of glucocortisol, which feeds back to the brain, damaging our three main mood cables and leading to many of the symptoms of anxiety and depression. Those with the long versions are less at risk of stress triggering the above. They also seemed to ruminate less about potential negative possibilities. Many feel that this is the main difference between the two groups.

This 'resilience' gene is part of a wider pool of probably fifteen genes which predispose to anxiety in particular. Although a constant background factor predisposing us to coping or not coping with stress, expression of this gene is completely dependent on how stress through epigenes activates it. We are all unique. How we cope with stress, and our resulting potential to develop anxiety or depression, is probably genetically set up at birth – to a level of around 40 to 60 percent. The rest is down to how environment, as we develop and mature, epigenetically expresses this potential. However, we can reshape these pathways by strengthening our cognitive brain's control.

How much does family environment affect the expression of our genes? We now know that a complex dynamic is involved. It was initially thought that the overall atmosphere in a particular home would be the only relevant factor. It now seems as though the position of each child, their individual personality, and the way each relates to the personalities of both parents and siblings, all go into the 'melting pot', with the final result intermingling with genes/epigenes to create individual brain pathways. This, together with genetic predispositions such as those already detailed, helps explain why some people, despite being reared in similar environments, may be more prone to anxiety, depression and addiction. Love is the most positive environmental influence. Resilience (our learned ability to cope positively with the stresses of life) comes next. Stresses such as rejection, the absence of love, and abuse are the most damaging.

Summary of Brain Pathways and How They Are Formed

1. The brain is composed of two halves, connected by a brain bridge (Figure 1).
2. The right brain is our creative side, looks at the bigger picture, puts things in context, and is in charge of our negative emotions. The left brain is our logical side, looks at the 'small print', and is in charge of our positive emotions.
3. We have an ancient and modern brain (Figure 2).
4. The Frontal Mood Department has four sections (Figure 3) – the Logic Box (in charge of planning and decision-making), the Emotional Control Box (in charge of monitoring and modifying emotions), the Social Control Box (in charge of empathy and making sense of our social world) and the Attention Box (in charge of focusing attention, particularly on our emotions, linking them with thoughts and physical reactions to our emotions).
5. The Attention Box has three key sections (Figure 4): Area 32 (which helps us make sense of our emotional state and that of others), Area 25 (which helps us become aware of sadness) and Area 24 (which helps us resolve emotional conflicts).
6. The Limbic Mood Department has four sections (Figure 5): the Stress Box (our stress system, and how we process and remember emotions, particularly negative ones), the Memory Box (manufacturing, storing and retrieving memories), the Pleasure Box (our pleasure sensations), and the Island (generating sensations like love, hate and disgust).
7. We have two main Mood Circuits linking logical and emotional parts of our brain (Figure 9): the Attention/Logical Circuit (conscious rational decision-making, ability consciously to direct attention towards thoughts and events internally or externally, future planning, monitoring of our emotional and behavioural circuit, the key player in the 'reappraisal' of emotions and behaviour) and the Emotional/Social Behavioural Circuit (social interactions and behaviour, background thoughts, stress response, the generation, monitoring and control of emotions, the physical symptoms created and the behavioural responses to the emotions generated, and the creation and control of mood).

8. We have different emotional brain pathways for fear (Figure 10), pleasure (Figure 11), sadness (Figure 12) and anger (Figure 13).

9. A key system is the mirror neuron system. This allows us to read other people's minds and hearts, and is at the heart of empathy. Another is the spindle cell system (Figure 14), which allows us to react emotionally to others.

10. The brain creates each person's unique pathway from birth to thirty. From then on, it also has the ability to change them through a process called neuroplasticity. This describes the ability of individual neurons to increase or decrease the number of connections with other neurons and strengthen or weaken the various pathways in the brain. It is the interaction of environmental factors and genes within each cell that drives this process.

11. It is the genes and DNA in each neuron that controls the formation of these connections, and is in turn influenced by the small chemical molecules, called epigenes, which have been found to switch our genes on or off.

12. Some of these epigenes, called DNA zippers (Figure 19), encourage the genes to become active; others, called DNA unzippers, close them down.

13. Genes increase the connections between neurons by increasing or decreasing levels of key protein in the neurons called BDNF (Figure 20).

14. Increasing or decreasing BDNF levels alters the connection between neurons and as a result can increase or decrease activity in the brain pathways they serve, in turn altering our thought, emotion and behavioural pathways (Figure 21).

3

The Therapy Pathways

Causes of emotional distress and life difficulties are complex and diverse, and so too are the solutions. There is no 'easy fix', and one should be suspicious of those who promise such. As somebody who has 'walked the journey' with many people suffering from depression, I have learned that each person is unique and special. Much damage has been done by not placing them at the centre of the therapy process. There is too much ill-informed debate about drugs versus psychotherapy, alternative versus conventional therapies, and psychiatry versus psychology. No wonder those in distress are unsure about whether presenting for help is worth the risk: there are too many vested interests, power struggles, 'big egos' and media 'experts'. We often forget what matters most: the person in distress.

Treatment of mental-health difficulties must be holistic: 'treating the whole person'. This doesn't mean treating psychological distress while ignoring clear physical difficulties and vice versa, nor imposing a highly selective therapy viewpoint which only partially deals with the problem. It means listening to the person in difficulty, empathising with their pain and distress, validating their emotions, and 'teasing out' individual issues unique to each person. It means presenting the various therapy options which are available and allowing them to choose the path *they* want to travel.

We must concoct different menus for each individual. This approach offers the best chance of recovery. The real journey in mental health is assisting people not just to feel better but to *get* better, not just to get well but to *stay* well. This has to be our goal. There are two key components: the person in distress must develop empathy with their doctor/therapist, and from the beginning must be *actively* involved in their own recovery.

Accepting that all therapies have a place, it seems sensible to assess each one scientifically. There has been an uneven playing field: some therapies, like drug therapy, have been 'analysed to death'. Others in the alternative health area (some of which are questionable scientifically) are accepted without a murmur. This does not, for example, mean that alternative approaches may not work for a particular individual. Rather, an honest appraisal of each therapy, supporting its inclusion in a 'holistic basket', is necessary.

The Empathy Therapy Pathway

The ability to sense where another person is at emotionally is a powerful healing tool. All possess this innate ability, but may not recognise it. When choosing somebody to help you with your distress, you must sense that this 'meeting of minds' is present. You must feel comfortable 'opening up' before entering into a therapeutic relationship. The mirror neuron systems of the person in difficulty and the therapist must be in harmony for this empathy to develop. This creates a secure environment, allowing the former to examine the causes and solutions of their problems. It is like two musical chords in harmony – a joint resonance of two brains and minds.

The brain empathy pathways involved (the stress box and the island of the person in distress) examine the facial and body 'language' emanating from the doctor or therapist. The same process is going on in reverse in the therapist. I have always believed that the empathy pathway is the cornerstone of successful therapies, particularly in anxiety and depression. Just naming a negative emotion weakens its hold on a person. Feeling free to ventilate allows us to examine and meet emotional demons. Within the brain, it opens up blocks in our logical and emotional pathways, clearing the way to analysing possible solutions.

This is a healing pathway, perhaps the most important step we will make in our journey back to health. Many never reveal their pain and distress. The mere thought of 'opening up' to someone fills them with foreboding. Attending a doctor or therapist is a step too far. If you feel like this, find one person, whether they are a family member or a friend, with whom you feel this vital empathy link, and open up to them. Remember that doctors and therapists are not the only ones who have empathy pathways.

The Lifestyle Therapy Pathways

The great strength of alternative medicine is its recognition of the importance of lifestyle factors in the creation and treatment of mental-health problems. Exercise, diet, supplements, stress management, and assessment of the place of alcohol and substances in our lives all play a major role. As a family doctor, I am increasingly convinced of the importance of lifestyle therapy pathways.

THE EXERCISE THERAPY PATHWAY: Simple exercise is one of the most powerful tools at our disposal in the battle to remain physically and mentally well. A rapidly increasing volume of evidence strongly supports this statement. Regular physical exercise has been shown to do the following:

- assist the obese in losing weight

- reduce the risk of cardiovascular disease (particularly heart attacks)

- help treat type 2 diabetes

- reduce the risk of, and aid the treatment of, osteoporosis

- slow down the emergence of Alzheimer's disease and dementia in the elderly

Regular exercise increases BDNF levels/dendrite connections in the neurons of key mood structures (logic, attention and memory boxes) and pathways. This is particularly important in depression. It increases activity in the serotonin and noradrenalin mood cables, and improves motivation by increasing activity in the dopamine mood cable. It also increases levels of endorphin 'feel-good' messengers in the brain, encourages the production of new cells in the memory box, and reduces levels of glucocorticosol. These combine to improve mood and general brain functions/memory, reduce stress and help keep us mentally well. In terms of our two mood circuits, exercise calms down the lower circuit and increases activity in the upper circuit.

There is interest in the effect of exercise therapy in reducing mental distress in people of all ages and the battle against chronic stress in our lives. What form is most beneficial, how often, and for how long, are questions that are exercising top research minds. The following is the general consensus:

- Thirty minutes of brisk exercise, preferably three to five times a week, is ideal.

- Longer periods do not confer extra benefits

- Any form of exercise is useful: walking, jogging, weightlifting, swimming

- Creative exercises like dancing and water aerobics are equally effective and have an extra social dimension

- If there are difficulties with motivation, building up to the above ideal in small daily increments is suggested

- A positive transfer of information (by doctor or therapist), that exercise will have a powerfully positive impact on the brain and mood, increases its effect

There are less obvious mental-health benefits to regular exercise, mainly in the social/empathy areas. Many with depression lose interest in meeting other people, due to fatigue and lack of enjoyment. If they interact socially during walking, jogging, dancing, swimming, going to the gym, and so on, this can only have a positive impact on them.

Exercise is the simplest and most powerful lifestyle therapeutic tool at our disposal. It is one of the first questions I ask at each visit: 'Are you exercising?' I cannot emphasise how important it is to the development and maintenance of good mental health.

THE NUTRITIONAL/SUPPLEMENT THERAPY PATHWAY: A vast amount of information has been generated on this subject, as a visit to any bookshop will verify, with many claims being made in relation to the treatment of mental-health problems. There is a clear place for proper nutrition as part of an overall treatment package, but too many claims are not scientifically validated. I counsel a healthy dose of common sense when reading much of the literature on diet out there. Having reviewed the research, I recommend the following:

- Have a sensible mix of fresh fish (particularly oily types like salmon, mackerel and tuna), eggs (especially free range), meat, vegetables, cereals, nuts, flax seeds and oils, grains and fruit.

- Prepare your own food, and avoid the world of fast food and highly processed packaged food.

- Eat – even if, when depressed, we can't see any point or pleasure in the task – as our brain cannot run without fuel.

- Avoid high-stimulant drinks like coffee and caffeinated soft drinks, which many people with depression and anxiety use in abundance.

- Avoid high-sugar 'hits', as bouncing our blood-sugar levels around is not helpful.

- Avoid the 'extreme diets' sometimes recommended by alternative 'experts', which often exclude key nutrients and supplements.

- `Avoid using food as a 'crutch' when you are feeling down or anxious.

- In the area of supplements, the main ones accepted as playing a role in the treatment of mental health are Omega 3 fish oils, and key B vitamins: folic acid, B6 and B12. All of these have been extensively investigated and there is substantial evidence to support their use as part of a holistic package, particularly in depression. I recommend a B complex once daily and Omega 3 oils (particularly EPA), in a 500–1000 mg dose.

- I am not completely convinced about the claims made in relation to minerals such as zinc, magnesium, selenium and so on.

- There is some evidence for the use of vitamin E in the elderly.

- There is some evidence that the supplement SAMe (S adenosyl l methionine) is of benefit in depression. This is a naturally occurring supplement found in high concentrations in the brain, where it plays an important role in the manufacture of the cell membranes of neurons. It has been given as a supplement on its own and is thought by some to be as effective as an antidepressant. There are side effects: agitation, insomnia and the risk of triggering manic episodes in bipolar disorder. It is also often given by injection, as there are concerns about oral preparations; it is expensive and can vary greatly in quality. It is not something I myself generally recommend.

- Pay special attention to the diet of young people, which is often high in quantity and low in quality at critical stages of brain development and the elderly where both quantity and quality may be lacking.

Why is nutrition so important to mental health? The smooth running of brain pathways depends on a regular supply of vitamins to help make vital neurotransmitters, like serotonin, and essential omega oils to manufacture dendrite connections and myelin. A healthy supply of proteins, healthy fats, and slow-release carbohydrates is also of benefit. It also seems that the food we eat has the capacity, like exercise, to increase or decrease BDNF levels in the neurons of the brain.

Many people suffering from mental-health problems eat poorly, worsening the brain-system dysfunctions underlying their conditions. It makes sense to reverse this pattern. But illnesses like depression are not treatable by diet alone; this is an unrealistic claim.

THE ROLE OF ALCOHOL AND OTHER SUBSTANCES IN OUR LIFESTYLE THERAPY PATHWAYS: It may seem unusual to include alcohol and illegal substances like hash, cocaine and ecstasy as part of a lifestyle therapy pathway, but dealing with the misuse and abuse of these substances in anxiety and depression is of great importance. Adult brain pathways are not fully formed till age twenty-five to thirty. Developing pathways are extremely sensitive to alcohol and illegal drugs. Misuse of alcohol is almost endemic in the twelve-to-thirty age groups, so these pathways are open to being disrupted – increasing the risks of illnesses like depression. Misuse of hash and cocaine, though less common, is prevalent and equally disruptive, increasing the risks of psychosis and depression. There is particular concern about their use among those under the age of fifteen.

When depressed as teenagers or adults, we may use alcohol or drugs to treat associated emotional and physical symptoms. This sets up a vicious circle: depression causes low mood, we use alcohol (a depressant in itself) to lift it, causing a further drop in mood, and so on. Or we may start with social anxiety and use hash to 'calm' our fears, messing up our mood cables as a result. We then become depressed, agitated and anxious, and the cycle continues. Without breaking this pattern, it can be difficult to improve mental health.

The use of illegal drugs has to cease permanently; otherwise, all therapies will struggle to have an effect. I have seen some transform their lives by facing their 'demons' in this area. It is particularly important for young people to take this step, as their brains are highly vulnerable to long-term damage as a result of substance misuse.

With alcohol, it depends on whether one is simply misusing it or addicted to it. I find that we are usually dealing with the former. In depression, I recommend abstaining for a three- to six-month period, or at least until mood is fully recovered. Many relate to alcohol's mood-lowering effects and abstain. If the person is addicted, consumption must cease permanently. In anxiety, I counsel caution in using it to 'numb' uncomfortable symptoms generated. Many Irish women in particular are using wine to deal with stress, anxiety and depression, and some are unfortunately becoming 'hooked'.

STRESS THERAPY PATHWAYS: Stress plays a major role in triggering illnesses like depression and anxiety. It is a significant issue in modern life: the pressures of housing, commuting, broken relationships, the recent economic downturn, with resulting unemployment, and the rapidly increasing pace of life are all taking their toll.

Any holistic package must include suggestions on how to deal with stress, and building in safeguards for the future. Reviewing stress factors in our lives often involves being honest with ourselves and those around us. We must not be afraid to make major changes in employment, relationships and financial matters.

Dealing with stress involves examining other lifestyle areas that have already been dealt with – exercise, nutrition and supplements – and being sensible in relation to the alcohol intake. Other useful suggestions can be yoga, meditation, reflexology, and spending time in parks and forests, on beaches, and by rivers and lakes. Safeguarding for the future usually involves recognising how frail we all are, trying to become realistic in our assessment of what we 'should' or 'ought' to be doing on a day-to-day basis, and continuing with the above lifestyle changes.

The Talk Therapy Pathways

Talk therapy, often called 'psychotherapy', is the treatment of psychological distress through talking with a specially trained therapist and learning new ways to cope, rather than using medication alone to alleviate distress. It is done with the immediate goal of aiding the person in increasing their self-knowledge and their awareness of their relationships with others. Psychotherapy assists people in becoming more aware of their unconscious thoughts, feelings and motives. Its long-term goal is to make it possible to exchange destructive patterns of behaviour for healthier, more successful ones.

There are many different forms of talk therapy, including counselling, psychoanalytic psychotherapy, cognitive behaviour therapy, behaviour therapy, inter-personal therapy, supportive psychotherapy, brief dynamic psychotherapy and family therapy.

COUNSELLING THERAPY: Simply talking about one's anxiety or depression helps ease emotional pain. Some people with these illnesses have experienced abuse, bereavement, addiction and stormy relationships in their past, or have difficulties coping with stress, either domestic or work-related. The aim of counselling is to help identify problem areas and examine possible solutions. It can be non-directive – where the person is encouraged to articulate their problems and work through them with minimal involvement from the counsellor. It may also be confrontational on a personal or group level. This is effective in addiction.

SUPPORTIVE PSYCHOTHERAPY is used in short-term stress situations and in the early stages of treating illnesses like depression. It is widely used by family doctors and psychiatrists. Supportive psychotherapy involves brief regular meetings with the person in difficulty, where they are encouraged to deal with short-term life or psychological crises. A classic example might be where somebody is started on an antidepressant but needs support and encouragement until it kicks into action. It is an ideal form of 'talk therapy' in many of the acute crises so often presenting to the family doctor/therapist – such as those associated with relationship breakups, work pressures, bullying and so on.

INTERPERSONAL THERAPY focuses on the importance of interpersonal relationships in our lives, particularly in depression. It helps the person understand and deal with conflicts and disputes within the relationship sphere. It can be a powerful way of improving mental health difficulties. It may involve problem-solving, dealing with areas like grief and introducing mechanisms of resolving future interpersonal issues.

FAMILY AND COUPLE THERAPY can be a powerful tool in dealing with mental-health problems – particularly in children and teenagers. This therapy focuses on the individual within the social context of the family. It sometimes regards the family as the client. Although this therapeutic process originally involved the inclusion of the entire family, today family therapy can be held in one-to-one sessions, as well as in family, group or couple sessions led by a trained psychotherapist. It can be helpful in depression, eating disorders, and family/relationship difficulties. It involves accepting that the person (e.g. a child or young adult) presenting with the initial problem is only the focal point of the whole unit. By working on relationships within the latter, this therapy can help resolve problems for the individuals.

PSYCHOANALYTICAL PSYCHOTHERAPY is the oldest form of psychotherapy; its origins lie in the pioneering work of Sigmund Freud and his rival, Carl Jung. Psychoanalytic psychotherapy focuses on underlying, often unconscious, sources of an individual's emotional or mental problems. It is based on the concept that much of our behaviour, thoughts and attitudes is regulated by the unconscious part of our mind and is thus not within ordinary conscious control.

THE PSYCHOANALYTIC THERAPIST assists the client in revealing their unconscious needs, motivations, wishes and memories in order to gain conscious control of their life. In doing so, the therapist enables them to become more aware of how those motivations influence their present actions and feelings and can perhaps find ways to resolve past issues. As well as inviting the client to talk, the therapist may also introduce other psychoanalytic techniques, including free association and dream interpretation.

The major function of the psychoanalytic therapist is to listen attentively to the client and to obtain verbal and nonverbal clues to their problems. The analyst must first understand these disguised communications and then transform them into information that is useful to the patient. The therapist asks questions, confronts distortions and enhances the listening experience to help the client share their thoughts and feelings comfortably. There is no specific time limit on psychoanalytic therapy.

Both patient and therapist form a therapeutic relationship to help the former explore their current mental-health distress difficulties and deal with them in relation to their family/childhood background. This will usually involve a commitment in time and money, sometimes lasting years. The therapist will usually have gone through years of training and self-analysis themselves. Although useful in complex areas like abuse, it is usually unnecessary in most cases of mental distress, where simpler forms of talk therapy are usually more appropriate.

BRIEF COUNSELLING THERAPY can make use of any of the above psychotherapeutic approaches but also involves specific techniques that have been shown to provide rapid relief for large numbers of people. Among these approaches are Narrative Therapy, Reverse Psychology and Solution-focused Therapy. These practices assist clients to identify occasions when stated problems are less dominant in their lives. Typically, brief counselling takes from one to five sessions. Employee Assistance Programs geared to provide brief assessments/interventions often fulfil a client's needs in just a few sessions. It is not unusual for community mental-health centres to offer Brief Counselling to new clients to encourage greater self-reliance and discourage dependence on a therapist.

BEHAVIOURAL THERAPY: Some consider this as a form of CBT but it actually preceded it. It works on behavioural responses rather than a person's thoughts and emotions. The theory is that if we alter our behaviour through a series of practical measures, it will result in an improvement in illnesses like anxiety (e.g. phobias) and depression.

COGNITIVE BEHAVIOUR THERAPY: In my opinion, no other form of therapy has such potential to 'revolutionise' mental health in Ireland. As part of a holistic package to treat depression, all forms of anxiety, eating disorders and addiction, CBT is unparalleled. In my first book, I dealt with the history of CBT and how the three 'megastars' in this area – Beck, Ellis and Linehan – developed their particular approaches. Although Beck is more in the public eye, Ellis was actually awarded the title of the most influential psychotherapist of the twentieth century – a field that included figures like Beck and Freud.

CBT STANDS FOR:
- COGNITIVE: mental processes such as thoughts, ideas, perceptions, memories, beliefs, and the ability to focus attention, reason and problem-solve.

- BEHAVIOUR: refers to 'what we do' and, just as importantly, 'what we avoid'.

- THERAPY: a particular approach used to deal with a problem or illness.

CBT IS BASED ON TWO SIMPLE, PROFOUND CONCEPTS:
1. Our thoughts influence our emotions, which in turn influence behaviour. So what we think affects what we feel and do.

2. It is not what happens to us in life that is important but how we choose to interpret it.

These form the basis of all therapy disciplines within CBT. The first is self-explanatory, but it is worth exploring the second. I often use the following example:

MARY invites six people to a dinner party but at the last moment cancels the event due to a family crisis. She sends a text to all six: 'Sorry for short notice. Have to cancel party tonight. I will talk to you tomorrow.' All six receive the same message. Not everybody interprets it the same way.

SARA takes it as an insult: 'How could she do that to me, not even a proper phone call, and no attempt to explain why she had to cancel. 'Typical'. She'd better not expect me at her next party.' Her inference is that Mary deliberately shunned her; her emotion is initially hurt, then anger, her behaviour to consider punishing Mary by avoiding further contact.

JANE starts to worry: 'I hope Mary is all right, it's so out of character, she seemed exhausted the last time I talked to her. Didn't her mother die of cancer two years ago? Maybe she's in trouble.' She rings a mutual friend to see if her worst fears will be realised. Her inference is that something terrible must have happened, her emotion is anxiety, her behaviour to seek reassurance that all is well.

CATHERINE, who six months before had got drunk at a previous dinner party, and, it was discovered later, had made a pass at the partner of one of her friends, becomes upset: 'I know Mary cancelled the party because of me, she must have decided that having me there would upset everybody.' Her inference was that nobody wanted to be at the same party as her because of her previous actions. Her emotion is shame, her behaviour to spend the rest of the evening replaying over and over in her head the events of the previous party, desperate to 'change parts of the tape' she wasn't happy with.

ANNE, already thinking of opting out, is also upset: 'I fully understand why Mary cancelled the party; she really didn't want me there. Nobody in their right mind would. I'd just be in the way. I wouldn't enjoy it anyway and would only spoil their night. Why would they want to talk to me, amn't I boring and useless? I feel so tired; I think I'll go to bed.' Her inference is to assume that Mary cancelled because she felt that Anne would spoil the party, as she is uninteresting and boring. Her emotion is depression, her behaviour to plan to avoid future parties and retreat to the safety of bed.

LOUISE also gets upset: 'After all I have done for Mary, the times I have had her and John over for meals. The one time she asks me over and she finds some reason to cancel the party. That's the last time they'll eat at my table.' Her inference is that Mary did not appreciate all the efforts she had put into being hospitable. Her emotion is anger, her behaviour to punish Mary by ceasing to invite her to further events.

HELEN is more pragmatic about the text she receives: 'Poor Mary, imagine having to cancel after all that preparation. She must be embarrassed to have to do so at such short notice. I'm sure it must have been something important for her to cancel. I must ring her tomorrow to check that all is well.' Her inference is that Mary would be upset that after all her hard work she had to cancel, and that there must have been a significant reason for the cancellation. Her emotion is concern, her behaviour to plan to contact her to offer support and empathise with her.

It seems that reconvening a new party is going to be an interesting exercise for Mary! In reality, it's unlikely that so many extremely 'negative' interpretations would occur over a simple party cancellation. But this example explains how our interpretation or analysis of events in our lives powerfully affects our emotional and behavioural responses to them. As we will see later, all of us bring learned thought patterns or beliefs along with us on life's journey, and through their lens make many of the above interpretations, particularly when we are under stress.

CBT stems from the interrelation between cognitions (how we interpret our environment) and behaviour. This interrelationship has been known about for centuries. The Greek stoic philosopher Epictetus (50–138 AD) stated: 'Men are not disturbed by events; they are disturbed by the interpretation of which they make of them.'

THE BECK APPROACH: His major contribution was to highlight how cognitive interpretation of events in our lives could lead us to be emotionally distressed – and to often unhelpful and self-perpetuating behavioural patterns. He felt that we all had *Core Beliefs* or ways of looking at the world, which lay underneath the above interpretations. We also had definite *Rules for Living* which arose out of the latter. In general, once he had identified the main emotion and behaviour, Beck would always try first to challenge our interpretations of events, getting us to dispute them using logic. Only if he was unable to reach the person would he move on to examine and dispute their core beliefs and rules for living.

Beck believed that depressed individuals, for example, have difficulties in the way they process and interpret external events. As a result, they may interpret innocent occurrences as reflecting badly on their self-esteem. They may view both themselves and their future as hopeless and as a result experience symptoms of depression. They may withdraw from people and situations that reinforce these assumptions. He also believed that what those experiencing depression perceive as true may not always be the reality, and that the behaviours and internal beliefs they have created to cope with this faulty thinking make the situation worse, thereby sustaining their depression.

Following on from Beck's original approach, Dr Chris Williams (who based his model on previous work by American CBT therapist Christine Padesky) developed a practical application of his work, the so-called *Five Areas Model* (Figure 24). This is a pragmatic and accessible model of assessment that communicates CBT principles and clinical interventions using simple language. One of the main problems that depressed and anxious people have is to be able to describe their problem in a way whereby they can see where they are going wrong. So much is going on in their mind that they find it nearly impossible to put these thoughts into a framework from where they can find solutions. The Five Areas Model shows them how to do this. It improves understanding of problems by breaking them down into five areas: thoughts, feelings, physical reactions, behaviour and environmental factors.

The main advantage of the model lies in its ability to help laypeople define aspects of their problem in CBT terms. This then facilitates them in more accurately examining what aspects are unhelpful and, using CBT techniques, hopefully change them, thereby solving the problem.

Unfortunately, its main disadvantage is that by basing the model primarily on a Beck approach to CBT, it doesn't provide a simple pathway whereby underlying schemas can be identified and addressed. The result of this is that problems have a habit of returning, albeit in a different guise.

For example, a woman develops a health anxiety that because her friend recently died of breast cancer, she might have it too. Using the Five Areas Model, she disputes this by rationally arguing that because her last mammogram was normal, she doesn't have cancer. Three months later, she develops another anxiety, only this time it's that her sore throat might be cancer.

And this continues on and on. Symptoms are addressed but the underlying problem is not resolved.

THE ELLIS APPROACH: Ellis's major contribution was to highlight that we all have underlying rational and irrational beliefs (known as rBs and iBs), and that it is through their lens that we assess events and their interpretation. *Rational beliefs* (which lead to healthy negative emotions like anger, concern and sadness) are self-limiting, problem-solving and empowering. They are a result of the person adopting a non-demanding philosophy and help us adapt to life's events. *Irrational beliefs* (which lead to unhealthy negative emotions like rage, anxiety and depression) are self-defeating, problem-generating and disabling. They inhibit our ability to cope.

He accepted Beck's concept of a triggering event and interpretation but was more interested in challenging the underlying belief system that he felt was driving the emotional response to the trigger. If our belief was a rational one, the emotion we felt was usually positive, and vice versa. His version of 'rules for living' was called the 'Big MACS'. He called his approach Rational Emotive Behaviour Therapy, or REBT.

THE LINEHAN APPROACH: Her major contribution was to highlight that, in cases of severe mental distress, we firstly have to help people to learn mechanisms to deal with their mental distress, before they can cope with the above approaches.

Linehan herself came from an Ellis background but developed her own approach, which she called Dialectical Behaviour Therapy, or DBT. This therapy has as its primary focus acceptance and change. It encourages people to find the balance between these two factors, and has four main components:

- Mindfulness Training (becoming aware of emotions)
- Emotional Regulation (reducing or eliminating negative emotions)
- Distress Tolerance (learning to tolerate painful emotions)
- Interpersonal Effectiveness (interpersonal-skills training)

Understanding CBT is as simple as 'ABC' (Figure 25):

A stands for ACTIVATING EVENT: the event that sets up a particular chain of thoughts, emotions and behaviour. It can refer to an external event, either present or future, or an internal one such as a memory, a mental image, a particular thought, a dream, and so on. A useful way of examining the activating event is to divide it into:

- The 'trigger', which relates to the actual event that starts the ball rolling

- The 'inference' we assign to the trigger, or how we view the event which has occurred. In many cases, this involves assigning a 'danger' to the triggering event. Why is it bothering us?

B stands for BELIEF, an all-encompassing term which includes our thoughts, the demands we make on ourselves, the world and others, our attitudes, and the meaning we attach to internal and external events in our lives. It is through these that we 'assess' the trigger and interpretation described in A. Beck called these 'core beliefs' (with accompanying 'rules for living'); Ellis called them 'rational and irrational beliefs'. I regard them as the lens through which we focus on our internal and external worlds. In practice, they often present as demands we make of ourselves – some reasonable, others not.

C stands for CONSEQUENCES: an all-inclusive term, which includes emotional and physical reactions experienced secondary to the emotions activated, and behavioural responses which result from A and B above.

Ellis created the 'ABC' model; it is an incredibly powerful and effective way of analysing our emotional and behavioural responses to situations. Let's examine an example of this in the following action:

John, who is due to sit his driving test in two days, becomes very anxious. If we were to do an 'ABC' on his problem, it would look like this:

A – ACTIVATING EVENT:

TRIGGER: His upcoming test
INFERENCE/DANGER: He might not pass his test

B – BELIEF/DEMAND: His internal thought/demand is 'I must pass my test; if I don't then I will be a failure.'

C – CONSEQUENCES:

EMOTION: Anxiety
PHYSICAL REACTIONS: His stomach in knots, a tension headache, sighing constantly to relieve tension

BEHAVIOUR: Stops eating (as a result of his stomach being upset, due to anxiety), wonders if he should find an excuse to cancel the test.

All three approaches taken by Beck, Ellis and Linehan consider the A, B and C but have a preference for concentrating on one over the other:

- Beck would primarily challenge the A, particularly the inference assigned by the person to the trigger. In this case, he would challenge John's thinking that he might not pass the test. If that was unsuccessful, he would only then move on to challenging the underlying 'core beliefs', if this was felt appropriate.

- Ellis would bypass this interpretation of the trigger and start challenging the B, John's unrealistic/unhealthy demand that he 'must' pass his test, and his susceptibility to being rated by himself and others. So John, in the example above, interprets his driving test (the trigger) as presenting a possibility that he 'might not pass', then evaluates the latter through his belief system that he 'must pass': an absolute demand. Additionally, that if he doesn't, others will think that he is a failure: a form of rating.

- Linehan would primarily focus on the C: self-soothing the anxiety symptoms (teaching him the skills to deal with his emotions, problem-solving, and behaviour). This would involve giving him a survival strategy to deal with the situation.

In practice, all three approaches will usually focus on unhealthy behaviour, which prevents the person getting to the 'root of the problem'. For example, if John cancelled the test, he would simply be avoiding the core issue, and the next time he applied he would find it harder to face.

There are occasions where one approach has been shown to be more effective than another, i.e. (as suggested by Enda Murphy to GPs) using Beck in panic attacks, Ellis in depression/general anxiety and Linehan in addiction. In the past, therapists using Beck's methods rather than Ellis's were 'elitist', often dismissing one another. Nowadays, differences between the two approaches have become more blurred and most therapists are happy to move from one to another, depending on the issue being dealt with.

If the person is having panic attacks secondary to depression, the CBT therapist might use Beck to deal with the former and Ellis the latter. So saying, most therapists like Enda Murphy (Ellis-trained) will have a natural preference for one method, with which they will be most comfortable.

In the past, CBT therapists did not usually begin by investigating the issues in the person's past that have led to their present distress. They preferred instead to help people to recognise current unhealthy thinking patterns and behaviour to deal with the problem in the present, if possible. Consider a motorist who has a flat tyre. Would it be better to teach him or her how to change the tyre, or to retrace their steps with them to see where they punctured it? The former is in general the more useful skill. It would only be necessary to retrace the route if one was developing repeated punctures. Ellis, in particular, felt that this was the best way to help people to move forwards; Beck less so, even though he felt that much of our negative thinking came from unconscious memories whose root was in their past. Much of his therapy dealt with interpretation of present triggers rather than internal belief systems.

Nowadays there has been a 'softening' of this approach, with most CBT therapists being more prepared to 'revisit' the past if it is felt that it will assist the person to move on. But the emphasis will always be on learning new methods to deal with the emotional distress that has led them to seek help, looking more to the future than to the past.

The biggest difficulty in both Ireland and Britain with this form of therapy is a shortage of trained CBT therapists; this situation frustrates family doctors and psychiatrists alike. Since it takes seven years to train a fully fledged CBT therapist – with each therapist only able to see a certain number of patients a year – it has seemed a hopeless situation for those in need.

Thankfully, a 'revolution' in thinking is occurring. It is increasingly accepted that many patients could be helped by simple CBT concepts, called Cognitive Behaviour Methods (CBM), delivered over a period of time by trained health professionals (e.g. family doctors) and possibly with the help of computerised programs. This, it is felt, could improve access to psychological therapies for a greater number of people.

Research evidence (see the technical section) is growing to support the view that a simple CBM model can, in many situations, be as effective as the full CBT package, and most people can be helped to overcome their distress through low-intensity interventions delivered by health professionals like primary-care providers.

In Ireland, Irish College of General Practitioners courses have been run since 2003 by senior CBT therapist/tutor Enda Murphy, bringing CBM to Irish GPs. He has already trained 311 family doctors in basic methods, and 25 (in Leinster, Munster and Connacht) in more advanced forms. I have been fortunate to be one of the latter, and found the courses to be invaluable. It is felt that a significant number of the cases of anxiety/depression a family doctor sees could be helped in this way, with the rest requiring a fully trained CBT therapist.

In the area of emotions, in CBT the term 'depression' has a different meaning to the illness of major depression. In this context, the term refers to 'feeling low' or 'down'. This may be for relatively short periods, only merging into major depression if it is present constantly for more than two weeks. It is also important that emotions are often called 'feelings' in CBT, and that it is quite normal for a negative emotion to be normal – such as feeling low or depressed for periods when grieving, or in many cases for no obvious reason.

CBT is extremely useful in the treatment of anxiety (whether acute, like panic attacks/phobias or chronic, like generalised anxiety disorder/ obsessive compulsive disorder), major depression, bipolar disorder, eating disorders, addiction, anger/jealousy/guilt difficulties, and helping reduce suicidal thinking.

There are a few 'ground rules', irrespective of the approach adopted that are important in CBT:

- We must validate and accept our emotions as having meaning for us, no matter how uncomfortable they are.

- We must examine unhealthy behaviour and be prepared to change it if appropriate.

- We all have developed (through our genes/personality/upbringing/life experiences) our own personal thoughts/beliefs/ways of looking at the world, and it is through this lens that we 'view' things that happen to us in life.

- In some cases, this may involve healthy thoughts/beliefs, which help us in our lives.

- In others, the view from our own personal lens can be unhelpful, causing us difficulties in our lives.

- Most of us only seek help when the consequences (or C) are causing distress in our lives. For example, I may be a perfectionist in thought/behaviour, but unless it is leading to emotional difficulties, there is no reason to intervene.

- Hard work is involved in making changes in our thoughts/behaviour. If we are not prepared to get 'stuck in', success is unlikely.

- If, on the other hand, we are prepared to make such changes where appropriate, with help, the benefits can be enormous.

I often use the following allegory (Figure 26). Frank, a farmer, for twenty years uses a particular track through a field to reach his cattle. The field is full of high grass and the path is terrible, full of ruts and water-filled potholes. He regularly falls, often arriving at his destination wet, with cuts and bruises, and usually cursing and swearing. He has become resigned to his fate, knowing that the worse the weather, the more inconvenienced he will be.

One day, a wise neighbour brings Frank over to another part of the field and suggests creating a new route. Frank, although bothered by having to wade his way through the long grass, decides to give it a go. It is difficult the first time, but he arrives unscathed. Day by day, with the support of his friend, he takes this new path. After ten days, the grass is beginning to become flattened down. By day fifty, a track is appearing; by day one hundred, a new pathway has been formed. The old path becomes overgrown, and Frank arrives at his destination no longer bleeding, wet and bruised, having found a useful new pathway.

The story doesn't end there, for the new path Frank has formed will in time become, like an old coat, worn and tattered, and ready to be discarded in its turn. It will become the 'old' path, and he will have to create new ones in the future. Life is a journey, and is all about finding new pathways, as one track is rarely sufficient. Pathway changes will often be necessary, and we have to develop the ability to adapt.

These are the skills we learn in CBT. Sometimes we have developed unhelpful and unhealthy mind/brain pathways, which lead to mental distress, but can see no other way forward. With the help of a therapist, we, like Frank, can make those first tentative steps towards making new pathways, and can gradually break down resistance to their formation, ending up with new healthy tracks, the old ones gradually disappearing. Although new tracks will greatly improve our lives, there may come a time when we once again have to make further pathway changes. If we have, with the help of the therapist, learned the appropriate skills, this should, with luck, not be a problem.

As with all therapies, CBT has its drawbacks:

- It requires genuine commitment from patient and therapist to succeed.

- The patient must be able to focus and concentrate on the process. If, for example in moderate to severe depression, they are unable to concentrate or are completely fatigued, not sleeping, and so on, they will struggle, and so may need drug therapy first.

- Some people will simply not 'click' with the approach and will seek another therapy.

- Some want a quick fix and are not prepared to do the hard work involved.

- Some with quite severe depression may have reduced function in parts of the brain crucial for the success of this therapy, e.g. Area 24.

- Some with major issues in their past, particularly abuse, may need more in-depth psychotherapy in order to move on.

- Some may be more amenable to drug therapy, counselling or other approaches.

SELF-HELP GROUP THERAPY is another powerful form of talk therapy. The real experts in depression, anxiety, addiction and eating disorders are the sufferers themselves. Members of groups like AA (Alcoholics Anonymous), GA (Gamblers Anonymous) and NA (Narcotics Anonymous) have for decades been helping each other to face up to the ravages of addiction. The concept of self-help has been incorporated into groups like Aware, which runs meetings throughout the thirty-two counties which are chaired by trained facilitators and also has a constantly monitored telephone helpline to assist those suffering from depression.

Other groups include Grow, No Panic, which runs help lines for anxiety sufferers, 'Bodywise', for eating disorders, and Recovery. At the heart of all these groups is the concept of 'unconditional self-acceptance'. The future lies, I believe, in using the web and monitored chatrooms, where people with illnesses like depression, particularly the under-thirties, can open up and share with each other how they feel. A particularly interesting project is being pioneered by leading psychologist Tony Bates and is aimed at reaching young people. It is called Headstrong and perhaps offers a vision of where we need to go. (It is reviewed in detail in the appendix.)

BIBLIOTHERAPY: Another variation of self-help, which dates back to the 1930s. The person with anxiety or depression visits the library to access self-help books (which have been carefully picked by experts) on these subjects. Bibliotherapy in its pure form is not confined to self-help books; the early work in this area suggested that the vicarious experiences that people often gained through fictional portrayals of various conditions resonated with their own life experiences and was therapeutic. A form of bibliography called the 'Books Prescription Scheme', whereby self-help books are prescribed for patients and provided through local libraries, is being piloted in Ireland through GPs in areas like the North Inner City.

THE TALK THERAPY BRAIN PATHWAYS have been the subject of intense scientific scrutiny over the past five years. For traditional therapists, the idea of elucidating brain pathways is anathema. They dismiss attempts to peer into the brain as reducing us all to being a mass of neurons/chemical neurotransmitters. Thankfully, modern psychotherapists accept that science is only confirming the core principles underpinning what they do. They are increasingly excited about new discoveries into how the brain and the mind are intimately connected, and about new insights into how the therapies they use work in the brain.

Neuroimaging, research into genes/epigenes and examining which internal cellular mechanisms in neurons are affected by therapies are a few areas of research that are helping us build up an impressive body of information as to how some psychotherapies work. They are opening up a real dialogue between scientists and therapists.

There is increasing interest in where psychotherapy works in the brain. Many therapists are coming around to the concept that the brain/mind has a built-in self-healing 'homeostatic' mechanism. Do talk therapies essentially encourage this homeostatic mechanism to swing into action?

Where would this actually take place? The likely culprit is the attention box, particularly Area 32 and Area 24. It is the ability of these areas to 'focus attention on emotional distress' that may trigger the brain's self-healing capacity. Area 32 may be playing a role in the empathic interplay with the therapist (whatever the talk therapy). It is felt to be increasingly involved, along with Area 24, in the capacity of the brain to focus on and resolve emotional conflicts/distress. It has close links with our logic box. Both have strong links with our memory box, so any change decided upon will be quickly stored away for future use.

This is felt to be the most likely reason for the effectiveness of CBT, and probably for all forms of talk therapy. It may also be the source of the brain's capacity to self-heal and recover from emotional distress, even in the absence of any intervention.

One mechanism that might underlie successful talk therapies involves how early life experiences lay down key 'emotional pathways', sometimes before our memory box is sufficiently formed to remember the details. These pathways (with the help of our spindle cell/mirror neuron systems) between our social/emotional behaviour boxes and stress box are formed in the usual way. Because the memory box is undeveloped up to the age of three, our memories are mainly unconscious emotional ones, and we have no context for them. These early experiences are not (as Freud once speculated) 'repressed': we just can't access them logically as our memory box was too immature.

As adults (during periods of mental distress) involved in effective talk therapies like CBT, the same pathways become activated by the therapist/patient empathy connections. The brain, through the above pathways, reproduces the original emotions, helping to focus attention on reassessing and reshaping them, and in this way encouraging self-healing. It is almost as if we revert to being the child, both emotionally and in terms of our brain pathways. We see through our mirror neuron system these emotional pathways reflected back to us through the eyes of the therapist, but can now use our logical brain to reshape them.

Is it the therapy or the therapist, or more likely the emotional chemistry between the two that underlies success? Time and research will hopefully answer this question. Talk therapies work on the upper brain circuit (particularly the logic, attention and memory boxes), eventually calming down the more active lower brain circuit (particularly the stress box). This is the basis of the top-down model, where talk therapies help the logical brain regain control over the emotional one, this itself being one of the tenets of maintaining mental health. This can be a slow process, which is why 'drug therapy', which is usually faster-acting, is often used in conjunction with talk therapy in areas such as depression. The final goal is self-healing – and often a sensible use of both approaches may achieve this more efficiently.

The Drug Therapy Pathways

No other form of therapy is the source of so much controversy, confusion and division. That a drug of any type could be helpful in the treatment of conditions affecting the mind seems anathema to many. These difficulties originated in the past when mental health lay firmly in the hands of a primitive form of institutional psychiatry, and in the poor quality of drugs available at the time. Medicine has of course advanced, but these memories remain. It is vital that we view drug therapy as part of a holistic package and not as the sole answer to mental-health problems. If used wisely, medicines are often extremely useful in the treatment of mental-health conditions. Some dismiss their use on the grounds that they are biological agents, whereas psychotherapy works on the mind. These people would do well to heed the words of the great research scientist Kandel: 'All psychological therapies have a biological effect on the brain, and all drug therapies have a psychological effect.' What Kandel was alluding to was that all therapies affecting the mind end up working on brain connections and pathways.

THE FIVE MAIN DRUG THERAPY GROUPS are antidepressants, minor tranquillisers, major tranquillisers, mood stabilisers and Lyrica.

ANTIDEPRESSANTS: Their primary function is to normalise depressed mood and improve the physical symptoms of depression. They are increasingly being used in anxiety. Issues like the placebo effect, concerns about addiction and suicide ideation, particularly in the under-twenty-fives, have all created a smokescreen around the real value and place of these drugs in a holistic therapy package. We will deal with these genuine concerns later; suffice to say, they have an important place in the treatment of depression in particular.

OLDER ANTIDEPRESSANTS: The most renowned group are the tricyclics, so called because there are three circles within their chemical structure. Their method of action is focused primarily on the serotonin, dopamine and noradrenalin mood cables. They are effective in depression but have undesirable side effects, including sedation, dry mouth, blurred vision, difficulty passing urine and impotence. Furthermore, some are extremely toxic and often fatal in overdose. This is a problem because although they are effective in severe depression, the person who is unwell is often suicidal, and prescribing them a drug like this will give them the means to kill themselves. Side effects like sedation can often simply replace the depressive symptoms, making it equally difficult for the person to function normally. Many people have stopped taking these drugs due to their side effects. Nevertheless, they were the drug of choice for decades in depression and have cured millions of patients. Some patients respond much better to these older drugs than to more modern ones, although this is the exception.

AMITRIPTYLINE is the most well-known and most widely prescribed tricyclic. It is extremely effective in restoring the mood system to normal. However, sedation, and a very high risk of fatality if taken in overdose, makes it a dangerous drug to prescribe, particularly if suicidal thoughts are present.

MODERN ANTIDEPRESSANTS: There are two main groups: the SSRIs, which stimulate the serotonin mood cable (their mode of action involves inhibiting the SERT molecule, which, as discussed earlier, is the focus of our resilience gene) and the SRNIs, which stimulate both serotonin and noradrenalin cables. Both work from the bottom of the brain up, calming down firstly the lower mood circuit, particularly the stress box, and eventually increasing activity in the upper circuit. (This is the opposite approach to that of the psychotherapies.) They are effective in treating depression, anxiety and eating disorders.

Here are some of the most common modern antidepressants in use:

1) FLUOXETINE (PROZAC): This SSRI has proved to be an effective and safe drug in the treatment of the illnesses mentioned above over the past fifteen years. It has been used in the under-eighteen age group, usually under the care of a specialist.

2) ESCITALOPRAM (LEXAPRO): This powerful SSRI is, at present, the first-choice drug for the treatment of depression and anxiety, gradually replacing its predecessor Citalopram (Cipramil). It has a favourable side-effect profile, with occasional nausea in the first week and menstrual changes in some women, but reduced sexual dysfunction compared to other SSRIs. It is generally fast-acting, well tolerated and effective in restoring normal mood and calming anxiety.

3) PAROXETINE (SEROXAT): This drug, a follow-up to Prozac, was initially greeted favourably. It then received a great deal of bad press because of its sexual and withdrawal side effects. It produces severe dizziness and disorientation when the drug is stopped, so care is needed to do this very slowly. This is the one SSRI that is completely contraindicated in pregnancy.

4) VENLAFAXINE (EFFEXOR): This SRNI targets both serotonin and noradrenalin cables. It is effective in treating depression in those with poor drive or motivation. It has similar side effects to the SSRIs but may also result in severe headaches and sweating. Those who are prescribed the drug have also experienced more sexual side effects. There are also concerns about its use in the elderly.

5) DULOXETINE (CYMBALTA): This is a newer SRNI, similar in type to Venlafaxine, but gradually replacing it. Its side effects seem to be less severe than those of Venlafaxine.

6) MIRTAZAPINE (ZISPIN OR MIRAP): This drug also targets the serotonin and noradrenalin cables but works through different mechanisms. It is a very useful drug but side effects like weight gain can be a problem. I find it helpful as an 'add-on' drug in 'small' amounts, to avoid the above side effects, in those who are having sleep or agitation problems in depression. It also lacks sexual side effects. This is only a sample of many drugs of this type. A list of all these drugs is available in the appendix, including advice on side effects, and usage in pregnancy, when breastfeeding, among the young and the elderly

7) AGOMELATINE (VALDOXAN): is a new drug due to be launched soon. It does not have the same mode of action as the SSRIs and SSNRI dealt with above. It blocks one specific serotonin receptor, and activates two melatonin receptors in the brain (for more see technical section). This leads to a lifting of mood, and improvements in sleep and internal body clock rhythms. It is reputed to have a good side effect profile in terms of sexual side effects and withdrawal symptoms. Time will tell.

MINOR TRANQUILLISERS include drugs like Xanax, Valium, Librium and Lexotane and are mainly used in the treatment of anxiety. They are not antidepressants and should never be used as such. They are highly addictive, have side effects like drowsiness, impaired concentration and tolerance (i.e. having to increase the dose to get the same effect) amongst others. They have some usefulness as short-term treatments for acute anxiety and to help alcoholics detoxify, but unfortunately in both cases they often end up as long-term crutches.

While much of the talk is about antidepressants, minor tranquillisers are much more widely abused. They work by calming down the stress box – the source of most of our anxiety.

MAJOR TRANQUILLISERS: These are unfortunately regarded as antidepressants in the media, even though nothing could be further than the truth. They were originally prescribed for the treatment of schizophrenia and have an important role to play in the management of this illness. Over the past few years, their use has widened to include the treatment of the psychotic side effects of drugs like hash and also the manic phase of bipolar mood disorder. The original major tranquillisers in use were Largactyl and Melleril; the modern versions are Zyprexa, Seroquel, Risperdal and Abilify. Major tranquillisers have significant side effects, including weight gain (particularly Zyprexa), drowsiness, cardiac problems (particularly in the elderly), muscle twitching in some, and a general flattening of affect. They are usually prescribed by the psychiatrist and only rarely by a GP – and with good reason. These are the drugs at the centre of the ongoing 'Toxic Psychiatry' debate.

They work mainly on the emotional limbic brain, the glutamate system and the dopamine mood cable. There is some evidence that early use of these more modern drugs in schizophrenia may prevent loss of dendrite connections in the logical brain. This is a very positive finding, but there are many side effects. Their usefulness has to be balanced against this. They have definitely helped many, particularly those with schizophrenia and bipolar mood disorder, but should only be used in long-term treatment under the careful supervision of a psychiatrist. They should be prescribed as part of a holistic care plan and should be reduced as soon as possible in order to minimise side effects.

There is a modern trend to use them on their own as long-term mood stabilisers, often in quite high doses in bipolar mood disorder. I am personally uneasy about this trend due to concerns about long-term weight/cardiac/diabetes issues in such cases. This has to be clearly distinguished from shorter-term use of these drugs to help 'bring down' a person with very elevated mood. In this situation, these drugs are very useful. I have particular concerns about trends towards using high doses of Zyprexa due to marked weight gain; I am, however, more comfortable with Seroquel. My one appeal is that they should not be included in the debate about usage of antidepressants, as I feel that this is neither their function nor their mode of action.

MOOD STABILISERS: These drugs are mainly used in the treatment of bipolar mood disorder. In this illness, changes within the neurons of our mood system predispose us to major shifts in mood. These drugs (many of which have been developed as anti-epilepsy drugs) work by stabilising the internal chemistry of the brain cells involved, and have transformed the lives of many people.

Drugs like Lithium and Epilim are very useful in situations where the predominant issue is elevated mood, and others, like Lamictal, where mood is depressed. Lithium seems to be extremely neuroprotective and strongly encourages dendrite connection growth pathways. It has a particular capacity to increase BDNF. We will be examining this in more detail later. Once again, they are not antidepressants but mood stabilisers. They do have side effects. Lithium and Epilim both cause some weight gain and should be avoided in pregnancy; the former can also cause tremors. Lamictal can cause rashes in some. As stated above, drugs like Zyprexa and Seroquel are also used by some psychiatrists as long-term mood stabilisers for management of elevated mood. While preferring the use of traditional mood stabilisers, I would be more comfortable with the use of Seroquel, which causes less weight gain.

LYRICA (PREGBALIN): This drug, which was originally used for chronic pain, has recently emerged as a treatment of general anxiety. It works very quickly (within a week) and has none of the addictive side effects of minor tranquillisers. It does have its own side effects. For those who would like to know more about its mode of action (and indeed about all of the above), see the technical section.

Drug versus Talk Therapies

There is no more contentious issue in modern medicine than the debate about drug versus talk therapy for the treatment of mental-health problems. In practice, Kandel's approach is more pragmatic and sensible. There is an obvious place for both drug and talk therapies in the treatment of many mental-health problems. When we examine how both therapies work in the brain, the picture becomes clearer (Figure 27). Drug therapies work more on the lower brain circuit; talk therapies on the upper. The use of both together often provides the best results. The common denominator is the ability of both to alter BDNF/dendrite connections and thus pathways in both circuits.

The Placebo Therapy Pathways

A placebo is a substance or procedure which a patient accepts as a medicine or therapy but which has no specific therapeutic activity for the condition. The placebo effect relates to the therapeutic and healing effect of an inert medicine or ineffective therapy. It occurs when a patient is treated in conjunction with a suggestion from an authority figure such as a doctor/therapist, or from information acquired, that the treatment will aid in healing; the patient's condition simultaneously improves. We have known for a century that a patient's expectation of the effectiveness of a particular therapy plays a role in either its success or failure. All therapies involve a placebo effect and it is in the brain where this effect occurs. Placebos are traditionally associated with drug companies, who compare them to active drugs in trials with a view to demonstrating the superior effectiveness of the drugs. Increasingly, however, the placebo effect is being studied in relation to non-drug therapies with a view to understanding how expectations, by stimulating different areas of the brain, can profoundly influence the therapy's effectiveness. In the last decade, research into the placebo effect by world experts such as Fabio Benedetti and Helen Mayberg has increased our knowledge of its importance and the mechanisms involved.

Research in this area has centred on pain relief, Parkinson's disease and depression. Of interest is the finding that the placebo effect 'mimics' the specific therapy under investigation. In relation to pain relief, it has been shown that endorphins (the natural pain-killing chemical neurotransmitters in the brain) are released as a result of this phenomenon. Areas of the brain involved in the anticipation and feelings of pain (such as the logic, emotional control, attention boxes, and island) are also involved. In Parkinson's disease, the dopamine system is strongly activated due to this effect. In depression, if we use placebos versus drug therapy, we find the serotonin system activated, along with parts of the brain involved in positive expectations.

The placebo effect is now seen as an important part of the therapeutic process. It enhances the actual active therapeutic effect of the treatment in use. We can learn much from studying this pathway. It teaches us that the more time we spend with a person as a doctor/therapist, the more we explain, empathise with and validate them, the more positive we are about the potential effectiveness of the therapy used, and the greater the possibility that this therapy will be effective. A key part of all therapies is the human expectation that their use will improve the person's situation. An empathic link with the 'healer' is vital for this to occur.

Difficulties with the placebo effect arise when it is applied to one form of therapy vis-à-vis another. Nowhere is this better illustrated than in depression. While drug therapies designed to treat this illness are obliged to go through trials to compare their effectiveness versus a placebo, other therapies, such as alternative ones, are not. This creates public confusion. We never consider that alternative therapies may also have a strong placebo effect and possibly little other therapeutic value. Some trials have been done in the area of talk therapies versus placebo in the treatment of mental-health problems; they are not, however, as well studied as drug therapies. The importance of this effect in psychotherapies cannot be overestimated.

Another key question is 'How long does this effect last?' In practice, the effect diminishes reasonably quickly with time, and the 'real' effectiveness of the therapy involved can then be ascertained. This can be a problem, as many mental health trials, particularly in relation to drug therapies, are of quite short duration. I feel that the combined roles of the empathy and placebo pathways are greatly underestimated in the treatment of mental health problems. In some senses, empathy lies at the core of the placebo effect. While it is almost impossible to put a figure on its role, it seems likely that 20 to 30 percent of the effectiveness of all therapies can be attributed to the placebo effect. The placebo effect is powerful proof of the plasticity of the brain – its extraordinary capacity to dynamically reshape its pathways.

The Alternative/Complementary Therapy Pathways

If one walks into any major bookshop seeking information on therapies available to treat the most common mental health problems, one would expect shelves of well-researched books written by expert doctors and therapists. Instead, we find large sections dedicated to a myriad of alternative therapies. This pattern is repeated in newspapers, magazines and radio and TV shows. Clearly, conventional therapies for mental distress are neither reaching nor assisting those in need. Those suffering from anxiety and depression are most vulnerable to the latest alternative 'craze' – desperately seeking help but afraid or ashamed to travel traditional routes.

When analysing alternative therapies for mental health, we must make some pragmatic observations:

- Many are effective because the therapist is able to spend more time with the person in difficulty and are more empathic and successful in convincing clients that their particular therapy is effective.

- As a result, the placebo effect may play a more powerful role in the therapy in question.

- Many alternative therapies have not undergone the extensive research or placebo trials which traditional therapies are obliged to go through.

- Where they have, results are often 'underwhelming'.

- There are risks in relying solely on such therapies without assessment by a trained mental-health professional.

- Assessing these therapies through good scientific research into their modes of action/effectiveness would be the ideal, together with regulation of many of the 'therapists' involved.

- All of us need to become more 'selective' in assessing books and literature on alternative therapies and their claims, examining the 'scientific basis' underlying them.

- We need to move away from the 'either/or' conflict between conventional and alternative therapies, to a modern approach, where both will have their proper place, based on sound scientific principles.

- Some alternative therapies are used in conjunction with conventional therapies. In such cases, we call them complementary.

- Some experts feel that the success of alternative medicine lies in the fact that it is treating the 'worried well', rather than those who may be medically unwell.

MEDITATION: Of the alternative/complementary therapies, this is the most interesting, most well-researched and potentially most valuable alternative on offer. It is also a therapy with a sound scientific basis which has helped us understand the workings of the mind/brain in a different way. I have no hesitation in recommending it to anyone who suffers from depression (primarily to prevent relapse), anxiety or other forms of mental distress. Many of us would also benefit from incorporating it into our everyday lives.

The reality is that meditation can take many forms – from peaceful contemplation while fishing on Lough Corrib, to watching a beautiful sunset and reflecting on the beauty of the world, or spending time in contemplative prayer (our ancestors used the rosary), and becoming mindfully aware of the present moment. Others might find that cooking or gardening, with focused attention on one activity, produces the same effects. All come under the wide umbrella of meditation. When discussing it as a therapy for stress, anxiety and depression, however, we are usually dealing with a more formal, structured form of meditation.

Meditation is a mental technique which involves focusing the mind on an object, sound, prayer, breathing, or conscious thoughts, in order to increase our awareness of the present moment, helping us to relax, reduce stress or enhance spiritual or personal growth. It was being practised in India as early as 5,000 BC and was a major influence in the main religious movements, particularly Buddhism, early Christianity, Islam and others up to the present day. Since the nineteenth century, it has become increasingly incorporated into the western psyche (with the arrival of Zen Buddhism, yoga and transcendental meditation). In the area of mental health, we have benefited from excellent research by Prof. Richard Davidson, who has examined what happens in the brain as a result of regular meditation. Thanks to his work, we now know that it shifts activity from the right side of the brain (the source of most of our negative thoughts and emotions) to the left. This explains the reduction in stress and negative thinking, and the increase in positive emotions like peacefulness, calmness, forgiveness, love, compassion and joy. His views have been supported by recent neuroimaging research on the both sides of the brain in relation to emotions. This has confirmed that the right side is the main player in our emotional world, with the left playing a lesser role. Although the right side deals with all emotions, it seems to focus particularly on negative ones, leaving the left side to deal with the easier, positive ones. Since the left side is strengthened by regular meditation, it is inevitable that peace and calm will follow.

If one examines the positive effects of meditation on our mood system, we find that it increases activity in our serotonin and dopamine cables, calms our noradrenalin cable and increases the supply of 'feel-good' endorphins in the brain. It also calms our stress system (thus reducing glucocortisol levels), increases our relaxant GABA neurotransmitters, increases melatonin (another calming neurotransmitter) and calms our lower mood circuit – the source of emotional distress in many mental illnesses.

Meditation performed over a long period of time can actually increase the size of parts of the frontal mood departments (particularly on the left side), memory box (right side) and island (right). The last of these plays an important role in self-awareness and emotions. This is another example of the brain's plasticity. This therapy actually encourages neuron dendrite connections in key parts of our brain to grow and develop. We also know that meditation reduces our heart rate, blood pressure and respiratory rate, with major positive effects on mental and physical health. Detailed analysis of the types of meditation available is beyond the scope of this book, but most will involve withdrawing into a quiet space, sitting in a straight-backed posture with legs folded, focusing on breathing, or repeating a word (mantra) over a designated period of time, dampening down the constant background chatter of our busy minds. While it is possible to learn these techniques on one's own, it is probably sensible to find an accredited meditation teacher or classes to help you become more adept.

Many people who are unfamiliar with meditation may assume that it makes the person 'sleepy and switched off', whereas in fact nothing could be further from the truth. It actually achieves the extraordinary feat of both calming the interior mind of the person and increasing awareness of their internal/external environment, improving their logical problem-solving capacity and focusing on important life issues.

Meditation has an important place in the treatment of illnesses like depression as part of an overall holistic package, and is perhaps an underrated therapy. I feel that it could play a major role in tackling depression-relapse prevention, dealing with uncomfortable emotions like severe anxiety and anger, and assisting in the reduction of craving in addiction and the treatment of personality disorders.

It has been partially absorbed into the world of CBT, where a form of meditation called Mindfulness Based Cognitive Therapy (MBCT) has been developed. This therapy uses the principles behind CBT, linking them to mindfulness, a form of meditation used in the East for thousands of years. MBCT was developed as a new approach to the prevention of depression relapses by Mark Williams, Jon Kabat-Zinn, Mark Teasdale, and Zindel Segal (see bibliography). We will be dealing with it in the section on depression.

I would like to pick out one useful mindfulness exercise that is often used in MBCT, particularly in depression. However, all of us could, I believe, benefit from this, the 'Three Minute Breathing Space'. This can be done at any time of the day but is of particular benefit if one is under a great deal of stress. It involves finding a quiet space and a comfortable posture, closing your eyes, and engaging with the following:

MINUTE ONE: Focus our mind on inner experiences, whether it is our thoughts, emotions or physical sensations. Don't try to change or challenge anything here, just become aware of them.

MINUTE TWO: Focus on the simple physical sensation of 'breathing', particularly on your abdomen rising and falling with each breath – again, not trying to control it.

MINUTE THREE: Increase focus or awareness of the body as a whole, including posture, facial expressions and sensations. Try to do this with acceptance and without judgement.

This is often called a 'mini meditation', and if there is one exercise that anybody with anxiety or depression wanted to take from this book, it is one of the simplest and most useful. If it is performed two or three times a day, the benefits are enormous. It is also an ideal simple therapy approach for those who do not want to travel the full meditation/mindfulness route.

YOGA: This is an ancient Indian therapy combining physical exercises, meditation and breathing techniques which has its base in ancient Hinduism. The name itself means 'union', referring to the union of mind, body and spirit. The combination of physical and breathing exercises can be used to reach a meditative state. In the West, it is considered to be a form of physical exercise by many, but the relaxation/breathing exercises/meditation side of this therapy can be useful as a complementary therapy in stress, anxiety and depression.

The main type used in the West is called hatha yoga, and it is composed of bodily postures called *Asanas*, breathing exercises called *Pranayama*, and meditation. Some of the exercises used in yoga have been absorbed into MBCT.

T'AI CHI: This is an ancient, gentle Chinese martial-arts system of physical and breathing exercises performed in an elegant sequence of set movements designed to increase the flow of vital energy, or 'qi', in the body. In some senses, it is a form of mindfulness in motion, reducing symptoms of anxiety and lifting mood, at least temporarily. Once again, it is helpful as part of a total preventative package in reducing the risk of recurrent depression.

HERBAL THERAPIES relate to the use of plant or plant extracts (leaves, flowers, roots, bark, and so on) in the treatment and prevention of illnesses. It is the most ancient and widely used therapy in the modern world. Most modern synthetic drug therapies (many of which originate from plants) have, in the main, one active substance. Herbal remedies contain any number of different active ingredients (sometimes up to hundreds), working in a synergistic or additive manner. This latter capacity makes them potentially useful but also more difficult to research and assess the side effects of. As with other alternative therapies, scientific research into the effectiveness and safety of many herbs is often lacking. This is of concern to family doctors because, although most herbs are safe, some have serious side effects, especially the potential to interact (sometimes fatally) with conventional drug therapies. Some Chinese herbs have been shown to be toxic to the kidney. Some ayurvedic herbs are contaminated with arsenic, lead and mercury.

ST JOHN'S WORT: This has been used for centuries in dealing with mental-health difficulties and is the most commonly prescribed antidepressant in Germany. It is derived from the beautiful shrub *Hyperforin perforatum*. Its main role has been in the treatment of depression and anxiety disorders. This herb has been extensively investigated to determine which of its many ingredients are most active. The two most commonly studied have been Hypericum and Hyperforin. The former was shown (through its effects on the hormone control box) to dampen down the glucocortisol cascade in depression. The latter was felt to increase activity in the serotonin, noradrenalin and dopamine cables – explaining the substance's possible role in the treatment of depression. St John's wort is more effective if the whole plant is used rather than isolated extracts.

If this 'natural herb' is so effective, why is it not more widely prescribed by family doctors? There are many reasons for this:

- There is a large variation in the quality of preparations of St John's wort available, with different levels, for example, of both Hypericum and Hyperforin. This lack of standardisation is a major problem.

- St John's wort has the potential to interact with a multitude of commonly prescribed conventional medications (oral contraceptives, lipid-lowering drugs, some blood-pressure tablets, anti-cancer drugs, and the blood thinner Warfarin), with possible life-threatening consequences. This occurs because it interferes with the liver's ability to break down such drugs.

- There is also a very serious interaction with SSRIs, which can be a problem, as many people with depression may not mention to the family doctor that they are using this herb. This can lead to 'serotonin syndrome' (this relates to a constellation of physical and psychological symptoms which arise from potentially fatal overactivity of the serotonin mood cable).

- There is a myth that St John's wort has no side effects. The general consensus is that there are fewer side effects than SSRIs, but this does not mean that there are none. There can be abdominal symptoms, confusion, tiredness, sedation, dizziness, some sexual side effects, skin rashes and excessive sensitivity to exposure to sunlight if fair-skinned, to name but a few.

- If used by mistake in schizophrenia, St John's wort can trigger psychosis.

- There is concern about its use in pregnancy, where it should be avoided.

There is little doubt that some have found this herb to be useful, particularly in mild to moderate depression. I have some patients who are quite happy using it. The latest regulations in Ireland recommend that the family doctor writes the script for its use. But many people get it without a script in other countries or online and do not inform their family doctor they are taking it. The average dose recommended is 300 mgs three times a day, but be aware of the differing amounts of active ingredients that may or may not be present. Do I feel that it should be a first-line therapy? Personally, I am concerned by the issues expressed above and would recommend considering other options. But if somebody is adamant about not using conventional drug therapy, it is the next-best option – only, however, if prescribed by their doctor.

VALERIAN: This pink-flowered herb has been used for hundreds of years as a sedative and is a commonly used natural remedy for anxiety, stress and sleep difficulties. It works in a similar manner to tranquillisers like Valium, probably by stimulating the GABA receptors in the brain. It can have side effects like drowsiness and headaches and should be avoided in pregnancy and breastfeeding. There have been rare cases of liver damage.

GINGKO BILOBA is a herbal remedy derived from leaves of the tree of the same name. It contains a number of antioxidants which are felt to improve blood circulation to the brain. It is claimed to be useful in reducing memory loss in dementia, of benefit in depression and in treating the sexual side effects associated with conventional antidepressants. It, like St John's wort, interacts with the blood thinner Warfarin and can cause bleeding and epilepsy in vulnerable people. There is little evidence to support any real effectiveness in the treatment of depression.

SIBERIAN GINSENG is thought to increase levels of serotonin, noradrenalin and dopamine and is thus useful in depression. However, one has to be aware of significant side effects, such as increasing blood pressure and heart rate (extremely dangerous to anybody with heart disease), and in high doses can reduce blood-sugar levels. Finally, it can cause drowsiness and headaches. It is not recommended in pregnancy or breastfeeding and should be avoided by those on Warfarin or aspirin.

For people wishing to travel the herbal route to deal with mental health problems, I would counsel caution. The only real herb shown scientifically to have a role, St John's wort, does not have any greater effectiveness than modern SSRIs. Simply because it is called a 'natural' remedy does not mean it is any safer or more effective than the often scorned but more reliable group of antidepressants discussed above. These products at least have the benefit of extensive research, standardisation and constant review. I am certainly wary of using herbal therapies without discussing it with your family doctor. If intent on their use, preferably attend herbalists with some medical background. Be extremely wary of combining them with any conventional medicine and always inform your doctor if using them on the side. Failing to do so may, in serious cases, cost you your life. I would be quite conscious of the possible dangers of toxic metals and other contaminating substances. Finally, if considering becoming pregnant, avoid all herbal remedies.

HOMEOPATHY: This controversial therapy is widely practiced. Its origins can be traced back to a German doctor called Samuel Hahnemann who created it in the late nineteenth century.

The concepts behind this popular alternative treatment are as follows:

1. If a substance produces certain symptoms in a healthy person, it will cure those suffering from an illness that has the same symptoms (the Law of Similars).

2. That the more we dilute a substance, the more powerful it becomes (the Law of Potentisation).

3. That the whole person (physical and mental), together with their individual symptoms and illnesses, must be treated (the Law of Individualisation).

While the third principle is easily understood and acceptable, the first two seem at first to make little scientific sense. Homeopaths believe that the more diluted a substance, even to a level where there seem to be no active ingredients left, the more powerful it becomes in the treatment of an illness. Nobody really knows how this therapy purports to work. The most common theory is that the substances involved interface with our vital life-energy forces, encouraging self-healing. The argument put forward by homeopaths is that it works at a quantum level and is therefore not accessible to scientific analysis. It cannot, therefore, be matched against conventional therapies. I have often reflected that the brain, with its trillions of synapses and countless internal chemical reactions, behaves like a giant quantum computer, but I cannot see why homeopathy alone can claim involvement at this level. It is likely that all therapies, even simple placebos, must involve quantum mechanisms.

In practice, despite huge popularity in Europe and the United States, homeopathy has little scientific backing. In 2005, the prestigious medical journal the *Lancet* reviewed all the trials involving homeopathy, concluding that it was little better than a placebo. Some reading this may have found this therapy useful. If so, just be aware that the reasons for its success may be different from the purported ones.

ACUPUNCTURE: This is another ancient therapy; it originated in China two thousand years ago and, like herbal medicines, has formed part of Traditional Chinese Medicine (TCM). It was also used in Japan and Korea before eventually spreading to the West in the past fifty years.

Acupuncture involves placing very fine needles into various part of the body, just under the skin. It is based on the concept that our bodies contain an invisible non-physical, vital energy force called 'qi' (a mixture of inherited energy and energy derived from air and food through our lives). This energy, in accordance with TCM, flows through a network of invisible channels called meridians that traverse the whole body. If qi is flowing normally through these meridians, we are healthy, but if blockages occur, we develop illnesses. When our qi is interrupted, exerting pressure (acupressure) or inserting needles (acupuncture) into particular sites on the skin along the line of these meridians clears this blockage, and we become well.

There are differences between Chinese (bigger needles, and more uncomfortable), Japanese (needles threaded through tubes, and less painful), Korean (emphasis on hand acupoints) and Western (combinations of all of the above) acupuncture methods. The most common reason for using acupuncture in the West is pain, in particular chronic pain, where it has been shown in many trials to be effective. It has also been used for a variety of medical conditions like diabetes, obesity and high blood pressure. It is widely used by doctors, therapists, pain-relief clinics and physiotherapists, and in many other disciplines.

Let us now examine acupuncture from a modern scientific standpoint. Does this therapy work, and if so, how? What role, if any, does it have to play in the area of mental health? Scientific research has failed to match the energy meridians with any obvious anatomical or physiological patterns in the body. It has, however, opened up new possibilities as to potential mechanisms of action of this ancient therapy. Apart from the effects at spinal-cord level in the area of pain relief, most modern research has centred on the brain itself, particularly the limbic mood department. This therapy encourages the brain to produce large amounts of chemical endorphins. These have two positive effects: relieving pain, and lifting mood and reducing anxiety. The most active area of the brain in this instance is the 'island', which is important in registering physical sensations from the body and converting them into relevant emotions. I have been intrigued by the description of many with depression, as being 'in pain' emotionally. The link between physical and emotional pain seems to be the island, particularly on the right side of the brain. Because acupuncture has been shown to be helpful in situations of chronic pain through the above mechanisms, it would make sense as a possible therapeutic option in depression. However, there is no evidence that this therapy on its own can relieve symptoms of this illness.

HYPNOTHERAPY: A controversial alternative therapy that involves a technique whereby one can induce an 'altered state of consciousness' in which our mind is no longer under the control of our logical, rational brain. In this state, the person's inner emotional world is theoretically exposed and, more importantly, 'open' to suggestion. At first glance, this would seem to be an ideal way to alter unhealthy emotional pathways. Many psychotherapists in the past have favoured this approach.

The scientific basis for hypnosis would seem to support its claim as a potentially useful therapy. It seems to switch off the logical, practical left side of the brain in favour of the more creative right side, making the person more open to 'creative' suggestions.

One has to approach this therapy with caution. It can be difficult to hypnotise some people and also to assess how 'suggestible' they are when in this state. Then one worries about the ideas that may be 'planted' in the subconsciousness of those involved. In depression, there seems to be little research evidence suggesting that hypnosis is an effective therapy. One would be particularly concerned about its use in schizophrenia. There seems to be more evidence of its benefits in anxiety but we need more research to justify its use. Another variation of hypnotherapy, called autogenic training, a form of self-hypnosis training, seems to offer some benefit in the areas of stress, anxiety and insomnia.

EMDR (EYE MOVEMENT DESENSITISATION AND REPROCESSING): I first came upon this therapy in Dr David Servan-Schreiber's fascinating book: *Healing without Freud or Prozac*. He described its use in treating victims of the horrors in Kosovo who were suffering from post-traumatic stress disorder (PTSD). The theory was based on the concept that we reorganise our emotional memories during our dream sleep (called 'REM' or 'Rapid Eye Movement' sleep). In PTSD, however, our emotional memories remain frozen. If we ask the person to recall the memories while getting them to follow the movements of our finger moving quickly over and back in front of their eyes, we mimic this process of REM sleep, allowing them to logically process them for good.

This has been a controversial therapy, with strong views being expressed by many therapists, both for and against it. The general consensus is that it is probably no more effective than many talk therapies like CBT, and its mode of action is unlikely to be that originally suggested.

AROMATHERAPY: A therapy with roots in the ancient Persian, Greek and Roman eras. It is a 'scent-using therapy', using essential oils extracted from plants (leaves, flowers, roots, berries, and so on), which may be applied by massage or inhalation, or simply released into the atmosphere with a view to treating various conditions. The theory behind this therapy is simple: that the oils involved (absorbed either though the nose or skin) arrive in the brain, having effects on our stress system and mood. In practice, this information arrives in our limbic mood department – the most likely source of its effectiveness. There is some evidence that it acts as a 'relaxant', relieving symptoms of short-term stress, depression and anxiety. Overall, there is little evidence that it can make serious inroads into these conditions on its own. Some feel that it is no more effective than simple massage. I feel it is a helpful complementary therapy.

MASSAGE: A popular therapy whose roots go back to ancient civilisations in China, Egypt, Greece and Rome. There are a number of differing approaches, involving touching or kneading the skin, with a view to reducing pain, stress and anxiety. The effects of massage are at a local level in the skin and underlying tissues and the brain, where sensory information from the body arrives, particularly the limbic mood department. It has been shown to increase serotonin and melatonin levels, so can help with sleep difficulties, and reduces anxiety. It stimulates the brain's pleasure system, releasing endorphins and dopamine. By calming down the limbic system, it reduces our stress hormone, glucocortisol. This therapy is a useful 'complementary medicine' when combined with a holistic package, but is unlikely to lift depression on its own.

REIKI is another healing therapy with modern origins in Japan. It is based on the concept that all of us are infused with 'universal life energy'. The basis for this energy source lies in the alliance of the mind, body and spirit. We become ill when this energy flow is disrupted. The healer attempts to channel this force through themselves into the sufferer, thus restoring well-being. During a healing process, the therapist will place their hands in twelve different positions near the head and abdomen, to align them with this universal energy source, and then realign them to transfer it to different parts of the body of the sufferer. Unlike spiritual healing, where the healer directly transfers energy to the recipient, in reiki the energy transfer involves the latter. There is little scientific evidence to explain or validate this therapy.

THOUGHT FIELD THERAPY: Another controversial therapy developed by American psychologist Roger Callahan. This therapy involves recalling traumatic events or distressing emotions while tapping particular acupressure energy points in the body in a particular sequence. It has been used to treat depression, anxiety and addiction. Once again, there is little scientific basis for this therapy.

BIOFEEDBACK: relates to a therapy whereby we learn to measure and control the physical reactions (like our heart rate, breathing, brain waves, and so on), usually through the use of special machinery. For centuries, it has been known that Indian yoga experts could control their pulse rate, breathing, and even body temperature through similar mechanisms, and this is simply a follow on. This therapy is useful for stress and anxiety in particular. Sportsmen like Tiger Woods practise such techniques to help cope with the pressures of major competitions.

CRANIOSACRAL THERAPY: relates to the gentle manipulation of the skull and the sacral bone in our lower back to facilitate an unrestricted flow of cerebrospinal fluid (CSF). It was created by an osteopath in the 1930s who believed that minute movements of the above bones could improve our general health. The scientific basis for this therapy is completely unsound and there is no evidence that it is of assistance in mental health or indeed in any other illness. Any effects will be placebo in type, similar to, say, massage.

LIGHT THERAPY In winter, when the hours of daylight reduce, many with depression will find their condition worsening. Others will suffer from SAD. In both, light therapies delivered through special light-therapy units and dawn simulators have been found to be of great assistance. We will be examining this in more detail later.

CREATIVE THERAPIES: There has been a great deal of interest in the role of art, music, drama, and other pursuits as part of an overall holistic package. Their role, however, is often overlooked. It may seem strange to consider such everyday activities as therapies, but there is increasing evidence that activating the creative side of the brain assists those in mental distress with expressing their emotions.

ART THERAPY: Many of us have happy memories as children drawing, painting and modelling clay. But as life, with its cares and difficulties arrives, adults lose the capacity to express themselves in such creative ways. Art can be used as a relaxing hobby, a de-stressor in its own right. It may also be helpful as part of a holistic package to tap into our deep-seated inner emotional world.

MUSIC THERAPY: Following publication of my last book, I received a lovely letter from a lady suggesting including music as a therapy for depression. There has been much research into its potential to help deal with emotional distress in children and adults. Music on its own has not been shown to treat depression effectively but when combined with other therapies, such as CBT, it has been found to be a useful adjunct. It is also useful in reducing stress.

DANCE THERAPY: There has been a wave of recent interest in dance, fuelled by TV shows. Dancing has been an integral part of human social interaction since earliest times. There has also been an upsurge in scientific research into how dancing activates parts of our brain, with possible potential benefits for mental health. Like music, this therapy is unlikely to be effective on its own.

DRAMA THERAPY: has been in vogue for thousands of years. I often reflect that Shakespeare was the greatest psychoanalytical psychotherapist of all time, as he expresses through his plays the most profound understanding of the human condition. In modern times, there is an interest in how drama can assist us in tapping into our limbic mood system and expressing unconscious feelings. Once again, I feel it is complementary to other therapies.

Traditional Healing Systems

Traditional healing systems, in existence in the East for thousands of years, have been 'transplanted' to the fertile soil of Western culture in the last few centuries. Most alternative therapies have roots in these traditions. In the West, we have a conventional model with specific symptoms, signs and indeed therapies for illnesses like depression. Inherent in this model is an acceptance of the critical role of environment in its causation, and a clear distinction between spirituality and medicine. In the East, there is no such distinction, so illness and spirituality happily coincide, making it difficult to compare and contrast with Western medicine. To understand alternative therapies, we must examine these traditions, and their origins.

TRADITIONAL CHINESE MEDICINE (TCM) has existed in China for thousands of years. It is now practised side by side with conventional medicine in modern China. A patient may be given two separate prescriptions, one for a conventional therapy and another for a TCM therapy.

It started with the use of herbs, later combining with philosophical/religious ideas, particularly Confucianism and Daoism, leading to a more organised system of diagnosis and treatments, particularly the development of acupuncture and herbal remedies.

It has its roots firmly in Daoism – the idea of living in harmony with nature, all living things having their roots in a primal energy, or qi. This in turn is made up of two dynamic opposing forces known as yin and yang. These two creative forces are present in all living things, the body and the environment we live in.

- Within our bodies, various organs belong to the yin or yang groups. We are healthy when both are in balance.

- Qi surges through our bodies through twelve main channels called meridians. Illness appears when these meridians are blocked.

- There are specific diagnostic tests the therapist will perform to decide on the problem and therapy to be used.

- Treatments suggested will include a healthy diet, physical and relaxation exercises, acupressure and acupuncture, herbal therapies, and finally meditation. These are all aimed at restoring yin/yang balance and making qi flow freely.

If we analyse TCM scientifically, it is difficult to find hard data on the underlying concepts but there are still positives. I find the emphasis on diet, exercise, breathing, meditation and harmony with nature very helpful.

AYURVEDIC MEDICINE (AM): India is the source of this equally ancient system.

Ayurveda itself can be translated into 'life knowledge'. This therapy system is over two thousand years old, with roots in Hinduism. In earlier times, it focused on herbal and dietary/lifestyle approaches; latterly, it developed into a full-blown diagnostic therapy system of its own. Like TCM in China, it is practised side by side with conventional medicine in modern India.

AM is based on the concept that the body is seen as a mini-universe where fire, earth, ether, air and water combine to produce three 'humours', which define your particular 'type'. Your type can be one of three particular variations based on the ability of your gut to digest and absorb food known as *vata, pitta* and *kapha*. Depending on the latter, recommendations can be made on changing your diet/lifestyle to improve health.

There is also a spiritual dimension to ayurveda. As it is closely related to Hinduism, concepts of reincarnation and karma are an integral part of the therapy system. Karma relates to the belief that, through reincarnation, behaving in an incorrect manner in a former life may be a possible cause of illness in this one. Therapists in India absorb this possibility into their diagnosis and treatments. In terms of therapies, ayurveda involves the use of herbal remedies, diet, lifestyle changes, yoga, massage and meditation.

There is little scientific basis for the theory behind ayurvedic medicine. Like TCM, it has some useful tools at its disposal: diet, exercise, yoga, meditation, massage and some herbal remedies. One area of concern is the tendency of AM practitioners to use metal extracts in their herbal remedies. Users of this system should be aware of the possible risks associated with the use of such extracts.

JAPANESE TRADITIONAL MEDICINE (JTM) is an Eastern therapy system whose roots go back to ancient times. It was gradually modified through the centuries, evolving to the present format. Its earliest roots go back to Shintoism, when illness was thought to be related to annoying the host of spirits which they felt populated the world. It was then strongly influenced by the arrival of physicians and healers through Buddhism in the fifth and sixth centuries, and at a later stage by Western traditional medicine. Eventually a whole diagnostic system was developed and, as in India and China, it is now practised side by side with conventional Western medicine.

JTM has its own unique approaches and therapies, many of which are in common usage in the West. A key concept is that illness can be caused by one of four difficulties:

- 'Impurities'

- 'Unhealthy lifestyles' which interfere with natural harmony (for example excessive eating, drinking, smoking, stress, lack of sleep)

- 'Interrupting the flow of *Ki*', which is a similar to the vital energy qi already discussed in TCM. This can lead to a deficiency (*kyo*) or an excess (*jitsu*) of this energy in various parts of the body. *Kyo* and *jitsu* are similar to yin and yang in TCM; we are ill when both are out of sync

- 'Spiritual Influences' are similar to those already discussed in ayurveda, whereby karma can be the cause of illness in this life

JTM therapies include Japanese acupuncture, herbal remedies (called *kanpo* therapies), massage (particularly shiatsu), diet, Zen-type meditation, warming therapies using oils, and spiritual rituals (such as reiki). Once again, scientific evidence is absent for some of the basic ideas behind JTM, although there is plenty of evidence to support the lifestyle issues mentioned.

TIBETAN TRADITIONAL MEDICINE (TTM) originates in Tibet and is over 2,500 years old. It was introduced into the Western consciousness by the Dalai Lama, spiritual and political leader in exile of the Tibetan people. TTM has its roots in Tibetan Buddhism, an offshoot of Indian Buddhism, which began in India in the fifth century BC and was influenced subsequently by Chinese and Persian medical concepts. Its physicians are usually Buddhist monks. At its core is the concept of a healthy balanced life, again achieved through moderate behaviour, diet, emotional calm and spiritual health.

In TTM, illness is caused by 'human ignorance' due to 'lack of enlightenment', leading to three negative thoughts, which disrupt our peace of mind. These are as follows:

- DESIRE (Attachment): This relates to possessing material things, people, or the search for permanent happiness

- HATRED (Aversion): Disliking or avoiding things, people, pain or unhappiness

- IGNORANCE (Confusion): This relates to indecision, mental confusion and listlessness

These negative thoughts can affect three types of energy or 'humours' that play a role in how our physical organs and systems work, and patients are categorised into one of these types. In terms of therapies, TTM makes use of diet, behavioural changes, herbal remedies, meditation, spiritual healing and acupuncture. Science cannot explain the underlying basis for this therapy system, which has at its roots a spiritual approach. It has, however, been able to show the power of meditation in particular in strengthening mental and physical health.

It is interesting to compare these traditional systems to our Western one. In the East, these therapies have been incorporated into a way of life with a strong spiritual underpinning, whether it is Hinduism, Buddhism or Daoism. In the West, medicine has become very scientific in basis and is largely detached from either spirituality or the individual as a whole. Both East and West have much to learn from each other. Ideally, a symbiotic relationship between both is required. Nowhere is this more relevant than with regard to illnesses affecting the mind.

A New Holistic Mental Health Therapy Pathway

Is it possible to combine the therapies examined and merge them into a new holistic mental-health therapy pathway? This is without doubt an ambitious task. I feel, however, that, if examined from a scientific standpoint, it is possible to put together an effective and clinically acceptable package. This might form the basis of a completely new approach.

When discussing a holistic approach, there is one big difference between East and West. The spiritual and religious ethos the person lives in and subscribes to serves as a leading factor in the health, both physical and mental, of those adhering to Eastern medicine. In the West, by contrast, there is usually a clear line of demarcation between spirituality and medicine and so, when discussing this united model, we will endeavour not to include specific spiritual pathways. Rather, we will assume that healing will occur within the individual's cultural/religious ethos. We also have to accept that age and social/environmental circumstances are critical when laying out a particular pathway for mental-health difficulties. This is of significance when assessing therapy options for the young and elderly, both of which have to be approached differently.

If you are reading this book while suffering from mental-health difficulties, I suggest that you consider the following model carefully. Pick out areas you feel will be of most benefit. In particular, read carefully the 'foundations' and do not dismiss these and move on to the next stage. Without a solid base, most buildings will collapse; successful therapy approaches are no different. With these concepts at the forefront, and given our current state of scientific knowledge, I propose the following holistic therapy pathway portrayed as a pyramid (Figure 28). If we examine this diagram, there is no mention of alternative therapies; in practice, they are absorbed into the therapy blocks mentioned.

THE FOUNDATIONS: In order to rebuild mental health, successful therapy systems must be based on solid foundations. The two most important are empathy (including the placebo effect) and lifestyle changes.

EMPATHY/PLACEBO PATHWAYS: If you are suffering from mental distress such as depression, find a therapist, doctor or healer who can empathise with you. Without this trust and mirroring of minds, it will be difficult to find your own way back to health. The importance of empathy lies in the power of the emotional brain to overrule the logical one. When our emotional brain goes into 'negative mode', it is difficult to switch it off. Through empathy, we can verbalise our distress, allowing our logical brain the opportunity to rationalise these thoughts, reshaping brain pathways as a result. This process cannot be achieved alone. If you are in difficulty, seek out a sympathetic, empathetic healer. Silence means that emotional pain will flourish and prosper.

One way of looking at empathy is to consider, as in the case of somebody coming for help to a family doctor or therapist during a bout of depression, that there are two experts in the room. The person with depression is expert on what it is like to feel down, both physically and mentally. The therapist is probably not an expert in the experience of depression; but rather in helping the person with depression recover. When both share their respective experiences, a meeting of minds occurs, and together they can hammer out a solution.

The placebo effect, the belief that a particular therapy will be of help, is also important in all therapy systems, activating key parts of the brain in a positive manner. Successful therapies will involve activating such pathways, as distinct from the actual mechanism of the therapy itself. The placebo effect will usually wane after a variable period of time, usually one to two months. It is strengthened by empathy bonds with the therapist. Empathy and the placebo effect go hand in hand, accounting for a much greater percentage of successful therapies in both Eastern and Western medicine systems than is generally perceived.

LIFESTYLE CHANGES: This is an area of common ground between both conventional and alternative therapies and Eastern and Western approaches. It is the least discussed yet arguably the most important foundation for any successful mental-health therapy system.

DIET: The basis for many Eastern systems for thousands of years. Recently, there has been an explosion of interest in this area from the West, with a renewed emphasis being placed on the importance of a healthy balanced diet in the treatment of illness. Within the area of mental health, research continues into the importance of eggs (important for memory pathways), fruit, meat, vegetables, fish, the role of B vitamins, and Omega 3 fish oils.

EXERCISE: Eastern medicine has recognised the importance of exercise for thousands of years, integrating it into its approach. Western medicine has always supported exercise as being good for the heart and useful in reducing obesity. Yet it has only in the past decade begun to grasp, through research data, the importance of this therapy to the brain itself: particularly in depression. We now accept the great power of exercise to alter brain pathways epigenetically. I cannot recommend exercise strongly enough. It should be built in as both a treatment in itself and as a preventative measure for many mental-health problems. My recommendation (backed up by research) is that thirty minutes per day (at least three to five times a week) of some form of physical exercise is of paramount importance in the maintenance of good mental health.

RELAXATION THERAPIES: For thousands of years, the East has recognised the importance of therapies which calm and soothe the mind, and many of the best known of these are being absorbed into Western culture. Massage of all types, such as shiatsu, reflexology and Indian head massage, have a place in helping to reduce stress and calm down the emotional brain. Yoga is another excellent relaxation therapy, as is aromatherapy with or without massage. Breathing exercises, so often recommended by psychologists for anxiety, have also been widely used in Eastern traditions and are of great help to many.

MODERATION THERAPY: In the West, the idea of moderation being a form of therapy seems absurd. In the East, being moderate in all areas of life is an innate part of therapy systems, with many considering some illnesses as being created by lifestyles excesses. In Ireland, the concept of moderation is not easy to grasp. The concept of balance in our lives is one we would do well to import from ancient Eastern traditions, where they have grasped the importance of enjoying life's pleasures without having to gorge. Eating sensibly, getting sufficient rest and sleep, enjoying sex and alcohol sensibly, trying to be moderate in our desire for possessions, and avoiding unnecessary stress in our lives are all recommended ways of maintaining this life balance.

THE MAIN STRUCTURE: Let's now examine the main building blocks of our holistic pathway: drug and talk therapies.

DRUG THERAPIES: As discussed earlier, these include all forms of conventional and alternative medicines. In the West, this has always been the most controversial form of therapy for tackling mental-health difficulties. Yet for thousands of years, traditional-medicine systems have included herbal treatments as part of their package. What are herbs, if not a plant form of drug therapy? Part of the objections to drug therapy in the West is the perception that we cannot relieve mental health problems using medication. This of course implies that only 'talk therapies' can deal with such conditions. While sharing concerns about using drug therapy as a stand-alone treatment, I feel that many of these objections are based on misconceptions about the nature of illnesses like depression. They also ignore research into how therapies 'change' pathways in the brain, which we are only at an infant stage of understanding. There is great confusion amongst the general public about the place of drug therapy in mental health. Additionally, there are major divisions within the media itself; so where does the truth lie?

My own opinion, based on years of clinical practice and studying research data on the effects of all therapies on the brain, is that drug therapy has a definite role to play in treating mental illness as part of a holistic package. Removing it would condemn countless people to long periods of emotional and physical pain and suffering. Accepting this, I would be first to recognise the limitations of drug therapy as an isolated treatment. No pharmaceutical, herbal or homeopathic remedy can ever 'solve' complex mental-health difficulties. Without the solid foundations of empathy and lifestyle, drug therapy will struggle to be effective. Similarly, most people respond best to a combination of talk and drug therapy. The basis for using drug therapy, in whatever form, is to help the person with depression, for example, to deal with physical and psychological symptoms that can often be paralysing in nature. These often prevent the person in trouble from engaging with the crucial talk therapies many will need to access.

It is difficult for somebody who is very depressed, and may as a result be completely exhausted, and unable to concentrate, eat, sleep or memorise, to engage with talk therapies. However, if we ally drug therapy to a solid foundation, within four to six weeks many are well enough to become involved with them. The lower brain circuit responds best to drug therapy; the upper to talk therapies. The stimulation of both is ideal.

There will always be a role for drug therapies in Western and Eastern medicine systems. The sooner we stop isolating this one form of therapy and denigrating it, but instead build it into a solid holistic package, the more people in distress will receive the assistance they deserve. If you are reading this, suffering from an illness like depression and confused about whether to accept conventional drug therapies, I strongly advise you to make up your own mind about their usefulness. Do not allow others to deny you a useful tool on the road back to recovery.

TALK THERAPIES can, as part of a holistic package, transform the lives of many people with mental-health problems. At the heart of talk therapies lies the Rogerian concept that 'all that many of us need to deal with emotional distress is proper information and support'. Information on its own is very helpful but when combined with warm encouragement from a counsellor, therapist or family doctor, it becomes easier for the person to escape from the maze. The modern scientific realisation that various forms of talk therapy have the capacity to reshape brain pathways is exciting. This has allowed us to absorb talk therapies into our 'common holistic pathway'. As discussed earlier, talk therapies include counselling, CBT, interpersonal therapy, psychoanalytical therapy, brief interventional psychotherapy, self-help groups and family therapy.

Our holistic therapy pathway involves solid foundations of empathy and major lifestyle changes, with huge overlap between Eastern and Western medicine systems in relation to both. The twin pillars of drug and talk therapies sit comfortably on top of these foundations. Each person in difficulty will require different 'concoctions' of these therapies, all acting on final common brain pathways.

4

The Anxiety Pathway

Anxiety is a major cause of distress and emotional turmoil for many. It is also innate to the human condition. All of us experience periods of acute and chronic anxiety, usually caused by specific events, e.g. exams, interviews or financial difficulty. For a substantial number of people, anxiety can become an unhealthy phenomenon and can severely interfere with normal life.

The roots of anxiety can often be traced back to experiences in early life – a powerful example of epigenetics in action. There is conflict between talk therapists and doctors about the nature of anxiety disorders, both in relation to cause and treatment. Therapists regard anxiety as a normal emotion, and only intervene if it is causing the person difficulties in his or her life. Health professionals regard anxiety disorders as illnesses. So who is right? In practice, both are partially correct; it is a question of interpretation and language.

In a brilliant lecture at a No Panic conference in Dublin in 2008, Prof. Paul Salkovskis, a leading world psychological expert in the treatment of anxiety disorders, made some excellent observations I feel are relevant here:

- Anxiety is a normal reaction.

- Feelings of anxiety are normal under threat.

- Physical changes are a normal part of this anxiety response.

- Avoidance and escape to safety are a normal reaction to anxiety.

- Anxiety becomes a clinical problem only when it is severe and persistent.

- Anxiety disorders, in his opinion, are exaggerations of normal emotional reactions, not an 'inherited brain disease'.

- Anxiety disorders can destroy the hopes and dreams of many sufferers.

- Anxiety involves the whole gamut of genes, epigenetics and environment so let's examine the pathways involved.

The Anxiety Pathways

From Freud to the present, debate has raged as to whether anxiety is an inherited trait or a product of our upbringing. Thankfully, epigenetics has at last put this to bed. Our anxiety pathways are formed by a subtle mixture of genetic traits, with upbringing and environment playing an important role in increasing or decreasing the potential of these genes to switch on or off.

It has been known for some time that some babies demonstrate evidence of anxiety shortly after birth. As far back as the 1970s, psychologist Jerome Kagan controversially demonstrated that some babies were more 'inhibited' in their emotional responses. Later, he showed how some of these showed increased levels of shyness and social inhibition in comparison with babies who did not demonstrate these traits. For a long time, this was assumed to be a genetically inherited trait. Now it is recognised that whether or not this trait is expressed into adult life depends on the type of upbringing the child experiences.

In the first few years of life, the big players in our emotional development are the stress box in our limbic brain and the social control box in our logical brain. Our spindle cells and mirror neuron system also both play crucial roles in how our emotional pathways develop. The bonding hormone oxytocin, released in large amounts in the infant's brain by positive maternal interaction, also plays a part. In some cases, our stress box may be genetically more vulnerable from the beginning or, may be overactive, as in the cases of the babies mentioned above. In a secure, calm family environment, the spindle-cell system allows the social control box gradually to modulate the stress box, reducing the chances in later childhood and adult life of unhealthy anxiety developing. Where the child grows up in an anxious, perfectionist, abusive or emotionally cold environment, underlying traits may be highlighted. In such cases, the ability of the social control box to calm down the stress box is reduced, and the person may go on to develop anxiety difficulties. One fascinating possibility as to how this might work in practice involves our stress hormone, glucocortisol. Because the stress box controls our stress pathways, overactivity of this in childhood may be involved in unhealthy pathways being set up, by dampening down the normal control mechanisms of the spindle cells/social control box. It is now known that the latter are particularly susceptible to high levels of glucocortisol and that what happens to us in early childhood may have longer-term consequences than was hitherto thought.

Increasingly, we are learning how environmental factors like the ones mentioned above are combining with genetic traits through epigenetic mechanisms to form the crucial brain pathways underlying anxiety. For decades, psychologists have insisted that early childhood experiences are more important than genetic traits, and now we are beginning to see the potential mechanisms that are involved.

We cannot overlook, however, the influence that genetic inheritance has: our earlier example dealt with the resilience gene. There are, in many cases, strong family histories suggesting a genetic pattern to anxiety disorders, but it looks increasingly as if the triggering or not of resilience-type genes is highly dependent on upbringing and early environment.

As we advance through the various stages of life's journey, we find that modifying environmental influences can either strengthen or weaken anxiety pathways that have already been set down. This is done through epigenetics. Although pathways become fairly fixed by twenty-five, they remain wonderfully adaptive and can be modulated by positive changes in a person's environment and varying therapy approaches.

Many people with anxiety disorders can trace their difficulties back to childhood. People may develop anxiety disorders in adulthood for different reasons. Sometimes these disorders develop in response to powerful environmental triggers such as addiction, trauma, bullying and so on. A classic example is the common occurrence of panic attacks in people who have developed alcohol or substance problems. We may even begin to see it for the first time in the elderly for biological and social reasons.

When anxiety pathways are triggered, the stress box will be overactive, overruling the social control and logical boxes, triggering emotional feelings of anxiety, and the instinctive behavioural reactions of safety and avoidance. It also leads to our stress system releasing adrenalin in acute anxiety, and glucocortisol in more chronic cases. Both contribute to the physical symptoms lying at the heart of anxiety (Figure 29). It becomes obvious that the lower brain circuit is really running the show in anxiety; the upper circuit is struggling to regain control. This is a classic example of the power of the emotional over the logical brain. It explains why CBT in particular is so effective in dealing with most forms of anxiety; it allows the logical brain to rationalise the activities of the emotional brain.

The Role of Our Holistic Therapy Pathway in Anxiety

In terms of foundations, it is vital that one finds a therapist or doctor with whom one feels empathy. Self-help information is useful but limited without the advice and support of an expert in the field. In the area of lifestyle, exercise is of particular help to those who suffer from chronic anxiety. Nutrition is often overlooked in anxiety: many suffering from the condition struggle to eat properly. Supplements like Omega 3 fish oils are helpful. Moderation is another vital lifestyle issue, because many with anxiety disorders misuse and abuse alcohol (and occasionally drugs), leading to further problems. I also counsel against stimulants like coffee, caffeinated soft drinks and chocolate, all of which 'hype up' an already busy stress system. Reviewing the role of stress in our lives is another key lifestyle foundation. This may involve getting sufficient rest, sleep and breaks from our busy working or home life.

In the area of drug therapy, the standard drugs of choice for decades have unfortunately been tranquillisers, which are often quite addictive. They act on GABA receptors in the brain, particularly in the stress box, which leads to a calming of the whole lower brain circuit. They can be helpful in acute short-term anxiety situations but are felt to be more a hindrance than a help by most experts in the field.

Modern antidepressants, particularly SSRIs are useful in severe cases of chronic anxiety. With the exception of OCD, however, these are not advisable for long-term use in most cases, as talk therapies may be more useful. They are also recommended by some specialists for panic attacks, but CBT is generally a much better route to travel. Lyrica (Pregbalin), a new drug for use in general anxiety, looks interesting, but we will have to assess it over time to ascertain its safety profile and long-term effectiveness.

In terms of alternative therapy options, the two main drug therapies are herbal and homeopathic remedies. One of the difficulties with herbal therapies is the variation in quality and quantity of the active ingredients. The most common herbal remedy recommended for anxiety is valerian; there is some evidence that it has anxiolytic (i.e. anxiety relieving) effects. Others include St John's wort, chamomile and lemon balm. My concerns regarding homeopathic cures and their mechanisms have already been discussed, but there are some who will feel they are of assistance. My own opinion is that drug therapy, either conventional or alternative, has a limited role in most cases of anxiety, with OCD being the exception.

Massage in all its forms – reflexology, Indian head massage, shiatsu and aromatherapy massage – are all helpful in anxiety. However, I feel that their effects are more likely to be of shorter duration in comparison with conventional medicine. Meditation in its various forms, particularly mindfulness, is very helpful in dealing with symptoms of anxiety. Yoga is another beneficial therapy, combining exercises, relaxation techniques and meditation.

In the area of anxiety, talk therapies are often more helpful. Counselling can be of assistance, particularly if there are associated conditions present. Most psychologists would feel that the treatment of choice is definitely CBT in all its forms. As a general rule, panic attacks and phobias are best treated with Beck approaches; generalised anxiety disorder and social phobias with Ellis. All will involve behavioural changes. Group therapy and self-help groups like No Panic can also prove quite useful in this area.

Chronic Anxiety Disorders

Most of us undergo periods where we become anxious or stressed about specific issues and problems. Others, however, find their lives overrun with persistent, chronic anxiety. In some cases, this is undiagnosed, even unnoticed by the sufferer, who learns to regard it as 'normal'.

Generalised Anxiety Disorder

Seventy thousand people in Ireland are experiencing symptoms of this disorder at any one time. After writing about it in the *Irish Times* health supplement, I was astonished by the response – from women in particular (it affects twice as many women as men).

GENERALISED ANXIETY DISORDER: (GAD) is a state of chronic anxiety where the person presents with persistent feelings of:

- intense anxiety and foreboding

- excessive worry about their health, family or job

- a constant sense of impending disaster

This is often combined with the following physical or psychological set of symptoms, many more distressing than the above:

- Mental and physical fatigue, in some cases extreme

- Poor concentration

- Difficulties with memory

- Muscle tension

- Restlessness, tremors

- Sleep difficulties (in up to 70 percent of sufferers), often associated with nightmares and teeth grinding

- Indecisiveness

- Hyper-vigilance at all times

- Regularly avoiding situations in everyday life due to fatigue and worrying about one's ability to cope

- Never wanting to begin a new task and worrying that they will not have the energy to finish it; they thus become apathetic about such ventures, which in turn limits the richness of their life

- Irritable-bowel-type symptoms like abdominal pain and loose bowel motions

The sufferer is also vulnerable to bouts of acute anxiety, panic-like episodes, with the following typical physical symptoms:

- Tension headaches

- Constant sighing

- Palpitations

- Stomach cramps and disturbance

- Loss of appetite, with associated weight loss

Severe stress, particularly in relation to loss, major health or financial concerns, will lead to bouts of extreme inner anxiety. All the usual symptoms of GAD are, in such cases, magnified, the person becoming quickly exhausted. It is the mental and physical fatigue that is most underestimated and causes the greatest upset in the life of the person with GAD, and this is often the factor that prompts them to seek help.

Women, especially, begin to accept the above symptoms as normal, living in a twilight world of worry and exhaustion. The situation often worsens with age, and as the mounting stresses of life build up, it takes less and less stress to trigger acute bouts. Many misuse alcohol in order to cope. The wine epidemic amongst women so regularly mentioned by alcohol counsellors as a major issue in modern Ireland has some roots in this often unrecognised disorder. Most sufferers from GAD will experience at least one episode of depression during their life. The good news is that this condition, once recognised, is very amenable to treatment using our holistic therapy pathway.

The pathways leading to this disorder are probably set up from early childhood to produce an over-sensitive stress box which reads all situations through a lens of fear and apprehension. Increasingly, environmental influences are felt to be a major deciding factor as to whether GAD appears later in life.

If we take an overview of the psychological and neurobiological data to date, we can build up the following picture of this illness:

- Some of us are born with genetic predispositions to being anxious.

- Of these, some will be raised in secure, calm households where fear pathways are modulated and the risk of developing this disorder diminishes.

- Others will be raised in more anxious households, difficult social circumstances, or perfectionist, non-validating environments. By the time they are adults, these people develop a hyped-up stress box or fear system and a higher risk of developing GAD.

- In such cases, life's stresses and strains put pressure on coping skills, creating multiple opportunities for the emotional brain to be fearful and negative.

- Higher brain centres (social/emotional and attention/logic boxes) struggle to keep a check on fear pathways and are quickly overruled, so anxiety rules the roost.

- The stress box's state of constant hyper-vigilance leads to the stream of secondary physical symptoms so prevalent in this condition.

- Glucocortisol plays an important role in relation to many of the physical symptoms like fatigue, and high levels during episodes can lead to increased risks of depression, osteoporosis, heart attacks, stroke, infections and other problems.

- Acute stressors can further trigger this system, activating our automatic nervous system, releasing adrenalin and leading to typical symptoms of acute anxiety.

- Once this general anxiety pathway is set in motion from the late teens/early twenties onwards, our emotional brain/lower mood circuit will endlessly perpetuate the process unless we identify it and make relevant changes.

- This explains why matters deteriorate as we get older, as stresses build up and the GAD pathway strengthens.

- The positive news is that major changes in relation to thinking and behaviour can be made, reshaping this negative path and transforming lives in the process.

How can our holistic therapy pathway help?

FOUNDATIONS: Find a doctor or therapist you can empathise with. This is particularly important in GAD, as it can be a difficult condition to explain. Women find it difficult, and men virtually impossible, to admit that anxiety is taking over their lives. Being comfortable that one will be listened to and empathised with makes this much easier. Often, men will only admit that they are stressed – and even do this with difficulty. This is partly due to the way they are hard-wired. For a man to express anxiety implies weakness, and so it is common that anxiety, like depression, will remain hidden, buried under a sea of alcohol. But stress and anxiety, as CBT therapists will often point out, are simply two sides of the same coin, involving the same stress system in the body.

Start by detailing your physical symptoms and heightened states of worry and apprehension. If you get a cynical or negative response, look further afield. If you are experiencing these symptoms, you are not imagining them or going mad: you are simply suffering from GAD.

Lifestyle is an area where some alternative therapies can play a constructive role. I encourage regular exercise and emphasise the importance of diet. I am a strong believer in B vitamins and Omega 3 fish-oil supplements, particularly for fatigue. I am against any form of 'wonder diet', which is often counter-productive. All forms of massage and aromatherapy are of benefit but probably need to be performed on an extremely regular basis in order to be effective. Japanese and Tibetan traditional medicine systems stress the importance of moderation: nowhere is this more important than in GAD. The major danger is gradual reliance on alcohol as a coping or avoidant mechanism. This in turn can lead to addiction and depression. Similarly, the use of drugs, whether legal or illegal, has to be rejected for similar reasons.

Less obvious but sometimes just as problematic is a reliance on caffeine as a stimulant to ease fatigue in particular. Another crutch may be chocolate or high-sugar 'hits'. While these are relatively harmless in themselves, their use in GAD can become a problem as they hype up an already overactive stress box and system, worsening physical symptoms. Learning to be kind to ourselves is another key foundation, as many with this disorder blame themselves excessively. We also need to examine our lives in order to try to reduce unnecessary stress.

DRUG THERAPIES have a place in the treatment of GAD but are less effective than talk therapies. Below are the five main groups, three conventional and two alternatives:

(A) MINOR TRANQUILLISERS: These drugs combat GAD by acting on GABA receptors to relax the stress box and calm down the lower mood circuit. They have an immediate effect, which makes them popular with anxiety sufferers. Tranquillisers can be useful for short periods, but long-term use can lead to addiction, perpetuating the problem.

(B) ANTIDEPRESSANTS: The main drugs used nowadays are the SSRIs, of which Escitalopram is the most commonly used. These drugs have been shown to decrease symptoms of anxiety by increasing activity in the serotonin mood cable, which calms the stress box, pathways and lower mood circuit. Where there are profound physical symptoms such as intractable irritable bowel syndrome, complete exhaustion or associated low mood in particular, these drugs can be extremely useful. My own opinion is that they are useful in helping the person with severe GAD arrive at a point where they can become involved in talk therapies. When the latter takes over, they should be removed. In the case of long-term treatment, there is the issue of side effects, particularly sexual ones.

(C) LYRICA is a drug mentioned earlier which in the past has been used to treat chronic pain but is now used as a therapy to relieve symptoms of GAD. It is fast-acting and non-addictive. It has side effects yet seems relatively safe, but only with time will we able to determine its usefulness.

(D) HERBAL REMEDIES: We have examined in detail the pros and cons associated with alternative herbal remedies. St John's wort is used in some countries to relieve the symptoms of GAD; this comes as no surprise, as it mimics actions of the SSRIs. But as discussed, it has its own dangers and interactions.

(E) HOMEOPATHY: There are a number of homeopathy treatments available, all of which are probably having a placebo effect, although some people may find them of help.

TALK THERAPIES are particularly helpful in this condition. In general, psychoanalytical talk therapies and counselling have less to offer than more targeted CBT exercises. I have seen the latter transform the lives of those suffering from GAD. I remain to be convinced that hypnotherapy has more to offer than traditional talk therapies.

Let's now examine two examples. As with many other stories of anxiety we will explore, we will examine the role of CBT/CBM; but advise that one must work with a trained health professional like a therapist/doctor to learn how to apply such concepts to one self.

'I'm so tired'

Sue, a thirty-two-year-old primary-school teacher, is a mother of two who attends her GP with the classic opening line: 'I'm constantly tired.' On probing, she admits to being forgetful, lacking concentration, struggling to both start and finish new tasks, and grinding her teeth at night. She also admits to drinking excessive amounts of wine, especially at night, when her exhaustion becomes overwhelming.

Her doctor examines her and performs some blood tests. On her next visit, he explains that there is no underlying anaemia, thyroid disease or diabetes and she is not depressed. He explains that she is suffering from a chronic anxiety state called GAD. He advises possible lifestyle changes like diet, supplements, exercise, severely curtailing her alcohol levels, taking up meditation and yoga, using stress-reducing measures and so on.

Sue mentioned using some homeopathic and herbal remedies from the local alternative health shop. Both seemed to help at the beginning but effects rapidly waned. Her doctor suggests that the real way forward was to explore her thoughts, emotions and behaviour using some simple CBM approaches, and she agrees. He then asks for an example of something that would often trigger a bout. Sue describes how she becomes extremely anxious if one of her children becomes ill. He asks her to be more specific.

'Two weeks ago, Darragh developed a fever and I became extremely anxious,' Sue elaborated. Her doctor nodded. 'And what about him developing a fever bothered you so much?' he asked. Sue explained her primary worry was that he would become very ill; on further probing, her major fear was that he might die. 'So what demands were you making in relation to his fever?' he inquired.

On reflection, Sue replied 'I must be certain he does not get really sick or die.' 'If he did become very ill, then what would that say about you?' her doctor inquired. Sue replied that she would feel very bad about herself. 'Can you tell me how you felt physically when you felt anxious about Darragh?' he asked. Sue explained that she had felt her heart pounding, her stomach in knots, had developed a tension headache and started to feel exhausted. 'How did you behave when Darragh developed his fever?' he inquired. Sue said she stopped eating, became over-protective of him, rang the out-of-hours doctor on two occasions, and couldn't sleep.

Her doctor then explained the 'ABC' concept. Together, they put all the information she had provided into the following format:

A: TRIGGER: Her son developing a fever

INTERPRETATION/ DANGER: He might become very ill or die

B: BELIEF (OR DEMAND): She must be certain her son will not become very ill or die. If this happened, she would feel a complete failure

C: EMOTION: Anxiety

PHYSICAL SYMPTOMS: Stomach in knots, tension headache, palpitations, difficulties sleeping, difficulties breathing and so on. In particular, she becomes very fatigued

BEHAVIOUR: Stops eating, becomes over-protective of her son, seeks reassurance he is not going to die by calling the doctor on duty

Her doctor then explains that he is firstly going to challenge her behaviour, then he will challenge the demand 'her son must not become very ill or die; if he did she would have failed him and she would feel awful about herself'. He explains that being over-protective of her son will only exacerbate the problem. He goes on to show her the 'Big MACS' (Figure 30) and how they would use them to challenge her demand. He then challenges her 'B' as follows:

'M' stands for 'must'. He explains that people who suffer from anxiety live in the 'land of must', where they use absolute terms like 'ought to', 'have to', 'should', 'must' and so on in relation to much of what happens to them in their lives. He elaborates that when we use absolute terms like 'must', we are generally looking for one of four things: 100 percent certainty, order, security or perfection (often represented by the term 'control'). 'So which of these were you looking for in relation to his fever/illness?' he asked.

Sue, on reflection, decided that she was looking for 100 percent certainty and security that he would not deteriorate and die. He then asked her: 'Can we be 100 percent certain of anything in life? Can you be certain that you will be home in time to cook the family meal this evening?' They agreed that anything could happen; she could have a flat tyre or an accident, and so on. He went on to explain that most of the time we could be 'reasonably certain' that we can achieve stated objectives, but never 'absolutely certain'. 'So let's examine the demand you were making,' he went on. 'Do you think it is a healthy demand?' Sue decided it was not and replied that she would prefer that he would not get very ill or die, but could not demand that this would be so.

They agreed that it was better to have a 'strong preference' rather than the more absolute 'must' because it was a more 'realistic' statement.

'A' STANDS FOR 'AWFUL'. The doctor went on to explain that many who suffer from anxiety imagine the worst-case scenario: 'If you feel there is a tiny chance that something will go wrong and there is a much bigger chance that it won't, you will spend all your time and effort reflecting on the former.'

Sue immediately recognised herself here. 'I spend so much of every day worrying about all kinds of things that never come to fruition,' she commented. 'In that way, I am very like my mother, who always worried about our health.' He then asked her what it was about Darragh's illness that she worried about, and she replied that she often visualised him dead, even in the coffin. 'Do you feel that when he has a fever there is a high chance that something terrible will happen?' he asked. Sue replied that on looking at his fever logically, the chances of him having a serious illness or dying were very slight indeed.

'C' STANDS FOR 'CAN'T STAND IT', and is quite common in those who suffer from anxiety. Sue agrees that she regularly feels that she would not be able to cope if her son became very ill. 'I just would disintegrate and wouldn't be able to handle how I would feel.' 'Suppose Darragh did actually become very ill?' asked her doctor. 'Would you cope if you had to?' Sue replied that she would have to because it would be her duty as a mother, otherwise he might get worse. 'So you might not cope the way you think you should, but you would cope,' he queried. Sue replied that she would.

'S' STANDS FOR 'SELF/OTHER RATING': and lies at the heart of anxiety and indeed depression. This is where we not only judge ourselves but accept other's opinions of us as well. 'Where do you rate yourself between one and a hundred,' (Figure 31), the doctor asked. Sue replied that she in general would rate herself quite highly, probably around eighty, and felt that others rated her 'around the same'. The doctor continued: 'And if Darragh became very ill, where would you rate yourself?' Sue replied that she would drop her rating down to ten, with the same rating from others.

'And now for the most important message of the day,' said her doctor; 'can we rate a human being? What is this measuring tool?' Sue on reflection agreed that we can't, as we are too complex. He then went on to ask her if she would like to join a very special club called the 'Raggy Doll Club' (Figure 32). He went on to explain that this was a highly exclusive club of which he himself had been a member for many years. 'But there are two important criteria if a person is to be allowed in as a member. Firstly, we cannot rate ourselves, and secondly, we cannot accept other people's rating of us.' He went on to explain that the Raggy Doll Club was a concept created by leading CBT therapist Enda Murphy, loosely based on a former TV cartoon series. The Raggy Dolls were the 'rejects' in the basket that nobody felt were important, and the series was about their adventures.

He explained that he was a member – just a normal human being, and fallible, who tried to do his best. He accepted that he would make mistakes; on some occasions, he would get it right, on others he would not. All the time, he must accept that he couldn't judge or rate himself, no matter what happened. He also would not accept other people's rating of him. In life, he explained, we can rate our own behaviour, but we cannot rate ourselves.

Sue exclaimed: 'But who else is a member of this club, and how do I join? It sounds like a lovely place to be.' He smiled. 'The other members of the club are the rest of the human race. All of us are fallible, imperfect and at the mercy of the arrows that life throws. We have to learn to accept ourselves unconditionally. It is easy to join. Membership is free and makes us invulnerable to life's arrows.' Sue began to smile, realising the power of the allegory. 'I want to join,' she decided.

Her doctor explained that the example of her son's illness was a microcosm of what happens to us when we became ego-anxious. If she could apply the lessons learned, she could reshape her thoughts and feelings. She would have to do a lot of work over a period of time if she wanted to get better: 'The skill of life is not learning how to succeed, but how to fail.' Sue was enthusiastic and agreed to continue. He asked her to keep a notebook where she would document the periods when she would became very anxious, in the 'ABC' manner they had worked on earlier.

Six months later, after a series of such sessions, Sue was experiencing much less anxiety and fatigue and was recognising the triggers and demands much more easily. She had become much more realistic in the demands she placed on herself and had found herself (as suggested by her doctor) a real-life Raggy Doll with whom she regularly communicated when she found she was rating herself. She also learned about mindfulness and began to practise the three-minute breathing space regularly each day (see page 67).

Sue still suffers from GAD and acute stressors will still occasionally throw her off line, but overall she has reshaped her pathways and is now able to incorporate these ideas into her life. More importantly, she has a technique to deal with any issues that arise and can return to her doctor if she gets into difficulties. She has also built into her life some key lifestyle change: she exercises regularly, eats better and takes fish oils. She has significantly moderated her wine consumption, avoids caffeine, practises yoga, enjoys massage as a de-stressor, and has taken up painting to fulfil the creative side of her personality. Her yellow flag is slowly turning to green.

'I must be certain'

Carol is thirty-three and comes from a background where her widowed mother had struggled both with anxiety and in making ends meet. This has led Carol to being insecure, always struggling to be in control of every part of her life, particularly finances. This has led her into the world of GAD. She is married with three children and combines a busy home life with a part-time job as a receptionist.

She presents to her doctor complaining of a number of symptoms: extreme exhaustion, irritable bowel, teeth grinding at night with secondary facial pain, becoming increasingly forgetful, and difficulty concentrating. She has also lost some weight. A good friend has become concerned that she might be developing depression and suggests that she go for help.

Before arriving at her doctor, Carol has spent a fortune on alternative remedies, ranging from homeopathy and hypnotherapy to aromatherapy and reflexology but had slipped further into trouble. She had, on advice from an alternative therapist, tried St John's wort but had stopped following a negative reaction.

She opens up to her doctor and shares her fear that she has become depressed, detailing the therapies she has tried. She also requests some blood tests and wonders if medication is the way forward. He listens to her story, examines her and does some blood tests. He explains that he does not feel she is depressed, as her mood itself seems normal. She may be suffering from a more general form of anxiety called GAD. 'In relation to using drug therapy, it is something we can consider if other therapies are not helping or if depression itself were to appear. But because you reacted badly to St John's wort, I would be inclined to avoid it.' He gives her general lifestyle advice on diet, exercise, supplements, moderation in alcohol and yoga/meditation therapies. She agrees to participate in some talk therapy in the form of CBM exercises.

She gives him the example of hearing from a friend that a close associate had just been let go as a result of the recession, which made her feel very anxious. 'And what was it about this news that bothered you?' he asks. Carol explained that she began to worry that she would be let go. She elaborated that they would struggle to pay their mortgage, and might lose the house, and she could see them on the street if this happened. 'So what demand did you make in relation to this news?' he asked. Carol replied that she must not lose her job for all the above reasons. 'And what would it say about yourself if you did lose your job?' he inquired. Carol replied that she would feel like a complete failure and very bad about herself. 'So what did you do, when you started to become very anxious?' he asked. Carol admitted ringing a work colleague for reassurance, checking out insurance cover on their house, drinking wine to calm herself down, putting her dinner in the bin, and being able to get to sleep only after hours spent replaying numerous scenarios as to what would happen if she was actually let go.

Her doctor then explained the 'ABC' system and put the information that had been gathered into the following format:

A: TRIGGER: The news that an associate had lost their job

INTERPRETATION/DANGER: That she herself would lose her job, that they as a unit would be unable to pay their mortgage, and that they would lose the family home and end up homeless

B: BELIEF/DEMAND: She must not lose her job, and if she did, she would regard herself as a failure

C: EMOTION: Anxiety

PHYSICAL SYMPTOMS: Stomach in knots, tension headache, palpitations, difficulties sleeping, difficulties breathing, and extreme fatigue

BEHAVIOUR: Rings work colleague, checks mortgage insurance, stops eating, drinks wine to calm her down, has difficulty eating and sleeping

Her doctor challenges initially her behaviour, and then her unhealthy belief/demands, using the 'Big MACS' system discussed above, and explains how these things were contributing to her anxiety.

M: He challenged her need for 100 percent certainty she would never lose her job. Was her need for 100 percent security in relation to their financial situation possible in this or any other area of their lives?

A: He challenged her assumption that the worst would inevitably happen and that she was certain to lose her job, when there was no clear evidence to back this up. What would she do if she lost her job?

C: He challenged her view that she would not be able to cope if this actually happened.

S: Finally, he challenged the concept that if she did lose her job, this would make her a failure, by introducing her to the Raggy Doll Club.

Carol begins to see the pattern. As a result of this and similar sessions over the next six months, she reshapes her thinking and becomes less anxious and fatigued. Her doctor introduces the concept of mindfulness and gives her some tapes to practise with. She begins to perform the three-minute breathing space on a daily basis and finds it very helpful. This, together with all the other lifestyle changes above, transforms her life. She still gets anxious but is now able to use the 'ABC' system to challenge stressors that come along. She still uses alternative therapies but is more realistic about their place. She has also become a fully fledged member of the Raggy Doll Club.

In general, the person with GAD lives in a world where they make impossible demands on themselves, on others and on the world in general. They imagine the worst-case scenarios and cannot cope if all is not as it should be. Most importantly, they allow themselves to be rated either by themselves or others. This is the psychological source of their problems and the physical symptoms that follow, in particular fatigue.

Post Traumatic Stress Disorder

All of us will experience traumatic and stressful periods in our lives and manage them accordingly. But following particularly traumatic occurrences, some will develop chronic persistent anxiety, called PTSD (Post Traumatic Stress Disorder). This is more likely to occur following severe accidents (e.g. major road-traffic accidents), assaults, rape, war, and so on, and when there has been a definite threat to the life of the sufferer or his family. A diagnosis is made only when symptoms are present for over six months.

Following such events, the sufferer complains of constant 'flashbacks' and nightmares relating to the event and a tendency to avoid thinking or dealing with the matter. Muscle pains, headaches and panicky feelings are typical physical symptoms of this condition. Others may feel down, ashamed or 'guilty' that they have survived the event. Many find themselves feeling 'on guard' all the time, constantly scanning their environment for danger signals. Many have difficulties with sleep and use alcohol to blot out how they feel. PTSD can affect some people for the rest of their lives. But the central message of this book, that we can change our pathways, is particularly relevant here. How can our holistic therapy pathway help?

FOUNDATIONS: As always, finding a doctor or therapist with whom you find empathy is essential. Lifestyle changes like exercise, nutrition and moderation of alcohol are extremely helpful. In the area of alternative and complementary medicine, there are many therapies, like massage, yoga, pilates and meditation, which can reduce symptoms of anxiety but on their own will not deal with the problem.

DRUG THERAPIES: Once again, these have their place but will rarely, on their own, be sufficient in the absence of talk therapy. The two main groups in the conventional area are the SSRI antidepressants and tranquillisers. I have no difficulty with the first if the person is extremely distressed by the anxiety symptoms, but have major concerns about the latter, due to the risks of long-term addiction. Recently, the use of drugs called beta blockers (which were traditionally used for treating blood pressure and palpitations) has been found to be of assistance in eliminating distressing memories. It will take time to see if this option will prove beneficial in practice. In the alternative area, the usual suspects like St John's wort and various homeopathic remedies are used.

TALK THERAPIES: Counselling and other talk therapies can sometimes be of help, particularly in abuse situations. CBT, where we challenge the sufferer's thinking and behaviour, is the treatment of choice, as we will see in the example below. In the alternative area, the controversial therapy of EMDR is the most popular.

'I can still see the truck'

Michael is brought to the doctor by his wife Maria. She had tried every alternative remedy over the previous year to help Michael and was running out of ideas. He was tired of a stream of therapies, including energy-field therapies, reiki, homeopathy, hypnosis, craniosacral therapy, yoga (which he had found helped him relax, but did not deal with the problem), St John's wort, Chinese and ayurvedic herbs, even EMDR, and was finally happy to open up to his GP.

It became clear that his problems related back to a bad car crash five years before, when he had just left his wife and children off at the swimming pool. On the way back home, he was hit by a truck that suddenly went out of control. Luckily, he steered the car out of a head-on collision but spent two weeks in hospital with a ruptured spleen and everyone telling him that he was lucky to be alive. His doctor outlines the typical symptoms of PTSD and explains what has been going on. The most common flashbacks relate to seeing the truck coming straight for him, and he constantly agonises as to how close he was to being wiped out.

Michael is not keen on drug therapy and his doctor agrees. Together, they draw up the following plans. He will:

- exercise, eat well and cease using alcohol as a coping mechanism.

- continue his yoga and consider taking up mindfulness.

- agree to see a counsellor to discuss his problems.

- return later for a session of CBM to help examine his thoughts and behaviour.

Six weeks later, following some helpful sessions with a counsellor, Michael returns for a CBM session without Maria. They begin with a situation where his anxiety levels soar while he is driving his family around in the car. His doctor explains the 'ABC' system and together they draw up the following analysis of his problem:

A: TRIGGER: Driving his family around in the car

INTERPRETATION OF DANGER: That the same will happen again – another truck or car will go out of control and crash into them with terrible consequences (they will be killed or maimed)

B: BELIEF (OR DEMAND): He must be completely certain that this will not happen again

C: EMOTION: Anxiety

PHYSICAL SYMPTOMS: His stomach is in knots, tension headache, palpitations, difficulties sleeping, difficulties breathing, difficulties talking, and so on.

BEHAVIOUR: He remains in a hyper-vigilant state all the time when driving and avoids taking the family out on busy main roads. His mental radar constantly scans the road for potential danger. He has begun to drive particularly slowly to make sure he will be able to react in time when disaster comes, and freezes when he sees a truck coming. He has nightmares where he visualises it happening again.

His doctor initially challenges his behaviour and they agree that this behaviour is only consolidating the problem. They draw up a number of areas for him to work on in relation to this. They work on his unhealthy belief or demand using the 'Big MACS' and analyse how this is contributing to his anxiety. He challenged his need for 100 percent certainty that he must never have a crash again and gives Michael examples of how impossible a demand this is in real life. They decide instead to use the word *prefer*. This implies that there will always to be a chance, however small, that he could crash again. He then moves on to examine other areas of his life where he is demanding similar 100 percent certainty.

Following a number of visits over the next six months, Michael learns to cease looking for 100 percent certainty in relation to driving and indeed other areas of his life. He also ceases scanning his environment for danger and many of the other safety behaviours he had developed. In time, the image of the truck bearing down on him ceases, and he becomes more relaxed on the road. Thankfully, the queues behind him also cease.

Obsessive Compulsive Disorder

Obsessive Compulsive Disorder (OCD) affects between 20,000 and 30,000 people in Ireland. It is a most distressing anxiety disorder, causing immense difficulties to sufferers and their families and loved ones. Many people have periodic obsessive thoughts and on occasions behave compulsively, particularly those suffering from other forms of anxiety. OCD is different in that it takes over the life of the sufferer. It is characterised by persistent obsessions, with or without compulsions.

Obsessions are intrusive, anxiety-provoking thoughts, ideas or images. Compulsions are repetitive rituals or mental actions performed in response to obsessions in order to decrease anxiety and remove 'contaminants'. Eventually, those suffering from OCD build into their lives a complex series of avoidant and safety behaviours, which create their own set of problems.

People with OCD experience their disturbing thoughts and images as intrusive and troublesome but recognise them as products of their own minds. Although patients report a range of different kinds of obsessions and compulsions, there is a notable consistency of themes. A modern view of the compulsive nature of this illness is to regard it as a form of 'behaviour addiction' similar to other common addictions. Incessant thoughts and compulsions (which the person tries to suppress or avoid) cause major interference with the person's family and working relationships, not to mention their own psychological state. These thoughts are not simply worries about everyday life difficulties; they use up the person's mental energy by causing extreme feelings of anxiety. The tension is only relieved by 'doing what the thoughts demand', but this is incredibly tiring, as the thoughts are never-ending. These obsessive thoughts may relate to:

- Fear over health, particularly personal health.

- Fear of contaminating themselves (with dirt, germs, bodily fluids like blood, faeces or urine, sticky materials). There will also be an over-estimation of the degree of risk of the contaminant.

- Fear of harming themselves or, more distressingly, those close to them (i.e. a mother may worry that she will harm her children).

- Fear of hurting others. Some people, for example, have obsessive fears of committing a terrible act in the future. This may compete with fears that they may already have done something awful in the past.

- Sexual obsessions, such as fear of being gay or a paedophile.

- Religious obsessions, such as fear of offending God.

- Constant fear that something terrible is going to happen.

- Obsessional doubting: the fear of having failed to perform some task adequately and that dire consequences will follow as a result.

Examples of compulsive actions are:

- Cleaning (includes excessive hand-washing or home cleaning)
- Checking (might involve checking light switches or that the front door is locked over and over)
- Counting
- Repeating (words, images or numbers, in the mind)
- Arranging (making sure everything in the room is in exactly the right place, in order to remain in control)
- Making lists
- Hoarding (usually items that are of little intrinsic value)

Compulsions persist. In the short term, they seem to reduce anxiety but eventually they become the problem, as over time they become almost ineffective, so compulsive behaviour has to increase. This is typical of what happens in routine addictions. In OCD, however, this behaviour pattern is not associated with feelings of enjoyment or satisfaction, rather a sense of relief, even if it is short-term. Washing compulsions are commonly associated with contamination obsessions. For example, a person concerned about contamination from the outside world may shower and launder all clothing immediately upon coming home. The compulsion may be triggered by direct contact with the feared object. In many cases, being in its general vicinity may stir up intense anxiety and a strong need to engage in a washing compulsion. The obsessions and compulsions go hand in hand, as in the example above. The more the person engages in compulsive behaviour to counteract the anxiety caused by the obsession, the more embedded the obsession becomes.

In terms of safety behaviours, simple examples would be using tissues to avoid touching handles, touching people or things only if you are sure it is 'safe'. Avoidant behaviours might involve avoiding contact with toilet seats, handles or taps refusing to pick things off the floor, to name but a few. A simple example of avoidant behaviour can be seen in cases where the main obsession is a fear of germs or dirt. Here, the person may avoid leaving home or allowing visitors to come inside to prevent contact with dirt or germs. People with such contamination obsessions may wear gloves, coats or even masks if they are forced to leave their house for some reason.

OCD can affect both children (as young as ten) and adults. The typical age of onset is late adolescence to early adulthood, with a slight preponderance of women over men. Women have more contamination obsessions and cleaning rituals, while men have more symmetry, ordering and sexual obsessions. Men will usually start earlier in their teens and women may present much later. It is estimated that 2 percent or more of the population can be affected but, despite its prevalence, OCD may not be diagnosed for up to ten years. People who suffer from OCD are often deeply ashamed, going to great lengths to hide their ritualistic behaviours. It may be diagnosed when family members get tired of the impact of the patient's behaviours on their lives and force them to consult a doctor. In other cases, the person may come for help themselves. In some cases, the person will present with depression, a commonly associated illness, with up to 65 percent of sufferers developing it at some stage in their lives.

There has been extraordinary interest in the causes and brain pathways underlying this illness. It is now recognised as a classic example of what can happen when key brain pathways become disrupted. It is clear from the above that the person with OCD 'knows' that their thoughts and actions are not logical but still can't stop them. So as is usual in the area of mental-health distress, the problem lies in the inability of the logical brain to put manners on the more unruly emotional one. Much work has been done through neuroimaging and other research studies to understand this condition. The following have all been shown to be involved in the pathways underlying this illness: the social behavioural, attention and logic boxes, the dopamine mood box and cable, the pleasure and stress boxes and, to a lesser extent, the serotonin mood cable. A full explanation of the complex mechanism described here is best left to the technical section.

There appear to be genetic factors involved in OCD. The families of persons who are diagnosed with the disorder have a greater risk of OCD than do the general population. Childhood-onset OCD appears to run in families more than adult-onset OCD, and twin studies indicate that identical twins are more likely to share the disorder than fraternal twins. The concordance (match) rate between identical twins is not 100 percent, however, which suggests that the occurrence of OCD is affected by environmental as well as genetic factors.

In addition, it is the general nature of OCD that seems to run in families rather than the specific symptoms; thus one family member who is affected by the disorder may have a compulsion about washing and cleaning while another is a compulsive counter.

If one person in a family has OCD, there is a 25 percent chance that another immediate family member has the condition. It also appears that stress and psychological factors may worsen symptoms. A lot of work has been done to elucidate the genes involved, mainly focusing on serotonin and dopamine systems. But no definitive one has been found, so we are probably looking at a polygenetic predisposition. Obviously family upbringing will play a part in how such predispositions might develop and prosper. OCD is a chronic disease that, if untreated, can last for decades and can fluctuate from mild to severe, worsening with age. When treated with a combination of drugs and talk therapy, some patients go into complete remission. Unfortunately, not all patients have such a good response. About 20 percent of people cannot find relief with either therapy. Hospitalisation may be required in some cases. Despite the crippling nature of the symptoms, many successful doctors, businesspeople and entertainers with OCD function well in society. Nevertheless, the emotional and financial cost of the condition can be quite high.

Let's examine how our holistic therapy pathway can help treat this extremely distressing condition. The goal of treatment is to reduce the frequency and severity of obsessions and compulsions so that the patient can work more efficiently and have more time for social activities. Few OCD patients become completely symptom-free, but most benefit considerably from treatment.

FOUNDATIONS: The most important first step is to find a doctor or therapist you can empathise with. In all cases, I encourage regular exercise, emphasise the importance of diet and suggest adding B vitamins or Omega 3 fish-oil supplements, along with all the other lifestyle changes discussed in GAD.

DRUG THERAPIES: It has been recognised for some time that antidepressant drugs, particularly the SSRIs, are very helpful in treating the distressing symptoms of this illness. But they require very high doses and are probably only effective in 50 to 60 percent of cases. They take a minimum of eight to ten weeks in OCD to kick in. It was assumed initially that their mode of action was via the serotonin mood cable. It is now felt to be due to indirect effects on the dopamine system. Some feel that the eight-week lead-in is due to delayed activity in the social control box. Interestingly, drugs that affect the noradrenalin mood cable, while effective in depression, are not effective in OCD.

Small amounts of major tranquillisers like Seroquel, if used in conjunction with the SSRIs, increase the chances of drug therapy being effective. This is again due to effects on the dopamine system. If associated depression is present, the use of antidepressant drug therapy will have a dual function.

In terms of herbal treatments, only St John's wort is felt to be of any assistance in this illness. Because it has effects on serotonin and dopamine, it makes sense that it might be an effective therapy. There is indeed evidence that it may help some people, but we still have all the potential problems associated with its use which we dealt with earlier. I would counsel using SSRIs as a safer alternative. An importance note: if using it, please inform your doctor in order to rule out the risks of drug interactions. I do not feel that homeopathy has any place in the treatment of OCD.

TALK THERAPIES play an important role in the management of this illness but are often more effective when combined with drug therapy. Counselling, behaviour therapy and CBT are of most assistance. Counselling can be helpful to some patients concerned about the consequences of OCD in their personal and social life, and psycho dynamic psychotherapy for the relationships between their upbringing and specific features of their OCD symptoms.

Behavioural treatments using the technique of exposure and response prevention are particularly effective in treating OCD. In this form of therapy, the patient and therapist draw up a list or hierarchy of the patient's obsessive and compulsive symptoms. The symptoms are arranged in order from least to most upsetting. The patient is then systematically exposed to the anxiety-producing thoughts or behaviours, beginning with the least upsetting. They are then asked to endure the feared event or image without engaging in the compulsion that is normally used to lower anxiety.

For example, a person with a contamination obsession might be asked to touch a series of increasingly dirty objects without washing their hands. In this way, the patient learns to tolerate the feared object, reducing both worrisome obsessions and anxiety-reducing compulsions. A substantial number of patients respond well to exposure and response prevention, with very significant reductions in symptoms, but it is a long and difficult road, for both patient and therapist.

CBT is another talk therapy helpful in OCD. By challenging the thoughts, dangers, demands and behaviour of the sufferer, the therapist can often assist the sufferer to achieve a better quality of life. CBT teaches patients how to confront their fears and obsessive thoughts by making the effort to endure or wait out the activities that usually cause anxiety without compulsively performing the calming rituals.

There are similarities between phobias and OCD when one is looking at things from a CBT perspective. Those suffering from both usually worry they will get anxious if exposed to the trigger (i.e. a handle) and will engage in safety and avoidant behaviour to prevent this happening. It is this pattern that CBT hopes to alter. Let's examine two examples:

'I just have to be sure they're clean'

Martin presents to his family doctor with weeping, bleeding hands. His GP diagnoses dermatitis. Martin admits that he is constantly washing his hands during the day till they are clean'. On further discussion, he opens up to a nightmare world of obsessive thoughts that his hands and body are never fully clean; his skin problems are caused by compulsive washing. It had been going on for over ten years but he was ashamed to reveal his inner world for fear of ridicule. His doctor treats his dermatitis but suggests that Martin might be suffering from OCD. He gives him some advice on lifestyle, suggests starting on a course of SSRIs to help reduce the immediate symptoms, and refers him to both a local psychiatrist to confirm the diagnosis and a local CBT therapist for further assistance.

Martin is seen by the psychiatrist, who agrees with the diagnosis and use of drug therapy. He is then referred to an experienced CBT therapist. They decide to deal with a typical situation – when he goes to the toilet – and decide on the following 'ABC' of his problem:

A: TRIGGER: Going to the toilet

    INTERPRETATION/DANGER: That his hands will be covered with germs

B: BELIEF/DEMAND: Must be certain that his hands are clean

C: EMOTION: Anxiety

PHYSICAL SYMPTOMS: Stomach in knots, tension headache, palpitations, difficulties sleeping, difficulties breathing and so on. In particular, he becomes very fatigued.

BEHAVIOUR: Compulsive, ritualistic hand-washing

His therapist challenges both his behaviour and his demand for certainty. They decide that if he does not involve himself in ritualistic hand-washing, he will be faced with uncertainty and unable to cope with this. His therapist asks him for any other area of his life where he looks for 100 percent certainty/control and usually succeeds. Martin notes that he constantly arranges the dishes at home in an exact manner, feeling less anxious when he has done so. His therapist challenges the idea of 100 percent certainty, also introducing him to the Raggy Doll Club. He suggests that Martin asks his partner to start changing little things around the house, disrupting his ideas of 100 percent perfection with a view to reducing his demand for this.

Six months later, following many visits to the therapist and a great deal of hard work on his thinking and behaviour, he has greatly improved, with a drastic reduction in ritualistic hand-washing. His dermatitis has also cleared up.

'I am constantly late for work'

Julia comes to her doctor looking for help. She is in trouble at work due to being constantly late in the mornings and has been given a final warning. On further probing, she reveals that she locks the front door but has to return constantly to check it over and over again. This is to satisfy the obsessive thought that she had forgotten to lock it. Deep down, she knows it is just a thought but is unable to break the behavioural cycle. As a result, she has become incredibly stressed, anxious and fatigued and her mood is beginning to drop.

Her doctor diagnoses her with OCD. Explaining the diagnosis, he gives her advice on lifestyle and decides on a course of SSRIs. He also refers her to a psychiatrist and local specialised CBT therapist for further help. She finally gets to see the latter, and together they draw up the following 'ABC' of her dilemma:

A: TRIGGER: Locking the front door

INTERPRETATION OR DANGER: The door is not locked

B: BELIEF OR DEMAND: Must be certain the door is locked

C: EMOTION: Anxiety

PHYSICAL SYMPTOMS: Stomach in knots, tension headache, palpitations, difficulties sleeping, difficulties breathing, and so on. In particular, she becomes very fatigued

BEHAVIOUR: constant checking and rechecking that the door is locked

Her therapist challenges both her behaviour and her demand for certainty that the door is locked. He looks for other areas of her life where she demands certainty and is usually successful. He challenges the idea of 100 percent certainty. He also gives some behavioural exercises, where Julia has to learn to deal with uncertainty, thus reducing her demand for 100 percent certainty. She attends her therapist regularly over the next six months and begins to notice a real improvement. She is now in time for work.

Acute Anxiety Disorders

These include some of the most common conditions causing mental distress. They are generally poorly understood and poorly managed by laypeople and health professionals. These conditions regularly remain hidden, because many sufferers feel ashamed about disclosing them to loved ones or professionals. Their main unspoken fear is that they are going mad or that others will regard them as being so. Organisations like No Panic reach as many sufferers as possible and, through their helplines, encourage them to seek assistance. Despite this, there are tens of thousands of people in Ireland, male and female, young and not so young, who live in this twilight world. The tragedy is that acute anxiety disorders are eminently treatable, often with simple therapy approaches.

Panic Disorder (Panic Attacks)

Panic disorder affects an estimated 150,000 people in Ireland. It refers to a condition where a person:

- is suffering from recurrent episodes of panic attacks

- is spending a lot of time worrying about the recurrence of such attacks

- experiences a clearly recognisable first episode from which future episodes emanate

Historically, there is evidence of recognition of the nature of panic attacks by ancient Greeks as far back as the sixth century BC. Around 8 to 10 percent of the population will experience occasional panic attacks; only 5 percent will develop panic disorder. So what's different about the latter?

Research by psychologist David Barlow, a world expert on the subject, suggests that apart from genetic predisposition, there are two psychological vulnerabilities at work in this condition:

- A generalised vulnerability to anxiety created during childhood (e.g. overprotective parents)
- A specific psychological vulnerability, where we learn as children that some situations are dangerous even if they are not

Panic disorder develops when a person with these vulnerabilities experiences major stress and a first panic attack. This activates the above-mentioned vulnerabilities, making them more sensitive to internal or external cues associated with the episode.

Panic attacks may present with the following symptoms:

- profuse sweating
- palpitations (fast heartbeat)
- dry mouth
- weakness
- headache
- chest pain
- hyperventilation (rapid, shallow breathing)
- trembling or shaking
- fear of losing control or 'going mad'
- dizziness
- a choking sensation
- a feeling that you are going to die

Many sufferers can identify with the above symptoms. They usually occur in bursts, are unexpected and at first glance have no obvious cause. They are frightening in nature, more common in women than in men and, thankfully, are treatable if the sufferer presents for help. The average duration of a panic attack is ten minutes. Panic attacks can also be brought on by alcohol or other substances and are often associated with other mental-health problems such as GAD and depression.

There has been significant research into the neurobiological pathways underlying panic attacks. The neurobiological theory (which fits with the psychological one) behind panic attacks is as follows:

- The person experiences symptoms of anxiety, triggered by the stress box sending information through the brain stem (particularly the noradrenalin and hormone control boxes), encouraging the adrenal gland to release adrenalin, which in turn gives rise to the initial physical symptoms of palpitations, and so on.

- The person's emotional and logical brain misinterprets the above, probably through the island or social behaviour box. The latter sends out instructions to the stress box that danger is present.

- This in turn sends the stress box into complete overdrive; the whole stress system starts firing acutely, with adrenalin pouring into the bloodstream and the arrival of a full-blown panic attack.

- The above process will come to a natural end after about ten minutes If attempts are made to stop, it lasts longer. When this occurs, the stress box calms down, the social behaviour box regains control, excess adrenalin is cleared out of the bloodstream and the physical symptoms of the panic attack subside.

- The memory box's main role is, unfortunately, to memorise the above patterns.

When treating panic disorder, there are two objectives:

- to assist the person in dealing with individual panic attacks

- to, more importantly, prevent them recurring

Let's apply our holistic therapy pathway to the problem:

114

FOUNDATIONS: Find a doctor or therapist who can empathise with you. In the area of lifestyle, diet, exercise, relaxation exercises and so on are generally more useful as generalised anxiety- or stress-reducing measures, rather than specific anti-panic ones.

DRUG THERAPIES: The use of tranquillisers has been a first-line approach in the past but has fallen very much into disfavour due to addictiveness and sedation issues. They are helpful in acute situations but quickly develop into a form of safety behaviour.

The other group of drugs used to prevent panic disorders are modern anti-depressant SSRIs. These are thought to boost the serotonin mood cable and have a calming effect on the lower mood circuit. These drugs do work and can be helpful in severe cases but it is now accepted by most experts that talk therapies, particularly CBT, is the better long-term treatment. If depression is also present, drug therapy has a more definite role. We have already discussed homeopathy and herbal therapies but the same rules apply as for conventional drugs.

TALK THERAPIES: While all of the talk therapies are assessed in the area of panic disorder, CBT is widely accepted as the therapy of choice and is borne out by clinical experience. While all the rest may have varying effects on underlying chronic anxiety, they do not have the same short- or long-term benefits in panic disorder. Let's examine a case and show how CBT can be of help.

'They are taking over my life'

Following a visit to the local A&E unit the previous night, John attends his local GP. 'They checked me out and explained that I was having a panic attack. This is the fifth time in two months. Can you prescribe something to prevent them? They're taking over my life.' His GP explains that John is suffering from panic disorder, describing the intricacies of the problem. He explains why drug therapy is not the ideal way to deal with it. If John wishes, he could show him a different way to deal with the episodes, and John agrees.

'Let's take the episode last night. Can you tell me where it happened and how it started?' begins his doctor. John clarifies that it had occurred in a friend's house, starting with his mouth going dry and feeling weak. 'And then?' asked the doctor. John explained that his heart started to 'jump out of his chest' and

115

his breathing became laboured and fast. He started to sweat, developed a headache and limb pains and felt that he was going to die. 'And what did you do then?' asked the doctor.

'I tried to make them go away,' said John, 'but they just got worse. Jimmy, my friend, thought something terrible was happening and called for an ambulance to have me brought to hospital. I spent hours there but got the all-clear. I was healthy.' The doctor wrote all of this down, explaining that it helped to put some order on the information given to him by John. His doctor then explained the 'ABC' concept, and together they put all the information into the following format:

A: TRIGGER: The presenting physical symptoms: dry mouth, weakness, palpitations

INTERPRETATION/DANGER: Was going to have a heart attack, a stroke or die

B: BELIEF (OR DEMAND): That the presenting symptoms must stop

C: EMOTION: Acute anxiety

PHYSICAL SYMPTOMS: Heart pounding, stomach in knots, difficulty breathing

BEHAVIOUR: Desperately tried to do breathing exercises, rushed out into the garden for air, agreed with his friend to call an ambulance, went straight to the local A&E, where he was examined. Had a chest X-ray/ECG performed and finally received a tranquilliser to calm him down

Finally, the doctor put down his pen. 'I think we have the necessary information,' he said. 'But before examining the above, which is more powerful, your logical or emotional brain?' he asked. John replied that it had to be the former and was surprised to learn that his emotional brain was much stronger. The doctor asked how John would feel if he was mugged. He replied that he would be terrified; his heart would be pounding, his stomach in knots, dry mouth, sweating and so on. 'And what would cause your body to behave like that?' asked the doctor. John didn't know so his doctor explained that these physical responses were due to an 'adrenalin rush'. This was caused by John's emotional brain feeling under threat and sending out information to his adrenal gland to release large amounts of this stress hormone into the bloodstream. 'What would happen to these symptoms if the mugger was chased away?' asked the doctor. 'I assume they would settle down,' replied John. The GP nodded. 'Now let's go back over the information you've given me,' he said.

Together, through an interactive dialogue, they work out the following:

- John's episode began when he started to experience the physical symptoms already outlined.

- He then interpreted them as dangerous, i.e. he might get a heart attack, a stroke or even die.

- He demanded that they go away. This made his emotional brain more edgy and it did the opposite.

- This triggered a panic episode with the acute physical symptoms outlined above.

- That the panic attack was only an acute bout of anxiety, fuelled by an adrenalin rush.

- Under normal circumstances, and had he not tried to stop it, the episode would have lasted only ten minutes.

- But because he had entered into safety behaviour by running off to A&E, the episode had persisted for more than an hour.

This led to the following conclusions:

- Symptoms of his panic attack were due to an adrenalin rush, which is uncomfortable but not dangerous. They would cease in ten minutes (despite periods of twenty to twenty-five minutes being quoted in the literature) if he did absolutely nothing. They lasted longer because he tried to stop them.

- The main reason the panic attack occurred was due to John interpreting initial physical symptoms of anxiety as dangerous, but since he hadn't had a heart attack, a stroke, or died, this assumption of danger was actually false.

- The main reason the panic episode persisted was John's safety behaviour.

- A panic attack is, at its most simple, anxiety about anxiety.

- Above all, symptoms of anxiety are uncomfortable but not dangerous. This is the key to losing the fear of panic attacks.

John agrees to try out the following strategy:

- The next time he gets a panic attack, he will purposely avoid safety behaviour. He will do absolutely nothing to stop it and will allow it to pass naturally in ten minutes.

- If in a public place, he will retreat to the quiet of the restroom and allow it to pass, perhaps texting symptoms of his attack to his GP.

- Do everything in his power to trigger panic attacks. He will be unable to bring them on, thus helping lessen his fears of getting one.

- Learn to identify triggering physical symptoms as being simply those of anxiety, 'uncomfortable but not dangerous'.

John returns eight weeks later and has had two further panic episodes but coped with them much better. He accepted them as normal, no longer trying to stop them, and can happily report that they cleared within ten minutes. He would now be comfortable even if one recurred. His doctor then discusses the importance of exercise, moderation, stress-reduction measures and other positive mental-health measures. Over the next six months, with the help of his doctor, John gradually begins to recognise initial triggering physical symptoms for what they are – routine anxiety symptoms he no longer regards as dangerous. His panic attacks fade away, and to date John has remained well.

Sometimes panic attacks will present as part of a more complex set of problems:

- MARY, a thirty-two-year-old mother of two, presents to her family doctor with panic attacks but on deeper probing reveals all the hallmarks of GAD. He helps her deal with her panic attacks, and then recommends she get further help for the underlying problem. Mary then has to decide if her chronic anxiety is causing enough difficulties in her life to warrant her making this step.

- BILL, a twenty-five-year-old postgraduate, presents with panic attacks but also reveals the depression he has been experiencing for the previous three months and his underlying suicidal thoughts. He had been misusing alcohol to lift his mood and his panic attacks deteriorated. His treatment will include getting help for his depression, reducing or stopping alcohol in the short term while getting advice on dealing with his panic episodes.

■ JILL is twenty-four and has buried the effects of an episode of sexual abuse at the age of fourteen. She is having alternating bouts of low mood and general anxiety, culminating in a period of severe panic attacks triggered by meeting the abuser briefly at a local supermarket. While with her doctor, she finds the courage to tell him. This begins a long journey, starting with learning to deal with her panic episodes and ending with a long period of counselling/psychoanalysis and considering facing down her abuser.

■ THOMAS is a thirty-three-year-old construction worker who has moved from being a binge drinker to becoming a binge alcoholic. He presents to his doctor with panic attacks. His GP explains that solving his problems will involve facing his addiction; otherwise it will be extremely difficult for him to eliminate the panic.

■ PAUL is a twenty-nine-year-old highly successful businessman. He has gradually slipped into a weekend cocaine habit. He presents to his doctor with a history of panic attacks, hiding his substance-abuse problem. As a result, he struggles to deal with these attacks and finds himself living more and more in a world of fear. It is not fully appreciated that drugs and panic attacks can often be constant companions.

■ JOAN is a sixty-year-old widow who has become increasingly anxious following the sudden death of her husband and the social isolation which followed. She is struggling to come to terms with his loss and is using alcohol intake to deal with periods of low mood. She begins to get panic attacks and becomes increasingly isolated as a result. She finally comes to see her doctor with her daughter, who is becoming worried about her. Her management will involve assistance to deal with her panic attacks, moderation of her alcohol, bereavement counselling, purchasing a pet dog (for company and as a guard) and trying to reintegrate her back into her local community.

If the person is determined to take the alternative-therapy route, I would avoid herbal or homeopathic cures for the same reasons that I am not in favour of conventional drug therapy. I would encourage meditation and mindfulness approaches as they help deal with the distress caused by panic attacks and hopefully reduce underlying stress and chronic anxiety. Any form of relaxation, breathing exercises or yoga can be of help but do not eliminate the underlying cognitive cause of the attack. I am often asked about hypnotherapy as a treatment and feel that it may have some effect but would like to see some conclusive research trials into the subject. Acupuncture is of little use in acute attacks but some find it useful as a stress-reducing therapy. Massage therapies are helpful in a similar way.

I have spoken to people, however, who have spent thousands of euros on multiple alternative therapies for a condition which is easily dealt with via a few CBT/CBM sessions.

Phobias

Phobias are one of the most common conditions affecting human beings. They can be defined as 'an excessive and persistent fear of particular objects or situations where exposure to either provokes an immediate anxiety response, leading to a tendency to avoid the phobic stimuli'.

Simple phobias include:

1. Exposure to animals or insects, such as cats, dogs, mice, spiders and snakes. A large percentage of the population suffers from varying forms of this. It is a remnant of earlier evolutionary times when spiders, snakes and large cats were something to fear and avoid. Most of the time, phobias are a nuisance but do not require intervention.

2. Exposure to situations such as confined spaces, heights, planes, motorways, blood and so on. Many fear heights and enclosed spaces (claustrophobia), and one of the most common modern simple phobias is fear of flying, which limits people and families from traveling abroad.

Generalised phobias include:

SOCIAL PHOBIA (often called Social Anxiety Disorder), a common, disabling condition where the person suffers from intense anxiety in social situations for a period of greater than six months. They experience a persistent fear of being judged harshly by others and are embarrassed by their own actions in social situations. These fears can be easily triggered by perceived or actual scrutiny by others. Symptoms of anxiety may be accompanied by blushing, excessive sweating, mind going blank, or stammering: which in many cases becomes the presenting problem. Some experts are happier with the term 'social anxiety disorder' as it is more self-explanatory. It is a classic example of ego anxiety. The most famous sufferer from this condition was Charles Darwin, who actually described many of the symptoms. Unlike other phobias, continuous exposure to social situations does not seem to lead to a lessening of the condition.

It is normal, particularly as teenagers and young adults, to become anxious in social situations. However, for 7 to 8 percent of the population, this social anxiety persists. We can learn about the effects of this disorder in people's lives by examining their thoughts and behaviour in social and working situations.

The key behaviour pattern is social avoidance, which worsens and perpetuates the problem. Sufferers fear and avoid situations such as group interactions, dating, restaurants, meeting strangers and countless other events. Paradoxically, many present as socially quite sophisticated. They are intensively self-critical of their 'performance' in public situations. Generally, people with social anxiety disorder fear and avoid social situations. These fall into two broad categories. Most people with social anxiety disorder fear situations from both categories:

PERFORMANCE SITUATIONS (e.g. situations that involve performing in front of others or being observed by other people)

Examples of feared performance situations in social anxiety disorder:

- Public speaking
- Talking in meetings/classes
- Participating in sports or working out in front of others
- Performing music or acting on stage
- Writing in front of others
- Eating or drinking in front of others

- Using public restrooms when other people are nearby

- Making mistakes in front of others

- Being in public areas such as a shopping mall or on a bus

SOCIAL INTERACTION SITUATIONS (e.g. situations that involve engaging or interacting with one or more people).

Examples of feared social interaction situations in social anxiety disorder:

- Going to a party

- Initiating or maintaining conversation

- Talking to strangers

- Inviting friends over for dinner

- Talking on the phone

- Expressing personal opinions

- Being assertive (e.g. refusing to give in to unreasonable requests, asking others to change their behaviour)

- Being in intimate situations

- Talking to people in authority (e.g. employers, professors, doctors)

- Returning items to a store or sending food back in a restaurant

Typical thoughts/beliefs might be:

- 'Everybody must like me'

- 'If all went well, nobody really noticed, and if it went badly it was my fault'

- 'I have nothing interesting to say, and I'm boring'

- 'I will make a fool of myself and they will all notice and judge me to be wanting'

- 'I will be paralysed with fear'.

The list is endless, as they have so many negative thoughts and beliefs about themselves.

They also learn safety behaviours if exposed to social situations. Again, the list of possibilities is extensive:

- Trying to remain anonymous by saying nothing controversial

- Staying close to the exit

- Trying to cover up blushing (e.g. with make-up) or excess sweating (particularly common)

- Avoiding eye contact

- Keep checking that you are coming across well (self-monitoring)

- Gripping glasses or cups tightly

- Continuously rehearsing what they are going to say

Some develop concomitant depression or use substances like alcohol as a crutch. In some cases, there may be a history of not fitting in socially or being bullied when passing through formative years. It is also the one anxiety disorder where the white flag of suicide may unfold.

After much research into the cause of this disorder, there is general agreement that the typical genetic/environmental/epigenetic mixture is at work. Those with an underlying genetic predisposition to the condition are influenced by upbringing and social environment. Resulting pathways are set down by the late teens. Personal experiences are thought to influence the development of social anxiety disorder. For example, negative experiences in social situations (e.g. being teased at school) may cause a person to fear or avoid social situations if being around people becomes associated with the negative experience.

In addition, an individual who is exposed to others with extreme social anxiety (e.g. growing up with parents who have social anxiety disorder) may learn to fear the same situations just through observation. The messages children receive from parents, teachers, friends and media (e.g. it's important always to make a good impression) may also affect the development of social anxiety disorder in some. Of course, negative social experiences alone are not enough to cause social anxiety disorder, and only a small percentage of people who have such experiences develop the problem. There are obviously other factors involved.

The good news is that this pathway can be reshaped, so we can learn and develop new skills to overcome an extremely distressing condition.

AGORAPHOBIA: refers to a fear of open spaces (*agora* is the Greek word for the marketplace). This phobia is often present in those who suffer from panic disorder. At any one time in Ireland, up to 20,000 people may be suffering from this condition which, like social phobia, leads to difficulties in the life of the sufferer.

It also refers to situations where we dread leaving the house, entering public areas like churches, supermarkets, cinemas, shopping centres and other crowded areas. In severe cases, sufferers find it difficult to leave their own room. It can be an isolating and paralysing condition. Behaviour involves safety seeking, such as requiring family or friends to accompany them or avoidant behaviour, where they find excuses to avoid the above situations.

At the heart of this phobia is the fear that, if they encounter the above, the result may be a panic attack; this makes them avoid such situations. In severe cases, the resulting isolation may trigger a bout of depression.

Most of us have irrational fears of objects or situations. It is only when these fears interfere with our normal everyday lives that we need to focus on them. Unfortunately, many are handicapped by these phobias. The tragedy is that phobias are, at their most simple, described as an 'anxiety about becoming anxious or panicky, when exposed to the phobic stimuli'. The condition is extremely amenable to simple CBT-type exercises.

There is increasing interest in the neurobiological basis of different phobias. The following is a summary of what we know to date:

- In simple phobias such as a fear of insects, the main parts of the fear pathways in operation are the stress box, island and attention box. The island has been shown to be a key player; the stress box less so. The logic box on the right side of the brain is strongly activated in spider phobia, which experts feel is the logical brain trying to come up with cognitive strategies aimed at self-regulating the fear triggered by exposure to the spider.

- In social phobia, the main player from early on in childhood seems to be an overly sensitive stress box. One of the functions of the latter is the screening of faces we meet, assessing negative cues (e.g. 'she doesn't like me'); in this disorder, it continuously overreacts. When in social situations, this in turn leads us to be overly sensitive as to how we perceive other people's assessment of us. This in turn triggers the physical symptoms associated with the condition.

- We know that the social control or attention boxes play a major role in how we learn to cope with our social world. As babies, infants and children, these boxes act as a constant balancing force over our stress box. But some will reach their late teens and early twenties and find, for many reasons, that this normal counterbalancing effect has been diminished and the social control and attention boxes struggle to counteract its negativity in social situations. The stress box, as a result, starts to misconstrue normal social meeting contacts before, during and after the event. Because it is the boss of our stress system, this ensures a regular flow of the physical symptoms of social anxiety.

Let us now examine our holistic-therapy approach in phobias:

FOUNDATIONS: Find a therapist or GP you can open up to and who will empathise with you. In terms of lifestyle therapies, general stress and anxiety-reducing measures like exercise, massage, yoga, moderation in relation to alcohol (which is often used as a crutch, particularly in social anxiety disorder), relaxation exercises, meditation and mindfulness are all useful but do not deal with the core underlying problem.

DRUG THERAPIES have been used for decades to deal with phobias but are of limited usefulness. Tranquillisers can be useful for short periods but long-term use leads to addiction, perpetuating the problem. One common example is using Xanax to help people travel by plane. Modern SSRI antidepressants can be useful in some situations, particularly social phobia and severe agoraphobia. Ideally, they should be used for shorter duration and in conjunction with talk therapies. Herbal remedies like valerian and St John's wort, and some homeopathic cures, may be suggested by some alternative practitioners, but once again I feel that their use is limited.

TALK THERAPIES: Talk therapies are the treatment of choice for phobias: particularly CBT in all its forms, including behaviour therapy. For simple phobias, they are extremely effective, and often only a few sessions are required. Social phobia is a more complex condition but will usually respond well to various behavioural approaches. Inter-personal therapy has been shown to have some effect as well. Agoraphobia has in the past been managed by progressive-exposure regimens, and these are now handled by simpler CBT measures.

Other forms of talk therapy, like hypnotherapy, may be useful but we still need more research to evaluate their place. Complex psychoanalysis is of limited help with phobias. Let's now look at some cases:

Fear of Flying: 'I will run amok.'

Sara is distressed when she attends her family doctor, presenting with a long-standing fear of flying. For years, her husband and two children have wanted to travel abroad for a holiday. But her fear of flying has prevented this from happening. For her fortieth birthday, her sisters decide to send her and her family on a holiday to Spain, springing it on her as a surprise. She now feels trapped, afraid to hurt them and ashamed to admit her phobia about flying, which she had always covered up by extolling the virtues of taking holidays at home.

Sara's eyes fill with tears, admitting that she envied friends who had travelled all over Europe. She had always wanted to see Rome but accepted that this would never happen. She then requests medication to help her get through this ordeal. Her doctor empathises but explores the possibilities. One would be to prescribe a short-acting tranquilliser, taken the night before and on the day of travel. A second, more rewarding approach would be to face once and for all her fear of flying, working with her doctor to understand and manage her phobia. This would open up a new world of opportunity to Sara and her family. She reflects on this and, with reservations, agrees.

'So what are you most afraid of when you think about flying?' her doctor asks. Sara replies that she is not really sure. 'Well, most people are afraid of either the plane crashing, or feeling trapped in a confined space. Which of these do you feel most applies to yourself?' he inquires. 'Well, I have never had any problems relating to the first, but feel very anxious when the door shuts, and I can't get off,' she replies. He then asks her to visualise being on the plane and the doors shutting. 'What do you feel will happen?' Sara replies that she could visualise becoming incredibly anxious, losing control and trying to open the doors in midair. 'They would end up putting me in restraints, turning the plane back. I can see it happening in front of my eyes. It would be so embarrassing for me and my husband.' Her doctor nods. 'I think we have the bones of the problem now, but it's useful to put this information down on paper in an organised manner.' He then explained the 'ABC' concept. Together, they put the information provided into the following format:

A: TRIGGER: Her upcoming plane journey

INTERPRETATION/DANGER: When the plane's doors shut, she might lose control and run amok, attempt to open them in midair and end up being restrained

B: BELIEF (OR DEMAND): Must be certain she will not be exposed to the symptoms of anxiety, with all of its potential consequences, like losing control and running amok

C: EMOTION: Anxiety

PHYSICAL SYMPTOMS: Stomach in knots, tension headache, palpitations, difficulties sleeping, difficulties breathing, and so on

BEHAVIOUR: 'avoidant behaviour' – seeking ways to cancel the trip to avoid having to face the dangers outlined above, considering tranquillisers to reduce the risks of becoming anxious or losing control of 'safety behaviour'

He then explains the difference between her emotional and logical mind: that anxiety symptoms are simply due to an adrenalin rush. This is 'uncomfortable but not dangerous'. He challenges her danger – her *visualisation* that she will become so anxious that she will try to open the doors. He gives her an analogy (courtesy of Irish CBT therapist Mary McCarron) asking Sara to visualise spilled milk. She visualises, as most people do, a full carton of milk falling on the floor, creating a complete mess. His doctor then explains that it was also possible that a tiny amount of milk could have been spilt, but most people will assume the worst-case scenario. It is the power of the emotional mind that brings this about.

Because anxiety relates to a fear of something that has not yet happened, her imagination, in the absence of any real experience, was overcompensating. By challenging and removing the danger in this way, she will stop demanding that she must not get anxious on the flight (a demand for certainty), and this in turn will reduce her symptoms of anxiety. He challenges her behaviour, explaining that using tranquillisers will only prevent her symptoms, and that looking for reasons to cancel the trip only adds to her anxiety memory bank.

Sara finally comes to accept that her fear of flying is not of the plane itself, but rather a fear that she will become anxious when on the plane. She is 'anxious that she may become anxious'. Sara returns at a later date, reporting that the plane trip went better than expected. She did become anxious but was able to deal with it, realising that the symptoms were uncomfortable but not dangerous. Following a number of such sessions, she becomes much more comfortable with air travel. Most importantly she and her husband were now planning to visit Rome, by plane.

Fear of Flying: 'It will crash.'

Dave is a thirty-five-year-old successful business executive. He is highly regarded by his company boss and prides himself on always being in control of his brief. He has, however, one hidden weakness: a fear of flying. Matters come to a head when his company becomes involved in a project in China and decide that their rising star will be chief negotiator; this will involve regular plane trips to the Far East. As the date of departure looms larger, his anxiety levels rise and he begins to feel panicky. He attends his GP looking for assistance, anxious not to reveal his flying phobia to the boss. He seeks a tranquilliser to help him over his dilemma but is persuaded by his doctor to try another way of dealing with the issue. Together, they come up with the following 'ABC' analysis of his problem:

A: TRIGGER: Getting on the plane

INTERPRETATION/DANGER: Because he is on the plane, it will definitely crash

B: BELIEF (OR DEMAND): He must be certain the plane will not crash

C: EMOTION: Anxiety

PHYSICAL SYMPTOMS: stomach in knots, tension headache, palpitations, difficulties sleeping, difficulties breathing, and so on

BEHAVIOUR: Avoids flying and looks for tranquillisers as a form of safety behaviour

Dave's doctor challenges his avoidant and safety behaviour and his demand that the plane 'must not crash'. They agree that his avoidant/safety behaviour is worsening the situation. His doctor then explores his desire for certainty. He firstly asks whether there is any such thing as a plane ticket guaranteeing that the plane won't crash. This demand is unachievable. There is therefore a theoretical possibility (if only a minuscule one) that it may crash. His doctor then explains, using the above spilled-milk scenario, that most people will assume the worst-case scenario. As a consequence, Dave 'in his mind' multiplies the possibility of the plane crashing to a level greater than the actual risk. He is looking for absolute certainty, but the more he demands this, the more uncertain he becomes, until all he can see is the plane crashing. His doctor also challenges Dave's belief that just because he is on the plane, it will inevitably crash.

His doctor suggests that a philosophy of looking for security, order, certainty and perfection in different areas of our lives only feeds the flames of uncertainty. With so many flames, it will be difficult to deal with his fear of flying as an isolated event.

He then examines other areas of Dave's life where he is looking for 100 percent certainty and has a reasonable chance of success, helping him to see how impossible a demand it is to satisfy in all cases. After a number of visits, where Dave gradually dismantles his desire for certainty in different areas in his life, demands for certainty in the area of flying begin to weaken, and his fear of flying gradually begins to disappear. Six months later, high-flying Dave is now a regular plane traveller.

Fear of Social Situations: 'I'm afraid to go out'

Jim is a twenty-five-year-old graduate who attends his doctor complaining of a number of physical symptoms. Following investigations, he is diagnosed with anxiety. On deeper probing, he admits to having great difficulties in social situations and to misusing alcohol on a regular basis as a coping mechanism. He also admits to periods of extreme anxiety in social gatherings and says that, since his late teens, he has dreaded meeting strangers, attending big family events, going to the theatre (which he loves) and having work meetings. He has admitted to one episode of depression at the age of twenty-one, but 'dealt with it himself'. He was highly critical of himself and his perceived social incompetence. His thoughts included the following:

- Everybody must like me or nobody must dislike me

- If all went well, nobody really noticed, and if it went badly it was my fault

- I have nothing interesting to say; I am boring

- I will make a fool of myself; they will *all* notice and judge me wanting

- I will be paralysed with fear

- I will blush or sweat excessively, and they will notice

- I will be unable to speak

His doctor explains that he is suffering from social anxiety, and recommends that he attend a CBT-therapist colleague. He also counsels avoidance of alcohol as a coping mechanism, citing the risks of addiction. Jim agrees to attend the therapist, who firstly gets him to fill out a social anxiety questionnaire examining his thoughts and behaviour in social circumstances. He then asks for a concrete example where he had experienced such anxiety.

Jim gives him the example of going into a pub to meet his friends the previous Saturday. The therapist explains the 'ABC' concept, and together they draw up the following:

A: TRIGGER: Going to the pub to meet his friends

INTERPRETATION/DANGER: On entering the pub, 'they' will be looking at him and they will see he is nervous or identify something wrong with him that will make them think he is a fool. They will see him blushing or sweating and, most of all, view him as he views himself

B: BELIEF (OR DEMAND): It must not happen. If it does, he would be a failure for letting it, and he must accept their opinion of him

C: EMOTION: Anxiety in relation to the first and shame in relation to the second

PHYSICAL SYMPTOMS: Stomach in knots, tension headache, palpitations, difficulties sleeping, difficulties breathing, and so on

BEHAVIOUR: Uses alcohol as a crutch, positions himself at the edge of the group, rehearses in his mind what he will say, grips his glass very tightly and keeps his jacket on to conceal his sweating

His therapist challenges Jim's thoughts and behaviour. How could he be 'measured' either by what his friends thought or what he himself actually did? The therapist introduced him to the Raggy Doll Club and its rules, i.e. 'We cannot rate ourselves or accept other people's rating of us'. He gave him shame-attacking exercises, specifically aimed at drawing attention to himself. Over the next nine months, and following many visits to his therapist, Jim continues to make good progress, is no longer as fearful of social situations, and gradually becomes a Raggy Doll.

Fear of Public Speaking

Owen is a thirty-year-old businessman who presents to his doctor complaining of stress and fatigue. It quickly becomes apparent that the symptoms appeared following his promotion to senior level three months before. Narrowing it down, he admitted to increasing levels of anxiety as he began presenting data on a fortnightly basis to differing groups within the company and some outside agencies.

A shy man, he had always found public speaking difficult since a particularly embarrassing experience at a school debate. As a result, he was spending the day before current meetings in a high state of anxiety, afraid that he would develop stage fright, and having difficulties eating and sleeping. He admitted using alcohol to reduce anxiety and spending increasing time practising presentations. He asks his GP for tranquillisers to calm him down for the duration of his speaking.

His doctor counsels avoidance of both alcohol and tranquillisers. He gives general lifestyle advice on diet, exercise and sleep and suggests CBT/CBM-type exercises to help deal with the problem. Owen agrees and over a few sessions they work out the following 'ABC' of his difficulties:

A: TRIGGER: Having to give a presentation in front of a group at work

Interpretation/Danger: He will become anxious during the presentation and clam up or make a fool of himself, with long-term career consequences

B: BELIEF (OR DEMAND): He must not clam up during the talk. 'They must not see me as incompetent'

C: EMOTION: Anxiety

PHYSICAL SYMPTOMS: Stomach in knots, tension headache, palpitations, difficulties sleeping, breathing and talking, and so on

BEHAVIOUR: Tries to avoid public presentation, continuously rehearses presentations for days before, uses alcohol as a crutch and would be happy to use tranquillisers in a similar way

His doctor then challenges his 'B' motivation: the demand that he must not clam up or be seen as incompetent. He introduces him to the Raggy Doll Club and its rules. He also challenges his behaviour, explaining how it was perpetuating the problem. After working with his doctor for some time and putting the suggestions into practice at work, Owen gradually becomes more confident and begins to lose his fear. He also learns to joke before each talk that he sometimes freezes, asking them to bear with him if this happens. This, he finds, removes a great deal of pressure. He was recently promoted as a result of his excellent presentations.

Fear of Leaving the House

Patricia comes to see her family doctor accompanied by her sister (who has, after months of urging, finally persuaded her to come). She admits to increasing difficulty in leaving her house over the previous six months. She has become very isolated and is losing contact with her friends (making up excuses as to why she can't come and see them). She admits to feeling like she's going mad and is ashamed about her behaviour. Her family is becoming increasingly frustrated with her belief that 'she was letting them down'. She had a history of panic attacks.

Her sister queried whether there was some drug therapy that would help her deal with her fear of leaving the house and mentioned the name of a well-known tranquilliser. Patricia herself, however, was adamant that she would not take tablets and asked if some form of counselling would help her. Her doctor agreed with her that tranquillisers were not the best approach and suggested some CBT/CBM exercises to assist her in overcoming her phobia about leaving the house. She agrees and, following a session, emerges with the following 'ABC' analysis of her problem:

A: TRIGGER: Leaving the house

INTERPRETATION/DANGER: She may get anxious or, worse, experience a panic attack if she leaves the house. 'What will happen if I do get a panic attack – get a heart attack, die or go mad?'

B: BELIEF (OR DEMAND): She 'must not' get anxious or have a panic attack if she leaves her house

C: EMOTION: Anxiety

> PHYSICAL SYMPTOMS: Stomach in knots, tension headache, palpitations, difficulties sleeping, difficulties breathing, and so on

> BEHAVIOUR; Avoiding leaving the house, making excuses to friends and family as to why she can't meet them, having somebody with her as a safety measure

Her doctor challenges her behaviour and explains how it is making the situation worse. He then challenges her 'danger' – 'What will happen if I get a panic attack on leaving the house?' and her demand that she must not get anxious. He starts by explaining the mechanisms underlying panic attacks (examined earlier) and how to cope with them if they occur. She gradually begins to understand that the physical symptoms of anxiety are uncomfortable but not dangerous. He introduces the idea of a behavioural exercise where she leaves the house and, on reaching grade seven out of ten in terms of anxiety, returns. By losing her fear of anxiety, she stops demanding that she must not be anxious if she leaves the house. With the support of her doctor, Patricia decides to investigate what actually happens on leaving the house and as a result soon loses her fear of leaving the house.

Fear of the Shopping Centre

Catherine, a mother of two comes to see her doctor complaining of difficulty visiting her local shopping centre. Recently it came to a head when she felt 'light headed' within minutes of entering the centre to visit her favourite store. She made excuses to her friend, and returned home. Since then, she had not been in the centre, becoming anxious if somebody suggested meeting her there.

She discusses it with her husband, and presents for a check-up, inquiring if she needed drug therapy or counselling to deal with her problems. Her GP examines and reassures her all is well from a physical point of view. He then suggests some simple CBM measures to deal with her fear of entering the shopping centre. Together they come up with the following ABC analysis of her problem:

A: TRIGGER: Entering her local shopping centre

INTERPRETATION/DANGER: She will become very anxious with distressing physical symptoms, these will get keep getting progressively worse until something terrible will happen

B: BELIEF (OR DEMAND): She 'must not' get anxious if she enters the centre – it would be just awful (for above reasons)

C: EMOTION: Anxiety

PHYSICAL SYMPTOMS: Stomach in knots, tension headache, palpations, difficulties sleeping, difficulties breathing, and so on.

BEHAVIOUR: Leaving the centre immediately she feels anxious, avoiding returning, making excuses as to why she cannot go there.

Her doctor then challenges her behaviour, and how it was exacerbating her fears. He then challenges her danger that she will get very anxious if she enters the centre, and her demand that she must not get anxious. He starts by explaining what the symptoms of anxiety are, that they are uncomfortable but not dangerous, and how to cope with them if they occur. This helps her cease demanding they don't happen if she enters the centre, as she will no longer fear the resulting physical symptoms, learning instead to accept them as due to a simple adrenalin rush which will pass.

She goes away to put it into practice, and decides to make a concerted effort to visit the centre on a daily basis. Although experiencing the uncomfortable symptoms of anxiety, she learns to accept them as normal. She now no longer demands that she should not become anxious if she enters the centre, and when she returns to see her doctor six weeks later, has made major inroads into her phobia. Her new problem is her husband is now worrying that she is developing a shopping addiction as a result of all the new clothes arriving in her wardrobe!

5

The Depression Pathway

It is important to distinguish between *normal depression*, usually designated as *unipolar depression*, and *bipolar mood disorder*, a completely different illness, but which features some of the same characteristics.

Simple Unipolar Depression

Periods of feeling down, sad or low are, like anxiety, innate to the human condition. All of us experience such periods following, for example, bereavement, the end of a relationship, the death of a beloved pet, major disappointment or loss, illness to ourselves or a loved one, or stressful periods in our lives. Such periods are usually of short duration and we quickly bounce back to our normal selves. But for hundreds of thousands of people in Ireland every year, this natural feeling of being low gives way to a much more serious mood state, namely *major depressive disorder*, which we will refer to as 'MDD' for the remainder of this discussion. MDD is the red flag.

Confusion surrounds the use of the word depression, regarded by therapists as a normal emotion, and the use of MDD, a biological illness with a classic combination of physical and psychological symptoms which, if undiagnosed and untreated, can lead to serious consequences. This difference is crucial because many people in the worlds of media and therapy blur this distinction. This has led to widespread uncertainty amongst those most affected. MDD can present at different stages and phases of our lives for completely different sets of reasons. Irrespective of the person's stage in life, it can cause untold chaos and suffering in the lives of those involved. The following list of symptoms provides a glimpse of what it is like to live in the world of serious depression:

LOW MOOD: 'I feel weighed down by hopelessness and sadness. It is a physical pain in my heart and no one understands how terrible it feels.'

John is a nineteen-year-old undergraduate student who has developed depression after moving away from his family for the first time to live in a flat in Dublin. He is successfully hiding it from his family and friends. Alcohol relieves the pain for short periods but its embrace is fleeting and illusory.

FATIGUE: 'The simplest of tasks drains me of all my energy. I just want to sleep all the time.'

Mary is a twenty-seven-year-old mother with two small children who has developed symptoms of depression following a series of stressful events, in particular the loss of a close friend to cancer.

ANXIETY: 'I am constantly on a high state of alert and always feel under pressure. I cannot cope when something goes wrong. I sometimes feel panicky for no obvious reason.'

Peter is twenty-two and has successfully hidden how he feels for the previous three years.

WEIGHT LOSS/GAIN: 'I'm just not hungry any more. Food does not look appetising and it's too much energy to eat. Hopefully I will waste away into nothing.'

Catherine is a single parent aged twenty-four. The stress of coping with a small child on social welfare, of living in a small, poorly equipped flat, with a partner who abuses alcohol, has triggered a bout of depression. She has lost more than a stone in weight. Her diet, which was already poor due to lack of money and lack of knowledge about nutrition, has now been reduced to coffee and cigarettes.

LOSS OF SELF-ESTEEM: 'I am ashamed of the weak, useless, boring, incompetent failure that I am. People hate spending time with me.'

Carl is a twenty-four-year-old mechanic whose quiet disposition and painful shyness has disguised his inner torment from those close to him. Depression affected him first at the age of seventeen and has been an unwelcome but frequent visitor since.

LOSS OF DRIVE: 'I don't enjoy any of the activities that I used to. It all seems like so much effort now, and I don't see the point.'

Maura is a twenty-four-year-old working mother who has developed depression three months after the birth of her first child.

POOR MEMORY: 'I have become increasingly forgetful and have difficulty remembering the simplest of things, like what I did yesterday.'

Noreen is a single, busy twenty-seven-year-old manager who is struggling to cope with her day-to-day duties due to depression triggered by a prolonged period of sustained stress.

REDUCED CONCENTRATION: 'I don't read any more. It's too much effort to make sense out of the words and it is becoming difficult to pay attention to anything.'

George is a seventeen-year-old Leaving Cert student who is struggling to study as he battles with a bout of unrecognised depression.

LACK OF PLEASURE (*ANHEDONIA*): 'I can barely manage a smile any more. I'm sick of people telling me to cheer up or saying "It can't be that bad". It is – and much worse than they can imagine.'

Paula is twenty-eight and has had bouts of depression for the previous five years. She was sexually abused at the age of nine.

SUICIDAL THOUGHTS: 'The world will be a much better place without me. I am a burden on everyone and they won't miss me at all.'

Jack is twenty-nine and has already quietly planned in great detail how he will end the pain. If his depression is not recognised and remains untreated, he may soon put these thoughts into action. This is made more likely by his dramatic increase in alcohol consumption to numb the pain of a recent break-up with his girlfriend.

To diagnose MDD, one must have a significantly depressed mood for over two weeks, combined with at least four of the above symptoms, particularly difficulties with sleep, appetite and fatigue, feelings of worthlessness, and anhedonia.

For those who have doubts about the physical and other consequences of this illness, the following risks should clarify the issue:

- 200 to 500 percent increase in the risk of heart disease

- Reduced defences against illness, affecting immune-cell receptors and their ability to respond to infection. This includes the ability to fight cancerous cells

- Poor bone formation, leading to osteoporosis (thinning of the bones).

- Increased risks of developing abdominal obesity and Type 2 diabetes

- Death by suicide, which occurs in up to 15 percent of those who have suffered recurrent bouts of depression.

The above explains why we call it major depression or the red flag. Before exploring the pathways and therapies involved, it is worth stating what MDD is *not*. It is not, as many people assume:

- an inherited brain disease

- a chemical illness of serotonin, the 'chemical' held responsible

- a purely psychological illness

- a weakness of one's personality ('Just pull yourself together, and stop whining')

- an exaggerated normal emotional response to difficulties in our lives

- a blockage of 'unseen and immeasurable' energy fields surrounding the body

- a description of the person: 'I am a depressive'

- a condition that all of us will experience at some stage in our lives. It seems to affect only about 15 to 20 percent of the community. All of us may have periods when our mood is low but only a specific group will suffer a bout of MDD

The Depression Pathways

Depression, or MDD, is a complex disorder that gives rise to a constellation of physical and psychological symptoms. It can occur at different stages of our lives for vastly different reasons and has puzzled researchers as to its underlying mechanisms. Once again, some may not be interested in the neurobiology which follows and wish to move on. For the rest, there are a number of important questions we must answer:

- Why do only 15 to 20 percent of us develop this illness? The rest of us will experience stress and regular periods of feeling a little sad or low. This is part of our human condition but does not develop into MDD.

- Why does this illness occur twice as frequently in women as men, particularly among women aged between fifteen and fifty, the usual reproductive period of their lives?

- Why does it occur in people over sixty-five who have no prior history of depression?

- Why is there such a high rate of recurrence? The more often we suffer an episode, the more likely we will have a further one.

- Why do women come for help, and men, particularly those under thirty, steadfastly refuse?

- Why is there such a variance in how sufferers will respond to treatment?

- Why is stress such a powerful initiating trigger for bouts of MDD at every stage of our lives? If the person suffers repeated episodes, why does it take increasing less stress to trigger an episode?

- Why is our logical mind and brain so incapable of switching off the emotional negativity pouring out from our emotional one?

- Why is there such a strong link between heart disease in particular and MDD?

In *Flagging the Problem*, I detailed how difficulties in the mood system in the brain lead to all the symptoms of depression. The main neurobiological findings can be summarised as follows:

- A breakdown in communication between our logical and our emotional brain.

- This allows our stress box in particular to pour out negative emotions, which flood our logical brain.

139

- This, in turn, will lead to our adrenal gland pumping out high levels of the stress hormone glucocortisol.

- This in turn damages our three big mood cables (serotonin, noradrenalin and dopamine) and boxes.

- This gives rise to most of the physical symptoms of depression, such as difficulties with sleep, appetite, drive, concentration, and so on.

While this analysis is of assistance in understanding how this illness affects us, it does not answer the question of 'why'. Up to a decade ago, it was felt that the underlying problem was a chemical one: we were lacking key neurotransmitters such as serotonin. Modern scientific research has, however, made this view outdated.

The modern twenty-first-century approach to MDD recognises that the condition has more to do with the following:

1. A malfunction within the internal workings of the neurons (and glial support cells) themselves and their connections (synapses) with each other.

2. As a result, there is a breakdown in some key brain systems and circuits.

3. In turn, this leads to mood, behaviour and thought difficulties. The physical consequences at the heart of this illness have already been outlined.

At present, a revolution in our understanding of the nature of this illness is occurring. This revolution is crucial in assisting us to examine the causes of MDD, answer some of the questions asked above, assess available therapies and, most importantly, develop new ones. Let's now examine two key components of this new understanding:

- The SECOND MESSENGER SYSTEM

- The MOOD SYSTEM

The role of the SECOND MESSENGER SYSTEM is an exciting development in our understanding of MDD. I will deal with it in detail in the technical section but I include here a broad outline of how it works.

Each neuron in the brain connects up with at least two thousand of its colleagues, busily sending neurotransmitters over and back across the small gaps, or synapses, between them. These little messengers *lock in* to receptors on the cell membrane. They have two main functions: to encourage the neuron to fire or not, and also to pass on information into the heart of the cell, where our genes reside. This second function is facilitated by the most extraordinary system within the body, the 'second messenger system' (the 'first messenger' being the little neurotransmitter itself). Figure 33 represents a cross section of the neuron. We can see the outer layer, where the neurotransmitter receptors are based; the middle layer, situated between the cell membrane and the third layer; and the third layer itself, the nucleus of the cell, where our chromosomes and genes/DNA reside.

The second messenger system transfers information between the cell membrane and our genes. It is composed of a series of chemical messengers which activate a choreographed sequence of reactions where each one 'talks' to the next. The second messenger system is extraordinarily complex. Within every neuron, this cascade of internal chemical messages activates our genes to produce vital neurotrophic (neuron-nourishing) proteins which have essential functions, central to our whole understanding of depression:

- to nourish and protect the cell;

- to regulate the number of connections each neuron has with its neighbours by increasing or decreasing the number of dendrites;

- to prevent the neuron from self-destructing and dying.

There are two major neurotrophic proteins produced as a result of the second messenger system. The first is BDNF, whose functions are very much connected with the first two functions. The second is called Bcl 2, whose functions also relate to the third. It is not important to know the actual mechanisms involved. (These will be explored in the technical section.) All that matters is that anything which interferes with our second messenger system will interfere with these vital nourishing proteins. Any decrease in functioning of the latter interferes with the structure, function and survival of the neuron.

The second messenger system is strongly influenced by:

- genetic/epigenetic and early environmental factors

- our sex hormones, particularly in women (oestrogen and progesterone)

- our stress hormone, glucocortisol

- the deleterious effects of alcohol and drugs, particularly in youth and old age

- vascular changes in the brain as we age

There is a large amount of research going on into this complex system (both the second messenger system and neurotrophic proteins) and the genes underlying it. When we have built up a total genetic and functional picture, we may see how individual malfunctions within this system can be triggered and perpetuated by environmental influences.

The malfunctions within this internal cascade of second messengers can lead to either deterioration in the function of, or the death of, individual neurons. This offers profound implications for our understanding of depression, partly because this system is influenced by such a wide variety of factors (which fits with what we know about depression) and partly because it provides an explanation for the second main finding: the widespread disruption of the brain's mood departments and circuits.

The role of the mood system in depression was described earlier; here, I would like to examine how malfunctions within the second messenger system affecting individual neurons can in turn lead to a breakdown within the brain circuits of which they are an integral part.

One of the most important findings in this area in the past ten years has been the discovery (through research into people suffering with recurrent bouts of significant depression) of a subtle loss of neurons, dendrite connections and even support glial cells scattered throughout key parts of the mood system. Of particular interest has been the finding of such brain-tissue loss in the logical brain (the logic, social behaviour and attention boxes: all key players in our ability to control negative emotions and thoughts). Researchers have discovered a similar loss of grey matter in parts of our emotional brain, particularly our memory and stress boxes. It now seems as if these losses of crucial neural connections, and indeed neurons themselves, most likely arise secondary to malfunctions occurring within the second messenger system, leading to a loss of the vital neurotrophic proteins already mentioned.

The result of all these changes is an inability of the logical brain to switch off the negative barrage coming from the emotional brain, particularly the stress box. This leads to the breakdown in the functioning of the two big mood circuits, the appearance of the dysfunctions in our mood system detailed earlier, and the arrival of the symptoms of major depression in our lives.

Let's examine the effects of all these changes and how they in turn affect our brain and mind pathways in depression.

The stress box lies like a spider at the centre of the web of depression pathways. It become overactive, producing (with the assistance of the island) most of the negative emotions of depression which cause so much distress. In particular, it pours out the feelings of overwhelming sadness which flow down our sadness pathway (Figure 12). This path winds its way through Area 25 and communicates with the emotional and social behaviour boxes, the key control areas of our logical brain. The final result is the creation of an extreme low mood, the key symptom of depression.

- Normally, Areas 32 and 24, together with the left logic box, are able to calm things down by focusing attention on the emotional state and helping to reappraise and modulate such feelings of low mood. In depression, for the reasons already outlined, this normal control is gone. We know, for example, that Area 24 may be reduced in size, may malfunction and may struggle to exert any control.

- The logic box on the left side of the brain suffers from 'power failure' in depression. This is the most-reproduced finding in this illness. It is a key player in helping us focus on positive emotions and thoughts, and works with Areas 24 and 32. It is therefore no surprise that this logic-box power failure is felt by many to be partly responsible for our inability to 'switch off' the torrent of negative emotional sadness and low mood emanating from the stress box, and the very distressing cascades of automatic negative thoughts in MDD.

- The social and emotional behavioural boxes normally try to exert a modulating effect on our negative emotions, but they too are malfunctioning in depression. In a desperate effort to calm things down, they become overactive, but they are unsuccessful.

- This breakdown in normal control of the stress box by the various departments of our logical brain leads to most of the symptoms of depression. Feelings of anxiety, negative thinking or reinterpretation of social interactions, behavioural responses to the latter, poor self-esteem and suicidal thoughts are all created by it.

- Another major symptom is the disappearance of joy from our lives. This occurs because we experience a dampening of our pleasure pathways, due to underactivity of our dopamine mood cable and pleasure box.

- The memory pathways also become disrupted. Reduced activity of the left logic box leads to difficulties with short-term memory, so we struggle to retain information recently gained. Our memory box itself becomes very disrupted by high glucocortisol levels, and as a result struggles to consolidate and retrieve longer-term memories.

- The three mood boxes and cables, due partly to a high glucocortisol barrage, become underactive, leading to physical symptoms such as sleep, appetite, concentration, libido, drive and, most of all, energy difficulties – all of which make MDD such a debilitating illness.

- High glucocortisol levels lead to other physical consequences, like heart disease, diabetes and osteoporosis, as already discussed. I refer those who would like to examine the above mechanisms in more detail to *Flagging the Problem*.

- It is useful to examine also the three phases of brain development and their role in MDD.

THE DEVELOPING BRAIN is the phase of brain development from the womb to age thirty. There are three stages to consider.

Within the womb itself, genetic and epigenetic factors shape brain pathways. This is the phase where the hard-wiring of the brain occurs, influenced by male and female sex hormones (testosterone and oestrogen). Many researchers feel that the developing brain at this stage can be affected by alcohol, drugs, infections and perhaps severe stress in the life of the mother.

There is a great deal of interest in the first three years of the life of the child in terms of the future development of potential depression and anxiety pathways. When a child is born, the key players in its life are the stress box in the emotional brain and the social control box in the logical brain. Our memory box is completely immature, so we do not remember these vital years. But our stress box does retain its own 'version of events'. The small infant and toddler is strongly influenced by what happens during this phase.

If, for example, the mother develops postnatal depression, the child may become withdrawn and less communicative, and may even reduce feeding. This occurs because the infant's mirror neuron system tunes in instantly to those in its immediate environment, sensing where they are at emotionally, without, of course, any conscious ability to understand why (see page 24). Thankfully, the infant's demeanour and behaviour quickly improves if the mother receives some assistance with her own mood.

If the small infant undergoes major stress, either directly or through the experiences of those closest to it, high levels of stress hormones like glucocortisol will be produced, giving rise to the development of early potential anxiety or depression pathways that remain buried in the unconscious mind of the child. In such cases, there may be genetic predispositions present, but environmental and epigenetic influences generate these pathways.

The result may be a predisposition in that child's future, whereby stress at a later stage, possibly in the teens, can unmask depression. Numerous psychotherapy approaches, from Freud onwards, have zoned in on this period, with the assumption that the source of a person's present problems may lie here. One interesting possibility as to how this might occur lies in the potential for high glucocortisol levels to damage our spindle cells and support cells, particularly in the attention box. Since these are such key players in how our sadness, anxiety and socialising pathways develop, any such damage could predispose us to depression. The most likely vehicle for such changes is the second messenger system.

As the child moves past three, there is a period of around nine years where there is significant activity in the developing brain, but it is a relatively peaceful time: the calm before the storm. For the first twelve years, brain development is partially under the influence of our serotonin and dopamine systems. So they are not only important neurotransmitters in themselves but key players in brain development. Again, this is probably mediated through our second messenger/neurotrophic system.

The thirteen-to-thirty stage is one of the most important periods in our life, in terms of both brain development and future depression. Just prior to this phase, the brain increases its neuron numbers, but from thirteen onwards it is all about pruning the connections between cells, increasing efficiency for future adult use, and starting with the emotional brain limbic mood department. This is driven by our sex hormones, which, as we have seen, communicate with our genes through the second messenger system. This is a period of massive change and adaptation in the life of both the young adolescent and the brain itself. During this phase, the person's emotional world is turned upside down as they and their immature brain struggle to deal with approaching adulthood.

After age twenty, attention switches to our logical brain, in the form of our frontal mood department. Here, further pruning and increased connections between the logical and emotional brains leads to the gradual development of maturity. Our logical brain is practically mature by twenty-five but a final spurt takes place around thirty. Depression frequently appears in the fifteen-to-twenty-five age groups, and it is easy to see why. It is often an incredibly stressful period for the emerging young person, who has to cope with their newfound sexuality, peer-group pressures, learning to mingle and socialise when often feeling awkward and vulnerable, and exposure to alcohol and illegal drugs before the brain is able to cope with them.

There seems little doubt that high levels of glucocortisol produced in response to the above, exposes those who are vulnerable to depression. The big swings in female hormones in particular may also play a role. We now know that oestrogen, through its effects on the second messenger system, has a positive effect on our mood, and progesterone a more negative one.

It is difficult to over-emphasise the role of alcohol and illegal drugs on the developing brain, particularly before the age of fifteen. They have a powerfully negative effect on the second messenger system, significantly increasing the risks of depression. We have been in the throes of an alcohol epidemic nationally for the past decade in particular and have been exposed to increasing usage of cocaine in the past five years. It is therefore almost inevitable that the incidence of mental distress and depression in this group will increase. Other important environmental factors are lack of exercise, poor nutrition and family breakups at vulnerable times in the life of the emerging young adult. Consumerism, materialism, sexual-identity issues and bullying all play their part too. In the case of young men in particular, uncertainty about their place in the brave new world of sexual equality, and the possible absence of spiritual meaning in their lives, may all contribute to the ascent of depression.

Equally, if we over-protect our children, teenagers and young adults, paradoxically we set up a risk situation. This is because we shelter them from 'real life', and when they are finally exposed to the rough and tumble of life's vagaries, the young person has difficulty coping. Stress-hormone levels rise for a completely different reason, but with similar results. The best advice for parents is consciously to decide from an early age to allow the child to experience stress in a carefully modulated manner. Let them experience pain and discomfort in a controlled environment every step of the way from early childhood to their twenties. If we teach young people skills like problem-solving, emotional coping, sharing, and learning to take responsibility for – and deal with the consequences of – their own decisions, we will have gone a long way towards improving their mental health.

Another fascinating aspect of this situation is that we in the West have actually created 'teenage culture'. As a result, we have separated the growing adolescent from what they need most: to work side by side with their adult parents, absorbing their wisdom and life skills first-hand. In the developing world, for example, young people learn vital life skills and knowledge in this way. We, on the other hand, separate them from us beginning in early childhood, allowing our educational system to shape them. We should try as much as possible to spend time with them doing normal household chores, sports and other activities, subtly passing on our experience and wisdom to them.

THE MATURE BRAIN relates to the phase between thirty and sixty-five, when our brain has finished its reorganisation. From a mood-system viewpoint, there is a healthy relationship between our emotional and logical brain and the right and left hemispheres, and the development of increasing 'wisdom', where we learn more quickly to get to the 'essence' of situations in emotional and everyday lives.

This is the phase where we develop careers, meet partners and make long-term commitments, have and rear children and engage in the many problems that life throws at us. The stresses in this phase are complex and change from decade to decade as we grow and develop as human beings. For women in particular, this can be an enormously stressful period, as they have to cope with rearing children and holding down a job, while all the time being exposed to pre-menstrual hormonal shifts, during and after pregnancy and again in the menopause (where the protective effects of oestrogen are removed). It is no surprise that so many women develop depression during this phase. Both men and women may have suffered bouts of MDD in their teens or early twenties but may develop them anew as the pressures of life expose them to high glucocortisol levels, triggering latent depression pathways. It is likely that the later one develops a first episode of depression, the greater the stress necessary to trigger it. This is probably because the genetic/epigenetic predispositions are weaker than in situations where it developed in the under-twenty-five age groups.

The most likely environmental triggers in the case of the over-twenty-five groups are loss and bereavement, relationship breakdowns, addiction problems, financial disasters, and mental or physical illness involving children, to name but a few. Once again, alcohol and drugs like cocaine can also act as a catalyst, either on their own or in conjunction with the above, to trigger bouts of depression.

THE AGEING BRAIN is the third and final stage in our journey. With modern neuroimaging and other research findings, we are building up a picture of what happens in our brain as we reach sixty-five and onwards.

Firstly, as we age, our neurons gradually start to shrink in number – in particular those in our three big mood cables (serotonin, dopamine and noradrenalin). This makes us less able to adapt to what life throws at us. Thankfully, most people will retain enough to get through this phase safely. But apart from the neurons themselves, many elderly people begin to develop atherosclerosis (hardening of the arteries) of both large and small blood vessels supplying key parts of the brain. We now know that blockages to small vessels leading to the left frontal mood department of the brain in particular can trigger depression, even in those who have never experienced a previous bout, and also that large blockages (as happens when we have a stroke) in the same area can have a similar effect.

These vascular changes are believed to damage the second messenger/neurotrophic systems within the neurons of our logical brain. This leads to a loss of normal control over negative thoughts and emotions emanating from the emotional brain. Vital pathways have been disrupted and damaged. Environmental factors can also play a role in overcoming our more vulnerable mood system during this phase. The absence or otherwise of loved ones, physical health, independence and self-esteem plays an important part in the expression of this illness.

Other illnesses affecting the brain strongly disrupt key pathways, often triggering depression. The best example here is Parkinson's disease, which disrupts the dopamine cable supply to the emotional and logical brains, producing depression in up to 50 percent of cases. Alzheimer's disease is also very destructive to key pathways, in particular to the memory box, and is also associated with the development of depression. There will obviously be a cohort within this age group who will have suffered bouts of depression throughout their lives. All the accumulated damage, plus the natural ageing process, increases the risks of further problems. Special mention has to be made of the capacity of alcohol to play havoc in the ageing brain. As with the developing brain, it can interfere with the normal functioning of key pathways and increase the likelihood of depression occurring.

We have examined the depression pathways and how they are triggered, as our brain develops, matures, and ages. Let's now examine how our holistic therapy pathway can treat and prevent this distressing illness.

The Role of Our Holistic Therapy Pathway in Depression

There are a number of important statements we must make before we examine this in detail:

- To treat this illness, the person must present for help.

- Depression is almost unique in this regard, as one of the cardinal symptoms is negative thinking ('I am of no value, untreatable, nobody else could possibly be of help, and anyway I don't deserve such help'), which often prevents people coming for help.

- Almost 50 percent with MDD do not present to any health professional for advice or assistance.

- The other 50 percent are self-treating and are often drawn into the world of alternative medicine without any real diagnosis being made, and often without knowledge as to whether a particular therapy has been scientifically researched or proven.

- Even when those in mental distress present to health professionals, there is often confusion in terms of diagnosis between chronic stress, general anxiety disorders, a short-term life crisis and genuine depression.

- This distinction is vital for the correct therapy pathway to be activated.

- Many of those who do not present for help will usually recover from individual bouts of depression, usually within (an extremely difficult) twelve months. Relapse is, however, very common.

- Treating MDD is vital when it comes to reducing the long-term physical consequences already outlined, to prevent 'as much as possible' the potential for relapses, to reduce the risk of suicide and to help the person and their family to have a normal, healthy life.

- Finally, there are two big goals that must be achieved at this stage: to treat the particular presenting acute bouts of depression and to put in place as much as possible measures to reduce the risk of relapse.

When examining the role of our holistic therapy pathway in the treatment of MDD, this last statement is of great importance. It is not enough just to help somebody recover from a bout; we must also try to reduce the risks of recurrence.

Foundations

With the emphasis on drug, talk and alternative therapies, foundations are often forgotten. But we must remember that, without good foundations, houses will quickly get into difficulties. This concept is equally applicable to depression.

Empathy is one of the most important foundations, and finding an understanding family doctor or other health professional is crucial. Empathy pathways have to be set up between the GP or therapist and sufferer, otherwise any intervention is likely to fail. Earlier, we explained how these pathways are activated and why they are so important in encouraging self-healing.

Exercise is another cornerstone of both treating acute episodes and preventing relapses. The simplest regime involves thirty minutes of reasonably brisk exercise for at least five days a week – I myself look for a daily commitment. The benefits of exercise in depression are so great that some rate it alongside drug therapy in terms of its importance. Since, as already discussed, there is a link between MDD and coronary heart disease, there are also cardiac benefits to the above regime. The major problem in practice is that sufferers with depression have extreme physical and mental fatigue and so find it extremely difficult to become motivated to engage with this crucial therapy.

Useful tips include:

- keeping a diary of how one feels before and after exercise

- remembering that our aim is not just to feel better but to get better

- simple CBM behavioural advice like 'if sitting, can one stand; when standing, can one take a step – then another – and another till we reach the front door; can we open the door; now we are out in the fresh air – can we keep going?'

- trying to engage in a form of exercise that one might enjoy – whether that be walking, swimming, dancing, weightlifting, or whatever else appeals

- don't be afraid to start with smaller periods of time, perhaps ten minutes a few times a day

- writing down and challenging the negative thought ('I can't exercise') can often be a useful tool. Remember, just because we have a thought, doesn't mean it's true

- sometimes exercise can be combined with other useful therapies like yoga and mindfulness, so we are achieving an even greater therapeutic benefit

- it can be helpful to ask someone to join you when exercising, as this has the extra benefit of social communication, which is so nourishing to mind and body

Nutrition is another important foundation. Many people with MDD eat poorly or not at all. This occurs because our depleted dopamine system prevents us from the normal enjoyment of food. Our brain requires key nutrients to survive and function, so a vicious cycle may occur: we become depressed, lose interest in food, stop eating or else eat rubbish; our brain becomes starved of nutrients and becomes more dysfunctional, our depression worsens, and the cycle begins again.

As with exercise, the person with depression may struggle to motivate themselves to eat the three meals a day required, may take high-stimulant snacks like chocolate and caffeinated soft drinks instead, and may use coffee as a stimulant or, if a smoker, increase usage. Once again, I strongly encourage a healthy diet as part of my holistic package. The following tips are useful:

- Eat even if we don't enjoy it; consider it medication – something we do to help us get better

- Divide the day into three slots and draw up a table for the week, giving ourselves a plus for each slot if we eat well and a minus if we don't, gradually increasing the number of pluses

- Concentrate on fresh food, cooked by ourselves, with the emphasis on fish, fruit, meat, nuts, vegetables, and avoiding coffee, chocolate and minerals

- Remember that, as depression improves, our appetite will return, and eventually we will enjoy food again

- Adding supplements like Omega 3 fish oils, which we discussed previously (in a daily dose of between 500 and 1000 mgs) and simple B vitamins can be of great help to a brain starved of these essential elements, particularly in cases where we have been eating poorly for some time

- Fish oils can have a secondary cardiac benefit and, as heart disease is more common in MDD, it is probably worth including them indefinitely in our diet

MODERATION THERAPY is another lifestyle foundation. In depression, this involves examining many often unhelpful areas of our lives. We have to mention the importance of alcohol in this illness. Many (particularly young men) use alcohol as a crutch in MDD. It gives them a temporary lift but their mood drops quickly, further increasing suicidal thoughts or actions. When taken in large amounts, it is very destructive to the developing brain, greatly increasing the risks of future depression arising. I am also becoming increasingly concerned about the numbers misusing hash, cocaine and alcohol, which increases destruction of the developing brain and indeed, as a cocktail, can cause fatal cardiac arrest.

RELAXATION THERAPIES as we discussed earlier, have a useful but relatively limited role in depression. Their main benefit is a short-term reduction in the anxiety symptoms so common in this illness. Meditation can be considered as another useful tool, particularly in the prevention of depression. We have already discussed this in detail earlier, and we will be discussing cognitive-based mindfulness later. However, I have reservations about the usefulness of meditation in acute depression and would counsel against it. It could worsen symptoms of negative thinking when we are particularly vulnerable.

STRESS REDUCTION: There is no doubt that stress plays a major role in triggering illnesses like depression. A key factor in any holistic package has to be a review of stress triggers that have led to the appearance of such illnesses, suggestions as to how we can deal with stress symptoms, and building in safeguards for the future. The following tips are useful:

- If there has been a definite stress trigger preceding a particular bout of depression, when feeling better it is vital that we examine it and make whatever changes are possible, in order to reduce the risks of further episodes.

- We should not be afraid to make major changes in employment, relationships and financial matters if these are felt to be of benefit.

- Examine stress-reducing measures like exercise, yoga, meditation, massage, and so on.

- Spend more time with Mother Nature and less in shopping centres.

- Stop putting unrealistic expectations in our way and accept that doing the best we can is all that is required of us in life.

THE PLACEBO EFFECT: We dealt with this in great detail in earlier chapters, but it is important to look at its place in MDD. Depression is an extraordinary illness in that the emotional brain convinces us that negative thoughts (such as 'I will never get better') are true, while knowing deep down that they are not. In reverse, there are few other illnesses where suggestions that a particular therapy (whatever its scientific truthfulness) can help us get better leads, in many cases, to an immediate, if temporary, improvement in symptoms. This is because the same areas of the brain involved in depression are stimulated by the actual thought that something positive is going to happen. We dealt with the pathways involved earlier.

Difficulties arise when we choose to compare some forms of therapy versus placebo treatments, but accept others as effective without any proper trials. In my opinion, this leads thousands of people to head down roads that will turn out to be expensive dead ends. The person in trouble will experience some form of placebo positive effect, almost no matter what the particular therapy concerned (this will usually have occurred in part due to the empathetic relationship developed with the alternative therapist in question), but this will usually wear off after one or two months. But this may be enough to convince the sufferer that it has been effective. The main issue here is that this may prevent the person from receiving the holistic package they really need, making relapse and further difficulties almost inevitable. So from the beginning, let us accept that:

- Every therapy has some form of placebo effect: an expectation that something positive will occur.

- In depression, this effect is more powerful, due to the underlying mechanisms associated with this illness.

- This is felt to be less so in the case of really serious depression, where the underlying system failure is so major that placebo pathways are less involved.

- The real effect of any therapy, if we wish to measure it scientifically, is the cumulative effect over a long period of time with the placebo.

- Few alternative therapies have been properly measured in this way, or else they have often failed to demonstrate effects greater than a placebo.

- A figure of around 20 to 30 percent is probably an average placebo effect in relation to all therapies.

- We should not diminish the importance of this powerful effect, which is driven by the brain mechanisms underlying hope and expectation. To do so would be to underestimate the place it holds in the journey towards recovery.

- A particular difficulty experienced by those researching drug therapies used in depression is that it is considered unethical to withhold treatment for any longer than six to eight weeks, which makes it more complex to tease out the actual placebo effect.

- It is probably more helpful as a result to compare different therapy approaches over a longer period of time in order to balance out this effect.

The Main Structure

Moving on, let's examine the role of the next two main planks of our holistic pathway, drug and talk therapies.

TALK THERAPIES

When dealing with depression, the opinion that drug therapy, on top of a solid foundation, helps us to feel better so that we can engage with the various forms of talk therapy to help us get better is indeed true.

There are many forms of talk therapy. We have examined most of them earlier, but some stand out as being of help in MDD. These include counselling, psychoanalytic psychotherapy, cognitive behaviour therapy (CBT), behaviour therapy, interpersonal therapy (ITP), supportive psychotherapy, brief dynamic psychotherapy and mindfulness-based cognitive therapy (MBCT), all of which would be classified as traditional mainstream therapies.

Counselling, CBT, ITP and MBCT would be regarded as the most helpful talk therapies in depression, and most research has been into CBT and IPT. We have already reviewed these therapies in detail but let us now briefly examine their role in depression.

- Counselling helps deal with stress, family or relationship difficulties, bereavement, abuse and addiction, all of which may play a role in the triggering and maintenance of depression.

- Interpersonal therapy (ITP) helps us deal with the role of interpersonal relationships in the triggering and maintenance of MDD.

- Cognitive behaviour therapy (CBT) helps us challenge the negative emotions, thoughts and behaviour that are so associated with depression, using Beck (e.g. the Five Areas model) and Ellis (e.g. the 'ABC' and Raggy Doll Club) approaches.

- Mindfulness-based cognitive therapy (MBCT) helps reduce depression relapses by teaching us to become mindfully aware of thoughts, emotions and behaviour in the present moment so that we can learn to recognise unhelpful patterns and gradually change them.

Let's examine the role of CBT and MBCT in depression in a little more detail. CBT is extremely useful in both the treatment and prevention of depression. The Five Areas model teaches the person to link together their thoughts, feelings, physical responses, behaviour and environment and shows how altering any one of these things in a positive sense can help improve the others. If, for example, I make a behavioural change, such as starting to exercise daily, this may in turn lead to my mood lifting, my fatigue reducing and my thinking becoming more positive.

The Ellis (symbolised by the Raggy Doll Club) approach helps us challenge the core negative belief that 'I am awful'. If I learn to accept myself without conditions, I have travelled a long way down the journey back to mental health. This too will challenge unhealthy safety and avoidant behaviour. I find this approach more helpful when dealing with depression.

MINDFULNESS-BASED COGNITIVE THERAPY (MBCT) may become increasingly important in the prevention of major depression. We examined earlier the place of meditation in depression. Eastern medicine has recognised the importance of this therapy in the area of mental health for millennia. In the past ten years, Western medicine has begun adapting these concepts into the CBT model and applied them to depression in particular. This has led to the development of MBCT.

If we have suffered from depression in the past, streams of distressing emotion, negative thoughts and resulting behaviour have usually become firmly embedded in our memory banks. These memory pathways can be easily triggered when internal or external events generate a similar mood, setting off a chain of emotions, thoughts and behaviour, and tipping us back into depression. This ability of the emotional brain to descend quickly into a flow of negative assessments about ourselves and the world is called 'rumination' and is felt by many psychologists to be a common reason for sliding back into the world of depression.

This makes sense because, as already discussed, each bout of depression seems to weaken the ability of our logical brain biologically to dampen down the negative barrage from the emotional one. In this sense, our mind and brain pathways are as one. The real battle in preventing depression must involve using therapies which target this tendency to 'ruminate'. We have already seen the power of normal CBT to help identify and actively challenge such thoughts and behaviour. In many senses, this is an active, 'hands-on' approach.

A second approach to the 'prevention' of depression is to use the skill of mindfulness to teach us to become increasingly aware of our thoughts, emotions and bodily sensations in the present moment. Through this awareness, we can learn to identify unhelpful thinking patterns, subtly breaking this negative chain of thoughts and emotions. A common ruminating pathway involves the criticism of ourselves that we are beginning to think and feel this way again ('Here we go again, what is wrong with me that I am unable to stop this happening, I am so weak and useless'). This harsh judgement of ourselves leaves us more prone to re-enter depression pathways.

This pattern develops because we spend most of our lives living in the world of 'doing versus being'. Unfortunately, the more we feel we have to do something to change the rumination barrage in our mind, the more we strengthen its hold. This is because our emotional brain is so strong. Mindfulness encourages us to be with our emotions and thoughts in the present moment, shutting down the negative ruminating pattern by focusing in on them, without actively trying to alter or change them.

This is why it is so essential that you are not in the middle of an active bout of depression while learning this technique or you might be overwhelmed by an awareness of the huge amount of negative thoughts flowing from your emotional brain. Rather, it is important to wait until you are well, and only then to learn the necessary skills to shut off at source these streams of negative thoughts.

MBCT is all about gradually learning, through graded mindfulness exercises (like the Three Minute Breathing Space detailed earlier), the capacity to identify unhealthy thoughts, emotions, physical feelings and behaviour patterns as they are at this particular moment of time (not in the past or the future), and to learn to accept and embrace them without harshly judging ourselves.

One of the most important benefits of this approach is the learned ability to accept individual thoughts (and emotions) as being just temporary, as experiences or events occurring in our mind rather than actual realities. This might be the most important single concept in the whole area of mental health, particularly in anxiety and depression. One of the most beautiful and visual ways of conceptualising this is to consider such thoughts and emotions as temporary phenomena like clouds floating across the sky, disappearing after a while, leaving behind a clear blue sky.

Techniques involved in MBCT are a cross between modern CBT and ancient yoga and meditation exercises. A number of such programmes have been developed. Ideally, they are best taught by experts and in groups. They usually involve focusing on mindfulness awareness of our breath, body, sound, touch, emotions and thoughts. A full explanation of all the techniques involved is beyond the scope of this book. Should you wish to learn more, I would highly recommend *The Mindful Way through Depression* (see bibliography), which is a superb book on this subject.

I would like to refer briefly to a meeting between Western scientists and Eastern experts in 2007. Participating in a day-long symposium entitled 'Mindful, Compassion and the Treatment of Depression' was the Dalai Lama and some Eastern colleagues, internationally acclaimed researchers Charles B. Nemeroff, MD, PhD, Professor Reunette W. Harris and Professor Helen S. Mayberg, MD, (department of psychiatry at Emory University), Zindel V. Segal, PhD, (one of the authors of *The Mindful Way through Depression*) and other distinguished guests.

The conference focused on the role of meditation in promoting cognitive, emotional and physiological states that protect against depression. This was within the broader context of whether developing mindfulness and greater compassion through meditation training in adulthood might help individuals compensate for the depression promoting effects of adversity, trauma and lack of nurturing early in life – all primary environmental contributors to major depression. Researchers presented data suggesting that mindfulness practices may help prevent the recurrence of major depression and that meditation practices, specifically designed to promote compassionate cognitions and emotions towards others, may have effects on the brain and body that are directly relevant to depression.

There is much to learn from this wonderful meeting of minds, with East and West both teaching and learning from each other. The conference emphasised the importance of empathy, the links between mind, body and spirit (whatever we perceive that to be), the role of stress, the importance of our social connections and, most interestingly, how both recognised the place of effective biological (drug) therapy in helping a person with this illness reach a place where talk therapies and mindfulness can be effective.

DRUG THERAPY plays a crucially important role in our holistic pathway in the treatment of depression. There are two main types used in mainstream medicine: antidepressants and mood stabilisers.

ANTIDEPRESSANTS: We discussed earlier the importance of the second messenger systems in MDD, and this allows us to reassess the importance of antidepressants. We know that they have an immediate effect (which starts to kick in after two to three weeks), improving many of the physical symptoms of depression (such as sleep, appetite, drive and concentration), and psychological ones such as low mood and anxiety. But we now know that there are delayed positive effects on the second messenger system/neurotrophic system, particularly in relation to BDNF, which seem to take up to six months or so to consolidate. This prevents the further shrinkage of neurons and their dendrites – a crucial piece of information which is often overlooked.

There are some practical observations to make here:

- If we start a course of antidepressants, we must accept that the course is for six to eight months if we want to achieve maximum effect.

- It is important to decide with your doctor just how long the course will last.

- The SSRIs are the treatment of choice in the majority of cases. They do have side effects like initial nausea (due to initial activation of serotonin receptors in the gut), sweating, tremors of the hands, and heavier periods in the case of females (through their effects on blood platelets). These often disappear after a while as the body adapts to the medication.

- Many people taking SSRIs for depression suffer from a loss of sexual libido, impotence and delayed or abnormal orgasm. For some, who may have had no sex drive due to their depression, this may not be a great problem. However, after several months of treatment, people will start to feel better and will regain their interest in sex. It is then that any sexual side effects caused by these drugs become an issue.

- If side effects do occur, they will disappear within a few days of finishing the course.

- If we stop taking these drugs suddenly, we will experience dizziness and a sense of spinning, which is relieved immediately once the course is started again. This is why it is so important to follow directions from your family doctor to the letter.

- When a course is over, your doctor will lay out how to come off the drugs.

- They are not addictive and generally do not cause drowsiness.

- They should generally, apart from Mirtazapine, be taken in the morning with food.

- Escitalopram (Lexapro) is the most commonly prescribed SSRI. It is extremely effective in most cases and generally well tolerated. I would regard it as a first-line option.

- The biggest problem in my experience is that many people are treated with doses that are too low and are not increased swiftly as required.

- If the SSRIs are not effective on their own, adding in small amounts of Mirtazapine can, in my experience, be of great help. If the person is still having problems, SRNI drugs that affect both serotonin and noradrenalin mood cables, like Cymbalta or Efexor, are the next options. Extra side effects like severe sweating and headaches can be a problem, and I find that Efexor has more sexual side effects than the SSRIs.

- I am more uneasy about using SRNIs, particularly Efexor, in the elderly due to potential cardiac and cerebrovascular side effects, although some may find them helpful.

- These drugs will only be effective in up to 70 to 80 percent of cases. Where they are not effective, a review of the diagnosis is essential, and applying other parts of the holistic pathway, such as lifestyle changes, mood stabilisers and talk therapies, will usually solve the problem.

- If you are misusing or abusing alcohol, hash or cocaine and do not inform your doctor of this, you will struggle to get your mood back up and are only fooling yourself.

- If you are under eighteen, drug therapy should ideally be started by a psychiatrist, and Prozac is the one most favoured in this group.

- In the elderly, drug therapy should be part of a total package, and should be started in doses half the normal level.

- In the case of recurrent significant depression, I feel that, due to the underlying neurobiological data already discussed, we should be considering using a mood stabiliser with an SSRI to reduce such risks.

MOOD STABILISERS are a second line of defence in more severe recurrent depression, often combined with antidepressants. Apart from stimulating the second messenger system to produce BDNF, which helps nourish the neuron and make new dendrites, they also increase Bcl, which prevents the neuron from self-destructing. The most common mood stabilisers are Lamictal and Lithium. Once again, we dealt with these drugs and their side effects in earlier chapters, and   they are also covered in the appendix. We will be also dealing with them further in the section on bipolar depression.

ALTERNATIVE DRUG THERAPIES relate to drugs other than mainstream ones that purport to be effective in the treatment of MDD. The two main groups here are homeopathy and herbal remedies. In relation to the latter, the main herb of choice is St John's wort, which we have discussed in detail already. Although it has shown to be effective in research trials, concerns about its interactions with other drugs, its side effects and the quality of the product limits its usefulness, with most experts feeling that modern SSRIs are safer. We have also dealt in detail with homeopathy, and the lack of any real scientific basis for this therapy. The main 'remedies' used here are *Arsenicum album, Ignacia psorinum, Pulsatilla, Natrium muraticum and Aurum metallicum.*

While many will continue to use alternative drug therapies, I counsel caution. My biggest concern is that a person with significant depression may not receive the vital help they need and may as a result waste time, energy and money on often dubious remedies, ending up in real difficulty. I recommend that you attend your family doctor before going down such roads.

Ancillary Therapies

This relates to those therapies, mainstream and alternative, that are also used to treat depression.

MAINSTREAM ANCILLARY THERAPIES include light therapy, sleep deprivation and brain-stimulating therapies like ECT, trans-cranial magnetic stimulation and deep-brain stimulation. I have dealt with the last three in my last book and suggest that those interested read the relevant section there. So let's now examine the other two.

SLEEP DEPRIVATION has been recognised for decades to improve mood in those suffering from a bout of MDD. Sleep is essential for normal brain function: it is when our brain (1) heals and repairs itself (through NREM, or deep sleep), and (2) reorganises and strengthens our memories (through REM, or dream sleep). In the first, the brain is quiet. In the latter, it bursts into activity, particularly in the second half of our sleep cycle.

These bursts of REM sleep, lasting about twenty minutes, are when we dream. REM stands for 'rapid eye movement'; during this phase, our eyes oscillate back and forth, and the movement ceases when the burst of activity is over. Dreams are created by our memory box passing information over and back to parts of the brain where previous memories are stored, and this explains their jumbled nature.

The average sleep cycle is eight hours. Both phases interchange throughout the night, and most REM sleep occurs in the second half. During sleep, our brain secretes melatonin (making us drowsy), generally switching off serotonin and noradrenalin systems. On waking, melatonin levels fall and serotonin/noradrenalin systems (making us alert) switch on. Sleep difficulties (particularly difficulty getting to sleep, broken sleep and early-morning waking) are the cardinal symptoms of depression. Many with depression note that their mood is low in the morning, and improves as the day goes on.

In depression, the serotonin system is already underactive, with a greater tendency to REM sleep when serotonin activity is switched off. Some feel that, in depression, the brain actually strengthens negative emotional memories while asleep. This occurs during REM sleep, which focuses in particular on emotional experiences.

Normal REM/NREM sleep patterns are disturbed, with more REM sleep occurring in the first half of the sleep cycle. There is a shortage of nocturnal melatonin (which is produced from serotonin), explaining difficulties in falling asleep or staying asleep. Because of the serotonin system's general nocturnal underactivity and the disruption of normal NREM/REM brain activities and reduced melatonin, many people with depression wake feeling very down and exhausted. If a person with depression takes a daytime nap, their serotonin system switches off, so they wake up even more depressed. This is problematic, as their behavioural pattern (due to mental exhaustion) encourages them to retire to bed, yet this worsens their symptoms.

An immediate way to improve low mood in MDD is a single night of total (all night) or partial (second half of night) sleep deprivation. This improves mood within hours. Although the effects of such therapy are helpful, it is not practical for use on its own. The brain needs sleep to repair itself and reorganise its memories, so chronic sleep deprivation would be toxic in the long run. Some have also combined it with light therapy as a possible approach when drug therapy is not possible.

LIGHT THERAPY is based on links between light and serotonin. In winter, due to a shortage of full-spectrum daylight, serotonin activity reduces, and the opposite is the case in summer. As a result, in winter months all of us feel flatter, crave carbohydrates and sleep more. Not surprisingly, 25 to 30 percent of people with depression see their condition deteriorate in winter.

One way of fooling the brain in depression is through the use of light therapy, either on its own or through a dawn simulator. Light therapy, particularly in the morning, increases serotonin activity and is a useful adjunct to other therapies. Light boxes emitting 2,500 to 10,000 lux of light (30 to 120 minutes, depending on appliance) are recommended for routine depression. Many of these boxes are small, portable and easy to use.

Dawn-simulator lamps (which I am a great believer in) fool the brain into thinking it is summertime. When set to come on an hour before waking, they gradually release full-spectrum light into the room, mimicking a summer dawn. This activates a reflex between the eyes and the brain, increasing serotonin and reducing melatonin activity, ideal for boosting mood. Some simulators will include an extra light-therapy attachment for those who would like to boost it further. Those who would like to acquire such devices should see the appendix.

ALTERNATIVE ANCILLARY THERAPIES include acupuncture, hypnosis, energy-field therapies, reiki and cranial manipulation, all of which we have already reviewed. There is little real evidence that any of the above have any real benefit apart from the empathy/placebo effects discussed earlier.

Application of the Holistic Therapy Pathway to Depression

When applying our therapy pathway to treat MDD, there are two key requirements:

1. Treating acute bouts when they arise;
2. Putting in place preventative measures to reduce the risk of further episodes.

The treatment of acute bouts of depression depends initially on the adage that the three main treatment priorities are diagnosis, diagnosis and diagnosis. This is of particular relevance where so many laypeople and media figures use the term 'depression' to describe everything from unhappiness to panic attacks. The most common cases of 'mistaken identity' versus MDD relate to chronic stress, generalised anxiety disorder and the normal causes of human sadness like grief and relationship breakdowns. I regularly see patients who feel they are depressed but are actually suffering symptoms from one of the above. We have already detailed these main symptoms. If in doubt I strongly advise visiting your family doctor. To qualify as true MDD, the symptoms must be present for a minimum of two weeks. In reality, most presenting to their family doctor will have been in trouble for months.

The next crucial step is to find a doctor or therapist who can empathise with you. In many cases, your family doctor is the obvious choice, as you will generally have built up a good relationship with him or her over a period of years. In other cases, you may have a good relationship with a counsellor or therapist and feel more comfortable in opening up to them. If that is not possible: start by sharing your distress with somebody close – a friend or family member.

After that, you must examine lifestyle – take nutrition, exercise (thirty minutes a day), supplements, ceasing alcohol for a definite period, as immediate steps to initiate. Your family doctor can out rule any other physical illnesses and do appropriate blood tests. With him (or her), you will have to make a decision as to whether you require drug therapy as a means of lifting mood and improving key physical symptoms like low energy, sleep problems, lack of concentration, low drive, reduced appetite and poor memory. In some cases, you may both decide that this will not be necessary and that a combination of lifestyle, stress-reducing measures (as already detailed), counselling if necessary, or some simple CBM techniques may be sufficient.

If (as will often be the case) you arrive in to see your family doctor feeling very down, exhausted and struggling to cope with the physical symptoms of this illness, you may decide on drug therapy to help restore normal functioning. The usual duration of such a course is six to eight months. Most will start to feel better with drug therapy within two to three weeks, and many will feel 'back to themselves' within six to eight weeks.

In my opinion, this is when the real work must begin. Lifestyle measures like exercise have to be emphasised, stress has to be analysed and appropriate measures have to be taken. Counselling or interpersonal therapy may be required, and negative thoughts and behaviour need to be challenged. This latter is best done using CBT/CBM methods, by working with either a GP or an appropriate therapist.

In some cases where drug therapy is needed and you are adamant that it is not an option, St John's wort is a possibility. But one has to take into account the concerns expressed about this form of treatment. Some may want to use homeopathic therapies. While I feel that there are major concerns about their scientific basis, some may find them helpful.

As the physical symptoms of the depression, and negative thinking, gradually improve, one can start to examine some helpful alternative therapies, like yoga, meditation, massage and so on, as useful stress-reducing measures.

There is one final step that I would recommend to all who are suffering from depression: to have one's cardiac risk factors like cholesterol, body weight, blood pressure, blood sugars, and so on, assessed at least once. This is because we now know that there is a significant link between MDD and coronary heart disease, for reasons we have already explained. This can be done through your family doctor. For women who have had a number of episodes of this illness, I would recommend having a DEXA scan of your bones, to rule out osteoporosis (thinning of the bones).

The statistic that only 50 percent of those with this illness will present for help, usually to their family doctor, is of great concern. We have to ask immediately: 'What happens to the other 50 percent?' Since up to 10 to 15 percent of the population will develop this illness (which corresponds to a projected figure of up to 400,000 in Ireland), a significant number in distress are not receiving the assistance they deserve. Why do so many not present for help?

The answer lies in negative thinking: they believe the thoughts 'We are of no worth', 'Nothing can be done to help us'; 'It's just the way we are'. This allied to a sense of shame and stigma attached to this illness, concerns that declaring it might have an impact on our jobs or career, and widespread confusion in relation to the different therapies, may lead to a great reluctance on the part of the person to come forward for help.

A person who is suffering from such negative thoughts should remember the crucial CBT concept: just because I have a thought, any thought, does not mean that it is true. Nowhere is this truer than in depression. You are like the rest of us, quite special: a 'Raggy Doll'. It is a false and unhealthy thought that you cannot be helped. In my experience, almost everybody can be helped, often with simple therapies and lifestyle changes. As to the shame and stigma concerns, one has to ask: 'Would you be as bothered about presenting with a similar physical condition like diabetes or high blood pressure?'

The prevention of further bouts of depression is the Holy Grail. For even when full recovery has been made, this illness tends to recur in a significant number of cases. The estimated risks of recurrence are 50 percent after the first bout, increasing rapidly after this to 80 to 90 percent after the third bout, if the first episode occurs in our teens, or if there is a strong family history. Between 50 and 85 percent of depressed persons will experience multiple episodes. The earlier we can treat an episode and put in place protective measures, the lower the risk becomes, as both mind and brain pathways become increasingly vulnerable to stress, the more episodes we experience.

Learning simple CBT/CBM concepts like the 'Raggy Doll' and applying it on a regular basis to many of the situations life throws at us can have profoundly positive effects on our mental health, as we learn to love and accept ourselves for the simple but wonderfully flawed human beings we are. These concepts can also be used to treat another common cause for depression relapses, namely underlying anxiety. Many are in a vicious cycle: anxiety wears them down, so they develop further bouts of depression and then recover, only to return to the world of anxiety again.

CBT can also be used as an adjunct to counselling for abuse, where we shed ourselves of the corrosive effects of hurt and anger, further triggering depression relapse. There is a significant role for meditation, particularly mindfulness-based cognitive therapy (MBCT), for those experiencing regular relapses.

The twin approach of 'active' CBT challenging negative thoughts and behaviour, and (seemingly) 'passive' MBCT assisting us to become more mindfully aware of our thoughts, emotions, physical reactions and behaviour may be the real secret to reducing the risks of MDD returning to our lives. We have already dealt with these in detail.

166

A sensible combination of these therapies will reduce the risk of depression relapses in a significant number of cases. But there is definitely a cohort of people with recurrent severe depression who will require maintenance drug therapy for long periods of time, and in some cases for life.

We have already examined the loss of brain neurons, dendrites and support cells in the logical and emotional brains, and the reality that repeated episodes of depression seem to increase the vulnerability of brain pathways to become dysfunctional as a result. We now know that drugs like the SSRIs have the ability, through their effects on BDNF, to nourish and protect the neurons of the mood system. Unfortunately, they do not, on their own, regenerate the tissues lost, but they do protect the remaining neurons. This is the basis for their use in the prevention of relapses.

One has to also wonder if we should, in such cases, be considering adding mood stabilisers. By increasing the neurons' production of neurotrophic factors like Bcl, we can help regenerate parts of the mood system and prevent further neurons from dying. I deal with this area in more detail in the technical section.

Combining a mood stabiliser like Lamictal with an SSRI-type antidepressant when depression, despite our best efforts, is constantly recurring is often of benefit. There is a huge amount of research into new therapies that will target the second messenger or neurotrophic systems, and maybe, in time, new therapy approaches will become available.

There are definitely situations where this approach is the road to travel, but the more we introduce lifestyle/CBT/mindfulness preventative measures at as early a stage as possible, the less likely it is that such drug-therapy combinations will be necessary. Also, I have no doubt that even where such drug therapy is being used in this way; the rest of the holistic path cannot but help reduce further risks of relapse.

There will be some who may feel that staying permanently on herbal treatments like St John's wort is the best route to travel. Although this may seem like the 'natural' route, there are significant side effects and drug interactions, which are not often discussed, and also concerns about the actual contents of many preparations, where many other herbs may be used. Once again, I counsel discussing it with your family doctor. Light therapy, in its various forms, can be a useful adjunct in the winter months to protect mood in those who note major drops at these times of the year.

Let us now meet a number of people presenting with depression at different stages of life and examine how their lives have been transformed by applying various parts of our holistic therapy path to their lives. As with anxiety, we do show the place of CBT/CBM in these stories; but once again advise that one must work with a trained health professional like a therapist/doctor to learn how to apply such concepts to oneself.

John's Story

'I feel weighed down by hopelessness and sadness. It is a physical pain in my heart, and no one understands how terrible it feels.'

John is a nineteen-year-old undergraduate student who develops depression after moving away from his family to live in a flat in Dublin. He successfully hides his depression from family and close friends. He uses copious amounts of alcohol to relieve the pain for short periods: its embrace, however, is fleeting and illusory. Thankfully, he opens up to a college counsellor. On his advice, John shares how he was feeling with his mum and dad. To his surprise, he feels better for doing so and, on their advice, he attends the family doctor.

He finds it difficult to explain how he feels but, with encouragement, admits to the exhaustion, sleep difficulties, anxiety, and loss of appetite, drive and concentration, which, along with a low mood, has turned his previous three months into a nightmare. He finds it helpful to discover that his difficulties with studying and retaining information are due to his memory and concentration being impeded by depression and that the suicidal thoughts he has been experiencing were also part of the condition. He has no plans to harm himself but has been distressed by the thoughts themselves.

John shares with his doctor that his mum suffered from depression in her earlier years, something she revealed following his own admission of difficulties. On probing, it becomes clear that he has become very isolated in Dublin. He has also begun to doubt (due to problems retaining information) whether he is suited to his course, and he is misusing alcohol to deal with his low mood.

Following discussion, the following treatment plan was drawn up, where John would:

- look for a special exemption from his course for the rest of the academic year on medical grounds

- do some simple blood tests to exclude any other physical reasons for his exhaustion

- start thirty minutes of brisk exercise every day, eat properly and take supplements prescribed

- cease taking alcohol until his mood has lifted

- begin a course of antidepressants to try to lift his mood and improve many of the physical symptoms of depression

- return again for follow-up, where further examination of some of his problems would ensue.

After four weeks, John was starting to feel a little better. His blood tests were normal, he was exercising (weightlifting and walking), was off alcohol, was eating a little better and was starting to sleep again. He had, with the help of his family doctor, organised his medical exemption, calming many of his fears.

After eight weeks, he felt more hopeful, his interest, energy and mood were better, and his suicidal thoughts had gone. Two problems remained: firstly, he was still feeling very negative about himself, and secondly, he was uncertain as to whether he should return to his course. His doctor recommended a guidance counsellor for advice on the road he should travel and did some simple CBM on his negative thinking. He started by asking for an example of the latter. John replied that he felt both ashamed and depressed because he had developed depression in the first place, had to pull out of college for the year and in his own words, had 'let everybody down'. His doctor asked him to choose which of these was bothering him the most. John replied: 'The depression.'

His doctor then explained the 'ABC' concepts to him, and together they drew up the following analysis of his problem:

A: TRIGGER: The arrival of depression in his life

INTERPRETATION/DANGER: Only 'weak' people become depressed, and other people, particularly friends and college acquaintances, would feel that he must be 'inferior' if he has developed these symptoms

B: BELIEF (OR DEMAND): Because he has developed depression, he is a failure and thus of no value to himself or others

C: EMOTION: Depression

PHYSICAL SYMPTOMS: All the physical symptoms already outlined.

BEHAVIOUR: He begins avoiding meeting peer-group friends, spends more time 'hiding away at home', stops socialising, avoids talking to his siblings, and spends more and more time on the computer.

His doctor challenges some of the above. Firstly, he explains how our behaviour can, in depression, further isolate us from the love and friendship of those with whom we normally associate with, worsening the illness. They agree that he will begin to change some of the unhealthy patterns he has become embroiled in.

He challenges John's unhealthy belief that because he had developed depression, he was 'of no value as a person'. He introduces him to the Raggy Doll Club (Figure 35) and its rules of admission: that we cannot rate ourselves or accept other people's rating. He helps John see that if he became a Raggy Doll, he could not rate himself because he had developed depression, or indeed for any other reason, nor could he allow other friends and colleagues to rate him.

The key message is that, if he could learn to become a Raggy Doll and accept himself without conditions, his negative personal assessments of himself would give way to more realistic ones. He would realise that he was a special human being, just like the rest of us.

He then gives John some homework. He asks him to begin doing some ABC's in situations where he found himself interpreting events (both internal or external) in a manner where he found his mood suddenly falling, and to return after a further two weeks to see how he has got on.

After another two visits, John is starting to feel much better, with an improvement not only in his physical symptoms and mood but also in his thinking. He has discussed his course decision and has realised that it was not the course but the way he had been feeling that was the problem. He is going to return to finish it.

After nine months, John is well, off all medication, exercising regularly, more careful with his diet and moderate in terms of his alcohol intake. He is back at college, involved in a lot more student activities and has a girlfriend. He has also, on the advice of his doctor, decided to join some of the student mental-health groups at college, where he learns about mindfulness and begins using it in simple ways in his life. He has put in place all the pieces to protect his mental health. Most importantly, he has become a Raggy Doll.

Mary's story

'The simplest of tasks drains me of all my energy. I just want to sleep all the time.'

Mary is a twenty-seven-year-old mother with two small children. She has developed symptoms of depression following a series of stressful events: her partner losing his job, leaving her as the main breadwinner, her mother developing early dementia, and finally losing a close friend to cancer.

Increasingly exhausted, she eventually breaks down in front of her family doctor on a routine visit with one of the children. She admits to her mood being down for six weeks before her friend had died, and having deteriorated since. She also admits to sleep, appetite, sex and memory/concentration difficulties and to a loss of enjoyment of her life. She was starting to have relationship problems as her negative rating of herself spread to her partner, whom she felt was responsible in part for the problem. She was also drinking more than usual, struggling to deal with the way she felt, and becoming increasingly isolated from close friends, as she simply did not have the energy to relate to them.

Her doctor examines her and arranges for blood tests to be done. He explains that her fatigue stems from depression and gives her some useful information. He sees her the following week, when her tests are reported to be clear. She is now happy to accept that her fatigue and other symptoms are due to depression, triggered by a number of life stress triggers and loss. They agree on the following treatment plan, where Mary would:

- take some time out of work on medical grounds in order to give her a chance to recover

- start exercising, improve her diet and take supplements

- cease taking alcohol until her mood has improved

- begin a course of antidepressants to improve some of her physical symptoms (particularly fatigue) and help lift her mood

- when she is feeling better, plan to get help from the local bereavement counselling service and, at a later stage, get some relationship counselling if she felt that this was necessary

- at a later stage, organise some community assistance for her mother

She returns after four weeks feeling a little better, with her mood definitely lifting, and some improvement in appetite and sleep, but her fatigue remains a major problem. She has managed to improve her diet but is really struggling with exercise. 'I can't motivate myself,' she explains. 'I plan to go for a walk every day but when the moment arrives, I just find any excuse not to go. I feel such a failure; I cannot even manage half an hour of exercise.'

After eight weeks, she is feeling much better; her fatigue is improving, but only gradually. She is now attending the bereavement counsellor, is off alcohol and is getting on much better with her partner, especially after having admitted her problem and looked for assistance. She is taking more care of herself, has booked in for weekly massages, is meeting up with some of her friends, with whom she shared her difficulties, and is receiving great support from them. She has enlisted help from her wider family, and they, together with local community services, have arranged for her mother to receive help. She no longer feels so isolated in relation to this issue.

She has two problems remaining, however. She still struggles with the fatigue and exercise part of her therapy and still feels very negative about herself, believing that she is a 'failure' for not being able to take regular exercise. At this stage, her doctor feels that she is well enough to do some CBM exercises with her and explains the 'ABC' approach. They use this on the above issue and together draw up the following analysis of her problem:

A: TRIGGER: Wanting to go for a thirty-minute walk to help her mood

INTERPRETATION/DANGER: She will be unable even to get started on the above due to fatigue and then feels she is a failure because of this

B: BELIEF (OR DEMAND): That because she is unable to exercise in this way, she is a complete failure and of no value to herself or others

C: EMOTION: Depression

PHYSICAL SYMPTOMS: All the physical symptoms already outlined

BEHAVIOUR: Stops going out for walks, making excuses as to why she is physically unable to do so.

Her doctor challenges some of the above. Firstly, he explains how, in depression, our behaviour, particularly in the area of exercise, can actually worsen the problem. By not exercising, we miss out on a proven therapy to help our mood and also isolate ourselves from the socialising benefits of meeting friends and neighbours when doing so. He gives her the following behaviour tips:

- to keep a diary of how she felt before and after exercise

- to start by breaking the exercise up into ten-minute slots and then gradually increasing the length of the sessions

- if struggling to get started, do the following good-humoured exercise: if you are sitting in the chair and unable to motivate yourself, ask yourself the following: Can you stand up? Can you then take a single step, then another, then another? Then, when you reach the front door, can your open it? You are now outside, off you go

- to remember the old Chinese proverb: 'A journey of a thousand miles begins with a single step'.

He then moves on to challenge her interpretation that she cannot exercise due to fatigue. Is this true or just a thought? Finally, he challenges her assertion that just because she is unable to exercise, she is a failure. He introduces her to the Raggy Doll Club and its rules. She is very affected by the latter and vows to become a member.

After nine months, Mary's life has been transformed. Her symptoms of depression are now just a memory, with even her fatigue clearing up. She is now exercising regularly and eating well. She has taken up yoga, is moderate in relation to her alcohol intake, is off her antidepressants, is taking supplements and is socialising again on a normal basis. She is back working, her relationship is back on an even keel, and she has come to terms with the loss of her close friend.

Paula's story

'I'm sick of people telling me to "cheer up" or that "it can't be that bad". But it is, and much worse than they can imagine.'

Paula is a twenty-eight-year-old single woman with a history of depression for the previous ten years. She was sexually abused by an uncle (who is now dead) at the age of nine. She has successfully hidden this from her friends and family, only confiding it to her older sister Ann after a night of heavy drinking, in an unsuccessful attempt to lift her mood. She has tried all types of alternative natural therapies and is afraid to go to her family doctor for fear he would suggest drug therapy, and due to her embarrassment about her previous abuse, which she had always felt responsible for.

She had found alternative therapists to be kind and understanding but had never admitted to the fact that she had been abused. Following brief lifts in mood, she would quickly return to the way she was. Finally, she breaks down in front of her sister Ann, the one person she feels safe with, and reveals the pain and distress of the previous few years. She also shares her fear of medication and her concern that if she admitted her symptoms to her doctor, he would feel that she was mad.

Ann empathises but convinces her to attend the family doctor, to whom Paula explains the way she is feeling. On probing, she admits to extreme fatigue, sleep, appetite, sex, memory and concentration difficulties, and to a complete loss of enjoyment of her life. She finds it easy to talk to the doctor and before she knows it has poured out to him the pain and distress of her previous sexual abuse. She also expressed her concerns about drug therapy (that they were addictive, that she would be on them for life, and that she would become a zombie on them).

Her doctor explains to Paula that all her symptoms were due to depression and that it was quite likely that the source of them lay in her childhood abuse. Together, they decided on the following treatment plan, where Paula would:

- start exercising, improve her diet and take supplements;

- cease taking alcohol until her mood improved;

- begin a course of antidepressants to try to improve her physical symptoms (particularly her problems with sleep, appetite, concentration and fatigue) and help lift her mood. Her doctor clarifies that this would be for a set period of time and also clears up many of the misunderstandings she has in relation to them;

- when feeling better, she would seek help to deal with the underlying history of abuse.

Paula returns at four and eight weeks to see her doctor and is now feeling better. To her surprise, apart from an initial nausea, which quickly subsided, she has experienced no significant side effects from the medication. She is now sleeping better, with fewer nightmares, is eating well, is exercising daily (something which she has come to enjoy very much) and has admitted to her doctor that it was the first time in years she had felt 'herself'.

They then decide that now she is feeling better, it is time to begin the crucial talk therapy necessary to help her get better. The doctor refers Paula to a counsellor who specialises in sexual abuse but continues to follow up with her in relation to her mood.

Six months later, Paula, on a follow-up visit, looks for further help as she has encountered a 'roadblock' in her work with the counsellor and it is starting to bring down her mood again. The problem turns out to be Paula's difficulties in dealing with the original abuse, which leads to her becoming increasingly distressed during counselling sessions. At this stage, her doctor explains the 'ABC' approach, asking whether she would like to use this CBM approach to deal with her hurt. She agrees. Together, they draw up the following analysis of her problem:

A: TRIGGER: The original sexual abuse

INTERPRETATION/DANGER: The abuser had betrayed her trust and she now regards herself as 'damaged goods'

B: BELIEF (OR DEMAND): That she was 'damaged goods' and, as a result, of no worth

C: EMOTION: Depression

PHYSICAL SYMPTOMS: All the physical symptoms already outlined

BEHAVIOUR: She increasingly avoids male company, leading her to become isolated

Her doctor challenges some of the above. Firstly, he explains how our behaviour can, in depression, further isolate us from the love and friendship of others, worsening the depression itself. They agree that she will begin to change some of the unhealthy patterns she had become embroiled in.

He then queries how her uncle's behaviour could make her 'damaged goods' or a failure. They agree that it would be better to say 'I have had damage done to me', rather than 'I am damaged goods', and introduces her to the Raggy Doll Club. He helps her to see that if she becomes a Raggy Doll, she cannot rate herself for having being abused by her uncle.

After a number of such sessions, she returns to her counsellor, the roadblock gone, and successfully completes the course. By the end of the year, she is off all medication, exercising, eating well and enjoying life for the first time in five years. She has taken up meditation on the advice of her counsellor, bought herself a Raggy Doll and, most importantly, finally surrendered to the embraces of a man she had been interested in but had been afraid to 'go there' with. She now has a much more informed attitude to the place of alternative and conventional drug therapies and their role in depression.

Thomas's story

'The simplest of tasks drains me of all my energy. I just want to sleep all the time.'

Thomas is a thirty-two-year-old, highly successful businessman suffering from undiagnosed bouts of depression for over a decade. His first bout came after a particularly stressful period in his life where the underlying anxiety that had been with him since the age of ten came to a head and his mood fell.

Since then, he has lived a double life. On the surface, those who knew him could never get over how cool, calm and controlled he seemed to be, no matter what business emergency arose. On the inside, though, he was in torment. For long periods, he would experience complete exhaustion, and the pain of low mood. Problems with sleep, appetite, sex, memory and concentration led to a complete loss of enjoyment in his life and increasingly negative thoughts about himself and his future, despite all his successes as a businessman. Suicidal thoughts and even some definite methods of ending it all were starting to dominate his thinking during recent episodes.

When his mood lifted, the gnawing anxiety and the demand for total perfection would return. This would eventually trigger negative thoughts, and his mood would fall again. As a man, Thomas felt that to reveal such emotional symptoms would attract derision, and he was therefore avoiding admitting his difficulties and accessing help. Only women, who were 'more emotional', could possibly admit to such feelings; 'real men don't'.

But the exhaustion became worse, and his partner, who has been with him for five years and yet is completely unaware of his difficulties, becomes concerned. Eventually, he agrees to come with her to the local doctor, looking

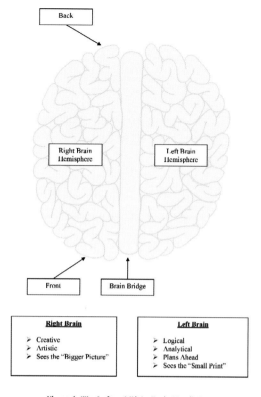

Figure 1: The Left and Right Brain Hemispheres

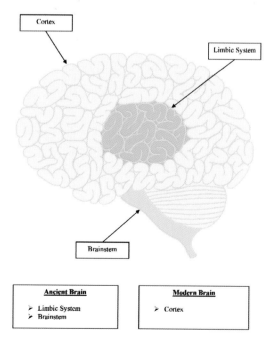

Figure 2: The Ancient and Modern Brain

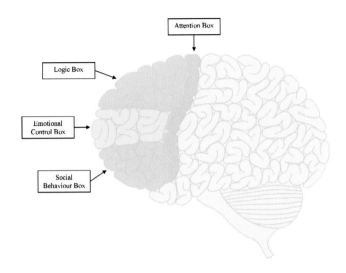

Figure 3: The Four Main Divisions of the Frontal Cortex Mood Department

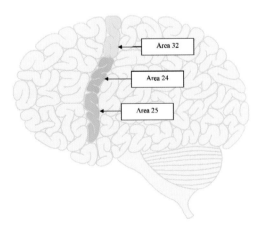

Figure 4: The Three Main Areas of the Attention Box

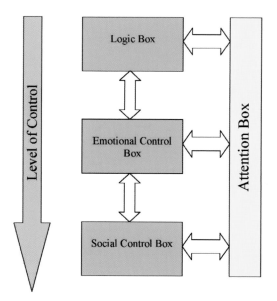

Figure 5: The Frontal Mood Department Hierarchical Structure

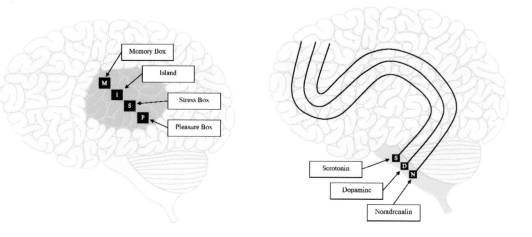

Figure 6: The Four Areas of the Limbic System Mood Department

Figure 7: The Three Mood Cables

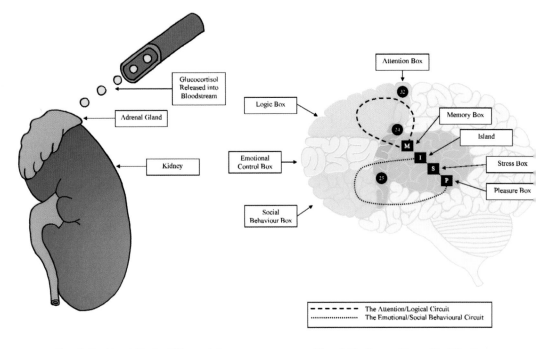

Figure 8: The Adrenal Gland and Glucocortisol

Figure 9: The Upper and Lower Mood Circuits

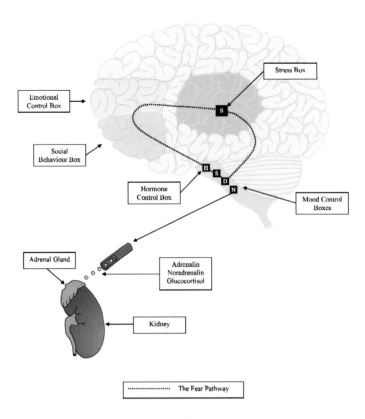

Figure 10: The Fear Pathway

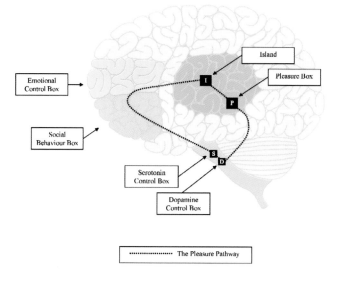

Figure 11: The Pleasure Pathway

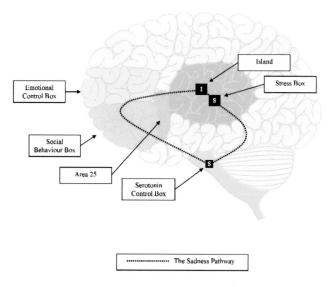

Figure 12: The Sadness Pathway

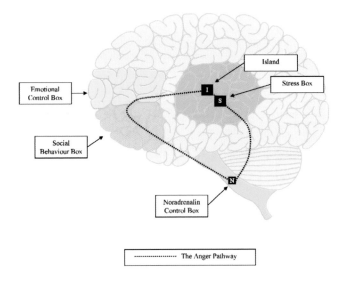

Figure 13: The Anger Pathway

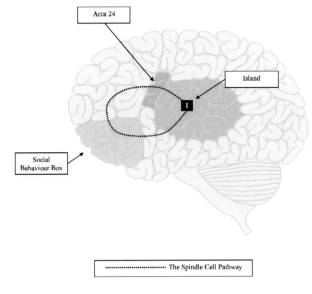

Figure 14: The Spindle Cell Pathway

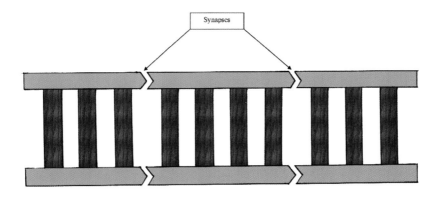

Figure 15: Railway Tracks

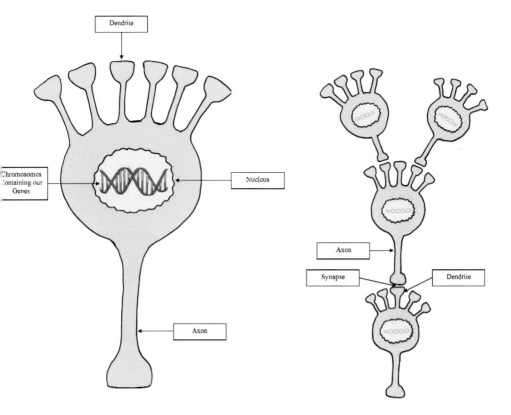

Figure 16: The Neuron

Figure 17: The Axon-Dendrite Connections

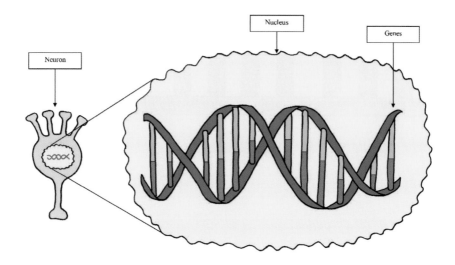

Figure 18: Our Genes

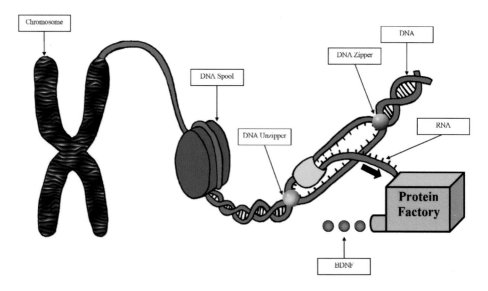

Figure 19: Epigenes

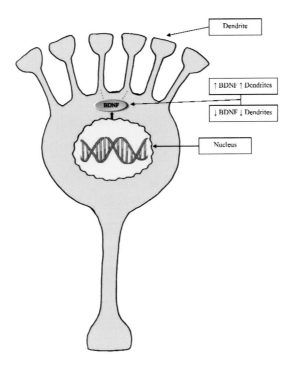

Figure 20: The Genes-BDNF-Dendrite Connection

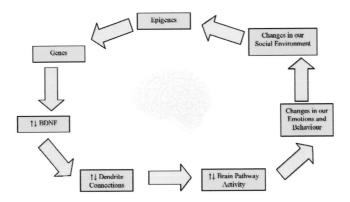

Figure 21: The Links between our Genes, Emotions, Behaviour and Environment

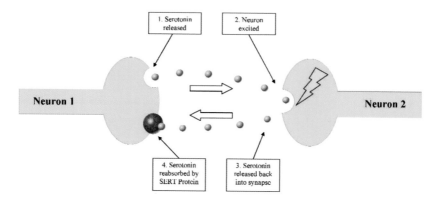

Figure 22: The SERT Protein

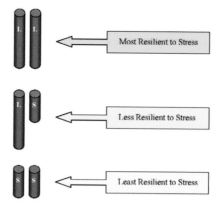

Figure 23: SERT Genes and Stress

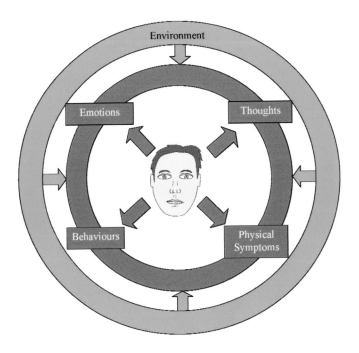

Figure 24: The Five Areas Approach

Developed by Dr. Chris Williams

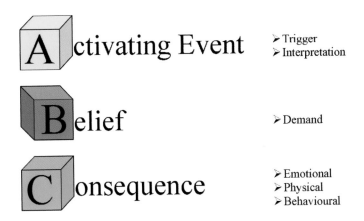

Figure 25: The ABC Model

Figure 26: Franks Path

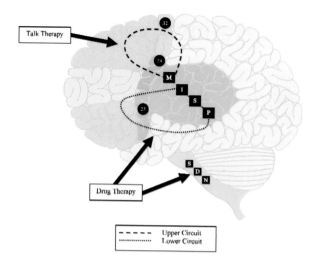

Figure 27: The Sites of Action of Drug and Talk Therapies

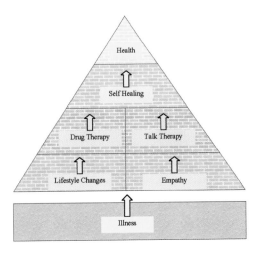

Figure 28: The Holistic Therapy Pyramid

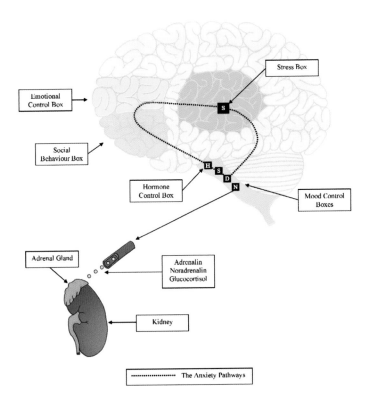

Figure 29: The Anxiety Pathways

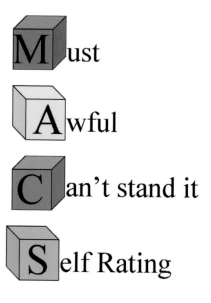

Figure 30: The Big MACS

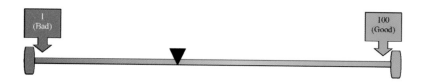

Figure 31: The Rating Scale

Figure 32: The Raggy Doll Club in Anxiety

**Based on the 1980's cartoon series "The Raggy Dolls", created by
Melvyn Jacobson and produced for Yorkshire TV**

Adapted for therapeutic use by CBT Therapist Enda Murphy

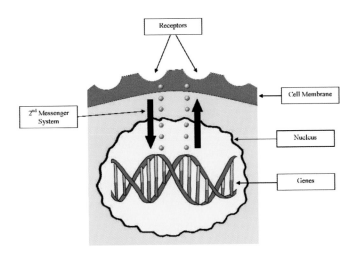

Figure 33: The Second Messenger System

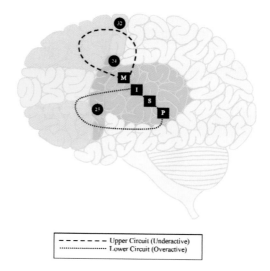

────── Upper Circuit (Underactive)
·············· Lower Circuit (Overactive)

Figure 34: The Mood Circuits in Depression

Figure 35: The Raggy Doll Club in Depression

Based on the 1980's cartoon series "The Raggy Dolls", created by Melvyn Jacobson and produced for Yorkshire TV

Adapted for therapeutic use by CBT Therapist Enda Murphy

for 'blood tests' to out rule diabetes.

Thomas explains his physical symptoms to his doctor but omits the emotional ones. His GP asks about any stress problems; Thomas denies these but mentions briefly his difficulties on occasion with concentration. His doctor decides to refer him for blood tests. A week later, he returns on his own for the results and, to his surprise, is told that he is completely healthy.

'But why am I so tired?' he asks. His doctor then suggests the possibility of depression, and initially Thomas is almost hostile. When his GP asks him to answer a series of questions to rule it out, he agrees. After replying yes to all twelve symptoms, he is forced to open up and admit how he is really feeling. He breaks down and pours out all the years of pain and hopelessness, and his increasing wish to end it all.

Following this outpouring, Thomas feels that a weight has been lifted off him for the first time in years. His doctor explains that his present symptoms are due to depression and that it was also likely that he had been suffering from anxiety since his teens – a primary trigger for his depression. He offers him the option of seeing a psychiatrist, but Thomas requests that his doctor, with whom he has shared so much, help him instead. So together they decide on the following treatment plan, where Thomas would:

- start exercising, improve his diet and take supplements

- cease taking alcohol until his mood has improved

- begin a course of antidepressants to try and improve some of the physical symptoms, reduce anxiety and help lift his mood

- share his depression with his partner, seeking her help and support

- once feeling better, get assistance to deal with both his negative thinking and his anxiety

- return immediately to see his doctor if he had any serious suicidal thoughts

- examine his work situation and, if appropriate, take a career break to give him time to deal with his problems

Eight weeks later, Thomas is feeling better: his physical symptoms are settling and his mood is improving. His partner turns out to be a rock of strength. He is now ready to begin the journey back to getting better. Initially, he attends a counsellor to delve into his past and identifies some issues to deal with. He also begins to work with his doctor on his negative thinking, in particular a return of the anxiety symptoms he has experienced since childhood. His doctor asks for an example of something that is making him anxious, and Thomas replies that he is worried because his boss is aware that he is suffering from depression, and he feels that his career prospects might suffer.

His doctor then explains the 'ABC' concepts to him and together they draw up the following analysis of his problem:

A: TRIGGER: Depression and his career

INTERPRETATION/ DANGER: That as a result of his admission of depression, his boss would consider him a liability and a weakness. He would cease to give him difficult tasks, as he would be concerned that Thomas would not be able to cope with them and would relapse.

B: BELIEF (OR DEMAND): His boss must not treat him differently. If he did, Thomas would feel a complete failure.

C: EMOTION: Anxiety and, on occasion, a drop in mood

PHYSICAL SYMPTOMS: Stomach in knots, tension headache, palpitations, difficulties sleeping, difficulties breathing, and so on. In particular, he becomes very fatigued.

BEHAVIOUR: Avoids any contact with his boss

His doctor challenges the above, in particular his behaviour in avoiding discussing the matter with his employer, explaining that this is only leading to a worsening of the problem. He also helps him see his physical symptoms of anxiety as uncomfortable but not dangerous. He then challenges his demand that his employer must not treat him differently. Does this demand prevent his boss treating him in this way? He introduces him to the 'Big MACS' – in particular to the 'land of must'.

Was there any law that gave Thomas the capacity to 'control' how his boss 'must' behave in this or any other situation? And wouldn't it be more acceptable to use the term 'prefer' rather than 'must'? One would obviously prefer that his boss would not treat him differently, but he could not control what he would in fact do.

He then queries how his boss treating him differently could make Thomas a failure, and introduces him to the Raggy Doll Club. He also shows how this demand increases his anxiety, making it more likely that his boss will treat him differently.

He asks him to begin doing some ABC's in situations where he finds himself interpreting events (internal or external) in a manner where he becomes anxious or his mood suddenly falls. This starts a process of teaching him to deal with his negative thinking, demands and rating, all of which is predisposing him to anxiety and depression.

Nine months later, following a lot of homework and visits, Thomas is back at work, feeling well, off medication, using alcohol in moderation, exercising daily, eating and sleeping better, enjoying life again, and learning to come to terms with his anxiety. To his great surprise, his boss turns out to be very supportive, and Thomas begins to suspect that his boss might have suffered from depression in the past himself. He has also become involved in a mindfulness program, finding this of great assistance in learning to let go of his negative thoughts and emotions. Most of all, he is now a fully fledged member of the Raggy Doll Club.

Susan's story
'I feel so guilty'

Susan is a twenty-six-year-old teacher who develops postnatal depression within four weeks of having her first baby. Following a normal delivery, she tries – unsuccessfully – to breastfeed. The baby fails to thrive, and Susan's mood begins to drop. She has no previous history of depression but her mother had suffered bouts after each pregnancy. Susan becomes increasingly exhausted, enduring sleep, appetite, sex, memory and concentration difficulties, and a loss of enjoyment in her life. She eventually breaks down in front of her practice nurse on a routine visit at eight weeks for childhood vaccination, and is referred to the family doctor. The nurse has also noted that the baby is not thriving and seems withdrawn.

Susan opens up to her doctor, in particular to her feelings of guilt that she 'should' be feeling wonderful but instead felt 'crap', as she put it. Didn't she have a wonderful husband, a beautiful baby boy, and no other problems in her life? She breaks down crying and admits that she cannot bond with her baby and is pushing her husband away, causing difficulties in her relationship. Her doctor explains that her symptoms are due to depression, the source lying in stress and hormonal changes which occur following pregnancy. He also notes that it is completely normal to feel lost and stressed in the postnatal period. Susan is very anxious not to use any form of drug therapy, despite her doctor's advice. He understands her reluctance, so they decide on the following treatment plan, where she would:

- start exercising, improve her diet and take supplements
- take a high dose of Omega 3 fish oils in particular
- accept that it is normal to feel stressed and 'flat' during this phase
- avoid alcohol until her mood has improved
- ask her mum to assist her with the new baby
- attend the practice nurse/GP regularly

Despite the above, after another three weeks, her mood is deteriorating and the baby is still not thriving. Her doctor once again suggests a short course of antidepressants, explaining that they are safe to take while breastfeeding and that it might be better for both the baby and herself, as the baby seems to be picking up on her depressed mood. She has a chat with her husband, and finally agrees.

Susan returns six weeks later: she is now feeling better and, to her surprise, is tolerating medication well. She is also sleeping and eating properly, and exercising daily. Her mood is almost back to normal, she is less anxious, and she is bonding with her baby son. Her thinking, however, remains very negative and she admits to her doctor that she felt guilty and down because she had developed postnatal depression and that her baby had failed to thrive. Her doctor explains the 'ABC' approach, suggesting that they use this approach to deal with her negative thinking; she agrees. Together, they draw up the following analysis of her problem:

A: TRIGGER: Feeling 'crap'

INTERPRETATION/DANGER: 'Because I feel this way, I am a bad mother and wife. I have nothing to be depressed about.'

B: BELIEF (OR DEMAND): I should not feel like this. I am a failure.

C: EMOTION: Depression

PHYSICAL SYMPTOMS: All the physical symptoms already outlined

BEHAVIOUR: Spends a lot of time ruminating on the above, has become over-protective of her baby, tends to develop a 'radar system' where she scans her environment and friends looking for confirmation that she is a 'bad mum', as all other mums seem to be coping better than her.

His doctor challenges the above. He firstly examines her behaviour, explaining how our behaviour in depression can actually worsen the problem. She agrees that constant rumination and scanning of her environment are not helping. He also explains the dynamics of postnatal depression. Most mothers in the period following the arrival of a new baby develop the 'blues', feel exhausted, stressed, anxious and overwhelmed. This is a normal state, but some mothers feel guilty and excessively anxious about feeling this way, viewing themselves as abnormal in comparison to other mothers. They start to feel more exhausted and down, starting the cycle of depression detailed in the 'ABC' above, and eventually become depressed about being depressed.

He then challenges her absolute demand that she should not feel this way. He asks 'How could developing the symptoms of depression make her a failure?' and introduces her to the Raggy Doll Club. She suddenly realises that she has indeed been very hard on herself and resolves to become a fully fledged member. After that, she never looks back. After nine months and a number of visits, she is off all medication, is exercising, is looking after her diet, has taken up meditation and yoga on the advice of her doctor, is back relating normally to her husband, and has now bonded fully with her son, who is thriving both physically and emotionally. She had also acquired a Raggy Doll.

Jane's story

'She has just lost interest in everything'.

Jane is a sixty-seven-year-old widow whose husband died three years previously. She is now living alone. In the past six months, her family have noticed her withdrawing, becoming more forgetful, losing interest in food and losing some weight. She doesn't seem to be enjoying anything, even the visits of her grandchildren, whom she is very close to. She has also stopped reading newspapers and novels (she had previously been an avid reader) and her family have noticed her drinking more.

Eventually, her daughter manages to persuade her to attend her family doctor. 'I am not sure if she is getting dementia, or just needs some blood tests,' she explains, 'but she is just not herself. Maybe it's just "old age".'

Jane's doctor has a chat with her, and following examination, sends her for some blood tests. On review, he is happy with most of her results, in particular that he has ruled out any thyroid gland problems, but he notes that her blood cholesterol and blood pressure are a bit high. He also decides that she displays no evidence of senile dementia but is suffering from depression. He explains that because she has no prior history of depression, the most likely cause of her illness is a mixture of the loss of her husband, combined with ageing changes in the brain and blockages in the small blood vessels supplying it, with her blood pressure and cholesterol findings contributing to the latter. Together, they draw up the following treatment plan:

- her blood pressure and high cholesterol would be managed with a combination of drug and dietary therapy

- start on a simple exercise daily regime and take some supplements as part of improving her nutrition

- cease taking alcohol until her mood has improved

- begin a course of antidepressants to try to improve some of the physical symptoms (particularly sleep, appetite, concentration and fatigue), reduce anxiety and help lift her mood

- when feeling better, she would attend bereavement counselling to deal with the loss of her husband

- consider attending the local community-care day centre, where she would mix with people of her own age and avail of useful services provided

- consider the possibility of getting a pet when she feels better

Six months later, Jane is a changed person. She is back to her old self, is eating and sleeping better, has ceased taking alcohol completely and her memory, concentration and reading have returned to normal. Physically, she has regained weight, her blood pressure and cholesterol are normal, and she is getting plenty of exercise and emotional nourishment thanks to her new dog Paddy, named after her late husband. She has finally finished grieving for him after some bereavement counselling and is back fussing around her young grandchildren. She has also made many new friends in the local community-care centre. She is still on drug therapy and may have to take it for some time, but she and her family are happy with the improvement in her condition. It wasn't just 'old age' after all.

Catherine's story

'I'm just not hungry any more. Food does not look appetising, and it's too much energy to eat. Hopefully, I will waste away into nothing.'

Catherine is a twenty-four-year-old single parent, living on social welfare in a small, poorly equipped flat, coping with a small child and a 'partner' who abuses alcohol (and her). The stress of this has triggered a bout of depression. She has lost more than a stone in weight. Her father (now dead), an alcoholic, had been physically and verbally abusive to Catherine and her siblings. Her mother had suffered from anxiety and postnatal depression.

Catherine has not known much love in her life and as a result has developed low self-esteem. Unfortunately, she has become infatuated with her present partner, a carbon copy of the father she both loved and hated. She becomes pregnant and has a baby girl. Following this, her partner's drinking and abusive behaviour has deteriorated. By the time the child is fifteen months, Catherine's coping mechanisms are exhausted, and she becomes depressed. As her mood falls, she begins to loathe herself, losing interest in her appearance, food and sex, and becoming increasingly isolated from friends and family. The more her mood drops, the more she relies on cigarettes and coffee to make it through the day. She drinks more and, on a number of occasions, becomes extremely drunk. This often ends in her partner becoming insulting and abusive. Her weight continues to fall, and she becomes anaemic as a result of a lack of iron in her diet.

On two occasions, she walked by the river bank, fantasising about how easy it would be to jump in, and that the world would be better off without her around. Her mother, increasingly concerned, offers to take the child for a period, and Catherine agrees.

Eventually, things came to a head: her drunken partner beats her up and she responds later that night by drinking half a bottle of vodka and swallowing twenty paracetamol tablets. Luckily, her sister calls to the house and finds her in a semi-comatose state. She calls the ambulance and Catherine is admitted to hospital.

After spending a few days in intensive care, she is assessed by a self-harm liaison nurse and social worker (but hides the abuse from both). She refuses to see a psychiatrist, receives some advice and is eventually allowed to go home. Thankfully, her mother insists that she goes to see her local doctor, with whom she has a good relationship, looking for further help.

There, she explains how she has been feeling for the previous few months, discussing her fatigue, lack of interest in food and sex, poor concentration and memory and thoughts of self-harm. On probing, she finally breaks down and reveals her domestic difficulties and abuse. She also admits to misusing alcohol and to her fear of becoming addicted, like her father. Her GP, who is concerned about her physical and mental health, explains that she is suffering from depression and offers to help. Together, they draw up the following treatment plan, where she would:

- start exercising, improve her diet and take supplements, in particular iron, B vitamins and Omega 3 fish oils

- cease taking alcohol until her mood has improved

- begin a course of antidepressants (to be dispensed by her mother) to improve some of her physical symptoms (particularly her sleep, appetite, concentration and fatigue) and help lift her mood

- see her doctor regularly for the following few weeks, in view of her suicide attempt

- when feeling better, get some counselling to help deal with her current social situation, and issues from her childhood

- also at a later stage, deal with her negative self-rating

- allow her mum to care for her child until she feels better

Eight weeks later, she is feeling much better, begins a course of counselling and has ceased drinking alcohol. She is eating well, regaining weight, exercising regularly and even considering stopping smoking.

After twelve weeks and some counselling, she faces down her partner, breaking off the relationship and returning to live with her mum until she sorts herself out. When he threatens her, she is strong enough to seek help, in the form of a protection order.

Through counselling, she begins to deal with issues from her past, even having a frank conversation with her mum as to why she had not stood up for her against her father's abuse. This resulted in an emotional and healing embrace.

After five months, she is back with her doctor, who is very happy with her progress. Her weight is normal and she is off cigarettes. She mentions feeling very negative about her decision to return to live with her mother, and that this was bringing down her mood. On further probing, this was just one of many negative thoughts which she was experiencing. At this stage, her doctor explains the 'ABC' approach and asks whether she would like to use this CBM approach to deal with this issue – to which she agrees. Together, they draw up the following analysis of her problem:

A: TRIGGER: Having to return to live with mum

INTERPRETATION/DANGER: This was a retrograde step, confirming what she and everybody else thought – namely that she couldn't cope

B: BELIEF (OR DEMAND): Because she had to return home following a failed relationship, she was a failure

C: EMOTION: Depression

PHYSICAL SYMPTOMS: All the physical symptoms already outlined

BEHAVIOUR: She was avoiding friends because she felt that they would only confirm her own assessment of herself.

Her doctor challenges the above. Firstly, he explains how her behaviour is further isolating her from the love and friendship of those she normally associates with. So they agree that she will begin to change some of her unhealthy behavioural patterns.

He then moves on to challenge Catherine's unhealthy belief that because she has returned home, this means that she is a failure. He introduces her to the Raggy Doll Club.

He then gives her some homework: to begin doing some ABC's in situations where she finds herself interpreting events (internal or external) in a manner where she finds her mood suddenly falling – thus starting the process of helping her deal with her negative thinking and low self-esteem.

After a year, Catherine's world has changed dramatically for the better. She is off drug therapy, is exercising and eating well, is off alcohol (and has decided, in view of her family history, to stay that way), is still off cigarettes, and is fully engaged in looking after her little girl. She is also planning to do a computer course and has become a fully fledged member of the Raggy Doll Club.

Noreen's story

'I have become increasingly forgetful, I have difficulty remembering the simplest of things, like what I did yesterday.'

Noreen is single, very busy twenty-seven-year-old manager who is struggling to cope with her day-to-day duties due to a depression triggered by a prolonged period of sustained stress. She has always suffered from anxiety and had a previous minor episode of depression in her late teens. Her mother and sister also have a history of depression. Following a difficult period at work, she begins to develop exhaustion, sleep difficulties, anxiety and loss of appetite, and poor drive, memory and concentration, which, together with her deteriorating low mood, makes her job almost impossible. She has always been an advocate of alternative versus conventional therapies and, with increasing desperation, tries one after another. But when trials of energy-field therapy, homeopathy, acupuncture, cranio sacral therapy, and reiki, among other things, were unsuccessful, she decides to visit her local family doctor for some blood tests.

When she explains her symptoms to her doctor, he agrees, but suggests that the most likely explanation was depression. Noreen dismisses this possibility, explaining that she was just a little bit stressed. Her GP gives her some information to read on the subject and arranges to see her after the tests.

When Noreen arrives home, she begins to reflect on his words, reads the booklet on depression, and consults with a close friend, who, to her surprise, agrees with her doctor's opinion. On her next visit, her tests are negative and she accepts his diagnosis but immediately states that drug therapy is not an option. She would be prepared to consider any other therapy: 'There is no way I am going to endure all those side effects or be turned into an addict,' she explains. He tries to convince her that this is not the case but still offers to do something to help her symptoms. After examining all the options, they agree on the following treatment plan, where Noreen would:

- start exercising, improve her diet and take supplements

- cease taking alcohol until her mood has improved

- begin a course of St John's wort (as a compromise alternative to a modern SSRI, explaining that it too has side effects and interactions) to try to improve some of the physical symptoms (particularly problems with sleep, appetite, concentration and fatigue) to reduce anxiety and help lift her mood

- take a period of time out of work to help her recover

- when feeling better, consider a session of counselling and a stress-management course, both available through her employers

- her doctor might do some work with her later on how her thinking patterns are underlying her anxiety and depression

After six weeks, she has some improvement in mood but, to her surprise, develops some side effects from the St John's wort – which she informs her doctor about. 'I thought it was completely natural,' she queries. He explains that it is still a drug very similar to the ones she wanted to avoid, and therefore had similar side effects. She decides to continue the course of St John's wort for the time being. She is eating better, is exercising and is off alcohol; she has also begun a course of reflexology and decides to take up some pilates classes. She returns to work after eight weeks, attends a work counsellor and begins the stress-management course, but she is still struggling with her concentration and memory and finds that her thinking is continuing to be extremely negative. She decides to revisits her doctor.

He suggests some memory work for her in the form of crossword puzzles, reading the paper (something she had ceased doing) and joining the library, explaining that her memory muscles were weakened by bouts of depression and needed exercise, both physical and mental, to strengthen them. In relation to her negative thinking, she offers a typical example: the previous week, her boss had avoided giving her a job she would normally have been asked to do. She has become quite down as a result.

Her doctor then explains the 'ABC' concepts to her, and together they draw up the following analysis of her problem:

A: TRIGGER: Her boss gives her colleague a work assignment that normally would be given to her

INTERPRETATION/DANGER: That he had purposefully avoided giving it to Noreen because he was aware that she had depression, was therefore untrustworthy and would be unable to perform the task

B: BELIEF (OR DEMAND): That because he did not do so, she was a failure, and felt bad about herself

C: EMOTION: Depression

PHYSICAL SYMPTOMS: All the physical symptoms already outlined

BEHAVIOUR: Withdrew into herself for the rest of the day, avoided talking to her work colleagues, left early and went home to bed

Her doctor challenges her belief that because her employer has apparently passed a task on to another colleague, this could possibly make her a failure and an awful person. He then introduces her to the Raggy Doll Club. He helps her see that if she becomes a 'Raggy Doll', she could not rate herself or be rated just because she had seemingly been passed over for some task, or indeed for any other reason.

Over the next few months, he works with her, using examples she provides him with, and using the 'ABC' concepts to help transform her thinking. This helps her deal with the barrage of negative thoughts underlying her anxiety and depression. After twelve months, Noreen's life has been transformed. She is no longer taking St John's wort and is exercising and eating well. As a result of her stress-management classes, and becoming a Raggy Doll, she is now less anxious and is coping much better with her work/life balance. On the advice of her doctor, she has taken up mindfulness meditation classes and, although she is still a fan of alternative medicine, she has accepted that conventional medicine has its place too.

Carl's story

'I am ashamed of the weak, useless, boring, incompetent failure I am. People hate spending time with me.'

Carl is a twenty-four-year-old mechanic whose quiet disposition and extreme shyness has disguised his inner torment from those close to him. Depression visited him first at the age of seventeen and has been an unwelcome but frequent visitor ever since.

He suffered from anxiety from an early age. On reaching his teens, he was badly bullied but managed to hide it from his family. His sense of self-worth took a major hit, and by seventeen his mood had begun to drop significantly, with fatigue, poor concentration and a host of other physical symptoms arriving in his life. But he bore them stoically: 'Wasn't he worthless anyway?' He came from a loving, caring family. His mother had suffered from depression following his birth and on a number of occasions since. His older sister was like her father, a complete extrovert – unlike his mum, who was of a quiet disposition. He had always loved cars and was happiest when he was tinkering with engines. Although an excellent mechanic, he still felt useless, finding fault with his own work at every opportunity.

Bouts of depression came and went, and he found solace in alcohol, which provided only a temporary relief. He found it difficult to relate to girls, feeling awkward and uncomfortable in their presence. Eventually, at the age of twenty-two, he met a lovely girl who helped him emerge from his cocoon. He started to feel better, and after two years they became engaged. Then, with the stress of trying to organise a new home and a wedding, his depression recurred with a vengeance.

Negative thoughts now rush like a torrent through his emotional brain: 'I am not good enough for her, she deserves better. She only agreed to marry me because she feels sorry for me.' Bit by bit, they wear him down and he becomes physically and mentally exhausted. He is making mistakes at work and receives a warning from his boss. He becomes withdrawn and morose and his drinking increases. As he starts to push his fiancée away, she feels very hurt and withdraws from him, unsure of what has changed. Eventually things come to a head and he breaks off the relationship, telling her that it is for the best: that she deserves more out of life than him.

Following this, Carl's mood drops further, he begins to feel hopeless and starts to plan his departure. On the night before he plans to end his life, something happens that will change his life. The girl who loved him had earlier that day come to see his mother, looking for some insight as to what she had done wrong in the relationship. As she was describing the sudden changes in his mood, his mother suddenly put everything together as a result of her own experience with depression. She shares her insight with Carl's fiancée. They both decide to tackle Carl that evening.

As a result of their intervention, and his mother's descriptions of her own battles with depression (and the love and warmth from them both), Carl opens up to the pain and mental distress he had been hiding. After some persuasion, he agrees to come with them to see their local doctor. That night, through their acceptance, he began his journey back to mental health.

Carl asks his fiancée to come in with him to see his GP, as he isn't sure he will be able to describe how he feels. Then, with her help, he pours out all the physical and mental symptoms he has been experiencing. His doctor asks some questions and slowly the pattern emerges: it had started with the initial bullying. He proceeds to explain that Carl is suffering from depression.

It turns out that he is not sleeping, is not exercising, is drinking too much, is eating poorly and is suffering from extreme fatigue. When his doctor inquires about suicide thoughts, Carl is silent, not wanting to upset his fiancée, but is relieved when his doctor explains that these things are normal in depression. He finally admits to his plans for suicide and feels much better for having shed light on this dark place in his mind. He also admits to being still affected by the school bullying, the memory of which remains.

His doctor then explains how depression can completely distort our thinking and lead to all the physical and emotional symptoms Carl is experiencing, and that appropriate treatment can successfully deal with the problem. Together, they draw up the following treatment plan, where Carl would:

- start exercising, improve his diet and take supplements

- cease taking alcohol until his mood has improved

- begin a course of antidepressants (to be dispensed by his mother) to try to improve some of his physical symptoms (particularly sleep, appetite, concentration and fatigue) and help lift his mood

- see his doctor regularly for the following few weeks in view of his suicide thoughts

- when feeling better, seek counselling to deal with both the bullying issues from his childhood and how depression is disrupting his current relationships

- at a later stage, work with his doctor to challenge his negative thoughts

Eight weeks later, Carl is feeling better, is exercising regularly and is eating properly. He is off alcohol, has reunited with his fiancée and is ready to begin counselling to deal with some of the issues from his early teens. After four months, and some counselling, he has begun to come to terms with the bullying and relationship issues, but he is still plagued by the thought that he is inferior and not 'good enough' for his girlfriend. His doctor decides to do some CBM exercises with him. His doctor then explains the 'ABC' concepts to him, and together they draw up the following analysis of his problem:

A: TRIGGER: His relationship with his fiancée

INTERPRETATION/DANGER: He is not good enough for her, and if she didn't marry him, she might meet somebody much more deserving

B: BELIEF (OR DEMAND): He is worthless and of no value

C: EMOTION: Depression

PHYSICAL SYMPTOMS: Already outlined

BEHAVIOUR: Tries to persuade his fiancée that she would do better with someone else

His doctor challenges some of the above. Firstly, he explains how, in depression, our behaviour can further isolate us, thereby worsening the problem, as in how Carl pushed away his fiancée. His doctor challenges Carl's unhealthy belief that he is a failure and of no value. He introduces him to the Raggy Doll Club.

He then gives him some homework: to begin doing some 'ABC's in situations where he finds himself interpreting events (internal or external) in a manner where his mood suddenly falls, thus starting the process of dealing with his negative thinking/low self-esteem.

Nine months later, Carl is well, off drug therapy and looking after his lifestyle. He has finished his counselling and, due to the work he and his doctor have done on his thinking, has become a true Raggy Doll. He is finally ready to marry the girl who stood beside him in his hour of darkness.

Jill's story
'Here we go again'.

Jill is a forty-six-year-old mother of two who holds down a part-time job in a local hotel and has suffered depression since the age of sixteen. She had a normal, happy childhood but found her early and mid teens to be a very stressful time, and her mood began to fall. She experienced multiple subsequent episodes of depression, including two postnatal bouts and one trip to hospital. She is becoming increasingly frustrated and hopeless because, no matter what she does, her depression seems to recur. Her husband has been wonderfully supportive but is finding it increasingly difficult to cope with her continuous relapses.

She has attended her family doctor and a number of different psychiatrists over the years, finally ending up on maintenance drug therapy in the form of a modern SSRI. She has also tried one alternative therapy after another, desperately looking for the 'magic cure', but despite this search she continues to relapse.

She finally comes in to her GP, feeling very down that once again her mood is falling, despite her maintenance therapy. She is not exercising and is eating poorly. She is drinking wine excessively and is struggling at work. She reveals that her suicidal thoughts are coming more to the fore and that the 'river' is very much in her mind. He empathises with her, and after a long discussion they draw up the following treatment plan, under which Jill agrees to:

- start exercising, improve her diet and take supplements
- cease taking alcohol until her mood was improved
- take a period of time out of work to help her recover

and her doctor will:

- refer her to a local psychiatrist, wondering if a mood stabiliser should be added to her medication
- possibly do some cognitive therapy and mindfulness work with her later, explaining how her thinking patterns have been acting as a triggering source for her depression

Ten weeks later, she has been reviewed by the specialist, who decides to put her on Lamictal (a mood stabiliser) also. She is now exercising regularly, is eating and sleeping better, is off alcohol, is no longer having suicidal thoughts and is generally improving. She revisits her family doctor, who is pleased with her progress. He feels that she is well enough to begin some CBM therapy. He starts by spending some time explaining that, just because we have a thought, this does not mean that it is true, and he gives her some examples. He continues that when we have suffered recurrent bouts of depression, we retain the memory of these negative thinking patterns. He gives her some information on the differences between CBM, which he suggests they begin, and mindfulness, which they might explore later. He then asks her to return to begin CBM. He explains the 'ABC' concepts, and they decide to do one on her commonest negative thought, namely 'here we go again':

A: TRIGGER: The thought that her depression is returning again

INTERPRETATION/DANGER: If her depression recurs, this will indicate that she is weak and useless, as she is unable to prevent it from happening.

B: BELIEF (OR DEMAND): She must not get depression again. If she does, it means that she is a failure.

C: EMOTION: Anxiety and depression

PHYSICAL SYMPTOMS: All the physical symptoms already outlined

BEHAVIOUR: Spends periods worrying about the possibility of a return of depression – and a fortune on a myriad of unproven alternative therapies.

Her doctor then challenges her unhealthy beliefs: firstly, her demand that she must not get depressed again, and then her belief that she is a failure and of no value. He introduces her to the 'Big MACS', challenging her demand for 100 percent certainty, and noting that it would be better to use the word 'prefer' instead of 'must'. He introduces her to the Raggy Doll Club. He then gets her to begin doing some ABC's in situations where she finds herself interpreting events (internal or external) in a manner where her mood suddenly falls.

Nine months later, and after a number of further visits to both her GP and her psychiatrist, she is much more confident that the risks of her depression recurring are receding. She is also more accepting of the fact that this could happen. Her doctor now introduces her to the concept of mindfulness. She quite quickly grasps the concepts behind mindfulness and its role in the prevention of depression. He recommends some reading material and a CD on the subject and explains the Three Minute Breathing Space meditation, saying how useful it can be in assisting us to become more aware of our negative thoughts and emotions.

Jill finds mindfulness and in particular the above exercise extremely useful. She starts to become more confident about coping with the normal stresses of life. She and her husband join a meditation group, gradually becoming more adept in day-to-day mindfulness. The addition of the mood stabiliser to her maintenance-drug therapy, together with becoming a Raggy Doll and her work with mindfulness, has transformed her life.

Jack's story (and the smile that saved him)

'The world will be a much better place without me. I am a burden on everyone and they won't miss me at all.'

Jack, a twenty-nine-year-old computer whizzkid, has already quietly planned in great detail how he will end his life. Because his depression has not been recognised and remains untreated, he is about to put these thoughts into action. This course of action has been made more likely by a dramatic increase in alcohol consumption to numb the pain associated with his recent break-up from his girlfriend.

He started to get into difficulties in his late teens and early twenties, struggling with bouts of major depression. Each time these occurred, negative thoughts roared in, swamping his logical brain. He has already taken an overdose in his mid-twenties following a night of heavy drinking.

When feeling well, he enjoys his work and is successful, but at a cost. Even when he seems to be completely on top of things, it requires a tremendous effort for him to remain so. The consequences of this are serious bouts of low mood. During these episodes, suicide thoughts come with increasing frequency, and more recently he thinks about the method he might use. The latter is assisted by information downloaded from an inappropriate site on the Web, where he finds his emotions and feelings of self-loathing mirrored.

He has managed to hide how he feels from those close to him, including his girlfriend Clare, who regularly feels upset and rejected by his sudden withdrawals into himself. Things come to a head when he lashes out verbally one night while going through a period of self-loathing, and the relationship ends.

He drinks heavily that weekend and his mood sinks further. The Monday following the departure of Clare, he begins preparations to end his life. He rings in sick to his workplace and calls his mother to tell her that he loves her. He texts Clare, apologising for his behaviour. He feels a huge sense of relief; the pain will be over at last. He leaves to travel to where he has decided to end his life, with what he needs in his backpack.

On his journey, by chance, he makes eye contact with a face in the crowd, a young mother gazing lovingly at the baby in her arms. Jack's eyes settle on the baby and then at the mother. She smiles at him and in that moment something lights up inside him. For a split second, the love of the mother for her baby, and the unaffected warmth of her smile, pierces the darkness and pain within like nothing else so far has managed to do. Suddenly an image of how his own mother would feel if he went ahead with his plans bursts into his consciousness. He sees her love mirrored in the smile of the mother with her baby, and the tears start to flow. Before he knows it, the phone is in his hand and he is calling her, pouring out his pain and distress. He has just begun one of the most important journeys of his life: the one back to mental health.

The following day, Jack, accompanied by his mum, comes to see his local family doctor and opens up to the decade of hell he experienced; the classic mixture of the physical (fatigue, poor concentration and memory, sleep, appetite and drive difficulties) and psychological symptoms (extremely low mood, anxiety, negative thinking and suicidal thoughts). His doctor is extremely empathetic, explaining that Jack's symptoms are due to depression and that he has taken the first and most important step towards recovery: sharing his pain. With Jack's help, he reviews his past, searching for any sources of his problems, but apart from a history of his mum having depression during and after his birth, there are no obvious causes. They did identify the role of stress in the generation and maintenance of his depression. Together, they draw up the following treatment plan, where Jack would:

- start exercising, improve his diet and take supplements
- cease taking alcohol until his mood has improved
- begin a course of antidepressants (to be dispensed by his mother) to try to improve some of the physical symptoms (particularly problems with sleep, appetite, concentration and fatigue) and help lift his mood
- see his doctor regularly for the following few weeks, in view of suicide thoughts
- agree to return to his GP if his suicide thoughts increase
- agree to have a specialist psychiatric assessment if his mood is not improving, or if his suicide thoughts became more persistent
- inform his employer's human-resource team of his illness and take a medical break to give himself time and space to heal
- when feeling better, access counselling to help deal with the difficulties created by his depression within his present relationships
- at a later stage, work with his doctor to challenge his negative thoughts

Within six weeks, and after a number of visits to his doctor, Jack is already seeing the benefits. His mood is up, his suicidal thoughts have begun to recede, his energy and concentration levels have improved, and his anxiety has lessened. He is exercising regularly, is eating properly, is off alcohol and has begun taking supplements. He has started the counselling provided by his company.

After ten weeks, he is feeling well enough to begin some CBM on his negative thinking with his doctor. Jack gives an example of one of the most common thoughts that have plagued him in social situations: 'If people knew how weak and useless I really am, they will, quite rightly, want nothing to do with me.' His doctor then explains the 'ABC' concepts to him, and together they draw up the following:

A: TRIGGER: Being in a room full of people

INTERPRETATION/DANGER: They recognise how weak and useless he is and will shun him as a result

B: BELIEF (OR DEMAND): I am a failure; they will view me the way I view myself

C: EMOTION: Depression

PHYSICAL SYMPTOMS: All the physical symptoms already outlined

BEHAVIOUR: Tries to avoid situations where he will meet friends and colleagues outside of his work, or if he does have to interact with them, he uses alcohol to help him cope.

His doctor challenges his unhealthy belief that he is a failure and of no value. He introduces him to the Raggy Doll Club. For Jack, this is a profound revelation. The Raggy Doll, like the smile from the lady who indirectly saved his life, touched something deep inside him. He really wants to join the club. His doctor asks Jack to begin doing some 'ABC's in situations where he finds himself interpreting events (internal or external) in a manner where his mood suddenly falls, and to return to see him.

Within a year, Jack's world has, like Alice in Wonderland, been turned upside down. His mood is fully back to normal, his physical symptoms have settled, he is back at work, and he is enjoying his life for the first time in a decade. He has also, on the advice of his doctor, learned to include some mindfulness exercises, like the Three Minute Breathing Space, finding them so helpful that he has embarked on a journey into the world of meditation. In his social life, there have also been major changes: he is now engaged to Clare. He mixes more with friends, and has learned to do so without the crutch of alcohol.

He still has a constant battle with the negative thoughts that keep rearing their ugly heads, especially when he is under stress, but with the help of his doctor and work on the 'ABC' concepts, he has gradually changed his unhealthy thinking patterns. He decides, with his doctor, to come off his drug therapy as a trial. Two years later, happily married and with his wife expecting their first child, Jack remains well.

There are some important lessons to learn from Jack's story:

- When we are very depressed, all seems bleak and hopeless, but, as in Jack's case, our lives can be transformed with often quite simple interventions.

- We can hide how we truly feel from those we know and love, often for long periods.

- When we find ourselves very depressed, in a dark place where suicide seems the only way out, we must remember all those who love and cherish us and whose lives may be destroyed by our planned actions.

- Opening up to our inner pain and hopelessness, as Jack discovered, can be the first step on a different journey: one that can transform our lives.

- That we all need to recognise the power within us to heal each other and that sometimes a warm smile or a kind gesture may be all that is required.

- The practice of mindfulness is extremely useful in preventing relapses of depression.

- As Jack also discovered, we are all Raggy Dolls.

Seasonal Affective Disorder (SAD)

For some people, particularly in more northerly climates, the darkness of wintertime creates a unique depression. People with SAD develop all the symptoms of depression, together with a craving for food, and accompanying weight gain and hypersomnia. There are some links between SAD and bipolar disorder.

Some experts maintain that darkness encourages the brain to make a neurotransmitter called melatonin. This has the general function of helping us to sleep at night. On the other hand, light encourages the production of serotonin. There is an important neural connection between the eyes and a part of the hormone control box which, as we discussed earlier, controls all our body rhythms and biological clocks. As daylight arrives every morning, it penetrates through our closed eyelids, activates this pathway (leading to increased serotonin cable activity in this box) and prompts us to wake up. When darkness falls, this neural pattern is reversed, and the brain produces melatonin to encourage us to sleep.

Artificial daylight (through our narrow-spectrum light bulbs) simulates much of this natural pattern. Real daylight is up to twenty times more powerful than artificial light, however. Melatonin and serotonin are intimately interwoven into the normal circadian rhythms of our lives.

SAD seems to be caused by an excessive production of melatonin and a lack of serotonin. Of great importance is the seasonal difference in the production of serotonin, with higher levels in the summer and lower levels in the winter. It may be that this exposes a general shortage of serotonin in those with this condition. This may explain why these people recover during the bright summer months and slip back into trouble in the winter.

It is also felt that a shortage of serotonin in the hormone control box in particular leads to a craving for carbohydrates, with resulting weight gain during SAD episodes. It is believed that the disorder is linked to problems with specific serotonin receptors.

We have already discussed the usefulness of light therapy and dawn simulators in depression in general. In SAD, this is especially the case, with up to 70 percent responding; the remainder may require serotonin-boosting drug therapy (SSRIs) as an adjunct. Talk therapies and alternative therapies have little function in this illness.

Bipolar Disorder (Manic Depression)

This illness is often confused with unipolar depression. In unipolar depression, mood can swing from normal to low and back again but does not become elevated. In bipolar, intermittent bouts of low, normal and elevated mood may be present.

The traditional view of bipolar mood disorder is that it is a completely distinct disorder from simple unipolar depression in its causes, genetics, presentation and treatment. While this is still the accepted norm, a body of opinion is viewing recurrent severe MDD and bipolar as part of a 'spectrum', varying from mania at one end to severe MDD at the other. This shift is happening due to the increasing overlap of neurobiological findings in both. Only time will reveal if this is true. Bipolar mood disorder can be divided into two main groups:

BIPOLAR DISORDER, TYPE 1: Here, the person will have suffered at least one manic episode, usually associated with periods of low mood or depression. They suffer the usual symptoms of depression already dealt with, including:

- Low mood

- Sleep difficulties

- Fatigue

- Low self-esteem

- Anxiety

- Suicide thoughts

Mania is the opposite of depression. It is defined as a distinct period of abnormally and persistently elevated mood lasting at least one week, which sometimes requires hospitalisation. During this period of elevated mood, the person will display the following:

- Extremely inflated self-esteem and mood

- Decreased need for sleep

- Talkativeness, and speech will often rhyme like poetry

- Racing thoughts and ideas

- High creativity

- Inexhaustible optimism, energy and enthusiasm

- Anger upon being challenged

- Indiscreet behaviour, with very poor judgement

- Insensitivity to the feelings of others

- Impairment of social function, particularly everyday activities

- Involvement in pleasurable activities with no regard for the consequences, such as spending sprees, shoplifting, reckless driving, excessive sexual activity or impulsive behaviour

A very unpleasant form of type one bipolar disorder is dysphoric mania. This is where the person gets a bout of depression during an episode of severe mania in which, instead of the person feeling 'on top of the world', they becomes extremely distressed, irritable and agitated, with racing and suicidal thoughts. It constitutes between 30 to 40 percent of instances of mania, is more common in women, is associated with a high suicide risk and a higher rate of familial depression, and will usually require hospitalisation. It can be a very distressing condition for both the person and their family. It can also be present in a lesser form as dysphoric hypomania, where depression is present during an episode of hypomania (see below).

BIPOLAR DISORDER, TYPE 2: Here, the person suffers mainly from bouts of depression, interspersed with periods of hypomania. Hypomania is a distinct period of euphoria lasting for at least four days. During this period of elevated mood, the symptoms of mania emerge, although they are not as obvious, usually do not cause major difficulties in the person's ability to cope with normal activities (in fact, many feel that they cope better during this period) and seldom require hospitalisation. The person will rarely suffer from delusions or hallucinations. A person with hypomania will have periods where they experience the following:

- a sudden increase in energy levels;

- racing thoughts;

- increased talkativeness;

- decreased need for sleep;

- irritability and annoyance if confronted;

- feeling on top of the world.

In future, we may be including a third type, namely anti-depressive triggered bipolar disorder, where a latent illness is unmasked by medication.

Bipolar disorder (BD) sometimes appears in the teenage years and, even when the condition is observed, it is often misdiagnosed as normal depression. Only when the periods of elevated mood are either admitted to or noticed by others, does the real diagnosis emerge. Bouts of low mood, periods of normality and occasional bouts of elevated mood merge to create the distinct pattern of this illness. Unfortunately, there is often quite a delay in diagnosis due to the erratic nature of the illness. In some people, the condition may (through a combination of not presenting early enough and a delay in accurate diagnosis) remain undetected for up to ten years. Only one in four bipolar sufferers are diagnosed within three years of onset of the condition. Over their lifetime, a bipolar sufferer will typically suffer eight to ten episodes of mood swings. Untreated episodes of mania may last from four to six months. In practice, mania symptoms are so severe that help is usually received quite quickly, so episodes may last only weeks. Episodes of hypomania are much more subtle and are of shorter duration, so they often go undetected. Bouts of depression, if untreated, can last up to nine months. One of the difficulties with this condition is that patients treated with antidepressants may develop a subsequent bout of hypomania or mania as a result of the medication. A particular concern is where a person with dysphoric hypomania presents with what may appear at first glance to be simple depression, and is treated with antidepressants. This can create more agitation, and suicidal thoughts or actions may increase.

The risk of suicide in general in bipolar disorder is greatest in the early stages of this illness (which is why early diagnosis is vital) and more often occurs in the depression or mixed-mania phases. There can be a delay of four to five years between the first and second episode. Following this, the length of time between episodes will gradually begin to shorten. In some cases, the severity of the illness, especially if it is untreated, will worsen. If one looks at the probability of recurrence, some estimate it at 50 percent for the first year, 70 percent by the fourth year, and 90 percent by the fifth year.

This illness is not as common as unipolar depression, and affects both men and women equally. The incidence of bipolar type one is 1 percent, and bipolar type two probably between 1 and 2 percent. Some experts believe that the true incidence of type two may be considerably higher.

The Bipolar Disorder Pathways

It is now accepted that MDD and bipolar disorder (BD) pathways are similar, as both involve:

1. malfunctions within the internal workings of the neurons (and glial support cells) themselves and in their connections (synapses) with each other

2. a breakdown in some key brain systems/circuits as a result of this

3. the mood, behaviour and thought difficulties and physical symptoms already outlined

Just as in MDD, it is now felt by most experts that BD is primarily a disorder affecting the second messenger system in the neurons themselves, leading to changes in the mood system, in a way that is similar to, but distinct from, MDD. We discussed the role of the second messenger system in bipolar disorder earlier (see page 140).

There is a large amount of research going on (some of it here in Ireland) into identifying the genes underlying BD, and the main culprits involved. When we have built up a total genetic picture, we can reveal how such genes lead to individual malfunctions within the second messenger system. We know that malfunctions within the internal cascade of second messengers can lead to either deterioration in the function of, or the death of, individual neurons, which in turn can lead to the widespread disruption of the brain's mood departments and circuits that is so prevalent in BD.

It is now felt that major stresses in early life, through epigenetic mechanisms, lead to a later triggering of BD. When the illness is actually triggered, it is felt that the second messenger system becomes increasingly maladaptive, making further episodes more likely. This system is also highly sensitive to sex hormones and glucocorticol, which explains why stress and pregnancy can trigger BD.

Abnormalities of this system in other parts of the body are the probable explanation for the concomitant presence of coronary heart disease and diabetes in both MDD and BD, probably through genetic links.

The role of the mood system in bipolar disorder is one of the most important findings in this area in the past ten years. Through research into those suffering from recurrent bouts of BD (and MDD), the subtle loss of neurons, dendrite connections and support glial cells scattered throughout key parts of our mood system, was discovered. It now seems as if these losses of crucial neural connections, and indeed of neurons themselves, most likely arise secondary to malfunctions occurring within the second messenger system, leading to a loss of the vital neurotrophic proteins already mentioned.

Of particular interest has been the finding of brain tissue loss in the logical brain, most notably in the logic, social behaviour and attention boxes (particularly on the left side of the brain) – all key players in our ability to control thoughts, emotions and behaviour. Similar loss of grey matter has also been discovered in parts of our emotional brain, particularly in our memory and stress boxes. This leads to a breakdown in both the functioning of these boxes and in key circuits connecting the logical and emotional brain, which results in the symptoms of BD. The result of all these changes in BD is a more profound disruption of the mood system than in MDD. We will discuss this in more detail in the technical section.

So, in summary, the bipolar pathway:

- is primarily genetic, triggered epigenetically on occasions by major stresses in early life;
- leads to malfunctioning of the second messenger system cascade;
- leads to disruption of key neurotrophic factors, particularly Bcl 2 and BDNF;
- leads to atrophy of neurons, dendrites and glial cells;
- leads to a decrease in key structures in the logical and emotional brain;
- disrupts the circuits between both;
- leads to the symptoms of BD.

The Role of Our Holistic Therapy Pathway in Bipolar Disorder

Foundations

The same rules apply in the areas of empathy, exercise and nutrition as in MDD. In terms of supplements, I would particularly recommend Omega 3 fish oils in BD, as they seem to have useful effects within the cell membrane/second messenger system and in the brain and heart. I would use up to 1000 mg of EPA, which I find to be useful in BD when taken in combination with other drug therapies. Moderation in the use of alcohol and drugs is another important area in this illness. It is crucial that we deal with this, as otherwise recovery will be blocked. Stress reduction is a vital area too, as stress is often a trigger for relapses. Meditation is useful, but only when mood has been stabilised. Relaxation therapies like yoga, massage and aromatherapy are useful short-term anti-stress measures when the person is stable. The placebo effect is less important in BD, owing to the more extreme neurobiological underpinnings of the illness.

Main Structure

Conventional drug therapies lie at the heart of the therapy pathway in BD, even more so than in MDD. Without them, recovery would be very difficult. Four groups of conventional drugs are used in BD:

LITHIUM is the most commonly used mood stabiliser, particularly in bipolar type 1. It has been extensively researched, with most of our information on internal cellular changes emerging from these findings. It has multiple positive effects on the second messenger system, which I will detail in the technical section, but the primary mechanism involves regulating Bcl 2 and BDNF. It not only safeguards neurons and dendrites but regenerates both in various parts of the emotional and logical brain, particularly in the attention box. Shown to be effective on its own in both the manic and depressive phases of BD, Lithium can be also used in combination with other mood stabilisers and antidepressants. It can cause weight gain (by stimulating appetite in the brain), slight tremors (alleviated by small amounts of beta blockers), is contraindicated in pregnancy (for the first three months) and requires regular blood-level monitoring to out rule toxicity.

ANTIEPILEPTIC-TYPE MOOD STABILISERS, which are routinely used in epilepsy, are also useful in BD:

EPILIM is an anti-epileptic-type mood stabiliser, extremely useful for treating bipolar type 1, and has similar effects on the second messenger system and BDNF and Bcl 2 as lithium, both medications being neuroprotective. It is primarily used in mania. Epilim can cause weight gain (by stimulating appetite in the brain). It is completely contraindicated in pregnancy.

LAMICTAL is another antiepileptic mood stabiliser, increasingly seen as an excellent treatment of bipolar type 2, and occasionally, when combined with anti-manic drugs, in bipolar type 1. Its great strength lies in its ability to prevent depression relapse. It does not lead to weight gain, can occasionally cause severe rashes and was initially thought to be safe in pregnancy (although now it is thought to increase the risk of cleft palate slightly). It can be combined with Lithium.

MAJOR TRANQUILLISERS have become increasingly popular as another type of mood stabiliser, but mechanisms of action are different to the above. They are used both to treat and to prevent mania in particular.

ZYPREXA is a popular choice but does have significant side effects, particularly marked sedation and extreme weight gain. It is quite effective and can be used in combination with any of the above.

SEROQUEL is another commonly used drug and one I personally prefer. It has fewer side effects than Zyprexa.

The main concern in relation to these drugs is their propensity to increase weight markedly. They lead to an excessive build-up of abdominal fat, which is the main cause of diabetes and accelerated atherosclerosis, with risks of heart attacks and strokes. They do so by stimulating appetite centres in the brain. BD is already associated with an increased risk of all of the above due to constant high levels of glucocortisol. Many experts are concerned about the overuse of these drugs because such side effects may accelerate these risks. If you are concerned about these things, never stop taking them unilaterally, but don't be afraid to discuss the issue with your specialist or family doctor, and make sure that you have regular checks on your weight, blood pressure, cholesterol and blood sugars.

ANTIDEPRESSANTS are of great help in MDD but their use in BD is more complex and controversial. The older antidepressants (Tricyclics) were renowned for tipping those with BD from depression into mania. The newer SSRIs are less inclined to cause this 'switch' but in the absence of a mood stabiliser can increase the risks of it occurring. Drugs affecting the noradrenalin mood cable, like Efexor/Cymbalta, behave like the older drugs and should be treated with more caution. The real problems occur when somebody who seems to have simple MDD is in fact a latent BD sufferer. In such cases, antidepressants may trigger a bout of elevated mood. They have a role in type 2 BD, but only if combined with a mood stabiliser, and should be withdrawn as soon as possible, to reduce the risks of a switch to mania.

ALTERNATIVE DRUG THERAPIES include herbal remedies like St John's wort and homeopathy. I strongly discourage the use of such remedies in BD. This is an extremely complex illness, which requires conventional specialist help. The use of Omega 3 oils is one area where both conventional and alternative practitioners agree. The consensus is that they are extremely useful as an adjunct, but probably not when used on their own.

TALK THERAPIES are also important in BD, but perhaps not as much as in MDD. This is due to the extreme biological nature of the former, where drug therapy is the cornerstone of treatment. Often, there are major issues in the life of the person with BD, and these may require counselling. Sometimes, this will involve relationship counselling or interpersonal therapy; other times, it may involve addiction counselling. In my opinion, there is little place for psychoanalytical psychotherapy. Of all the talk therapies, CBT is probably one of the most useful, but it can only be applied when the person's mood state has been stabilised. It can be used to assist with the negative thoughts and behaviours that might occur in the depressed phase of BD and in teaching others to recognise and moderate symptoms of elevated mood. Such work can only be done by a highly trained CBT therapist who has experience in the field.

Ancillary Therapies

This relates to those therapies, mainstream and alternative, which are also used to treat BD.

MAINSTREAM ANCILLARY THERAPIES include light therapy, sleep deprivation and brain-stimulating therapies like ECT, trans-cranial magnetic stimulation and deep-brain stimulation.

SLEEP DEPRIVATION has been found to be effective during bouts of depression in BD, particularly when combined with other therapies like mood stabilisers. We dealt earlier with its mechanism of action. It is still the fastest of all the therapies when it comes to lifting symptoms of depression, but in BD it runs the risk of occasionally triggering mania. This explains why some people with BD suddenly develop a bout of elevated mood following a sleepless night, in comparison to the capacity of a 'nap' to trigger a bout of low mood during the depressed phase.

LIGHT THERAPY was reviewed earlier in the sections on MDD and SAD. There is an extremely strong link between SAD and BD, so it is not surprising that seasonal shifts in light can trigger the latter as well. It is now felt that if depressive symptoms are deteriorating in the winter months, light therapy can be an extremely useful adjunct therapy.

ECT, TRANSCRANIAL MAGNETIC STIMULATION and DEEP-BRAIN STIMULATION have all been reviewed in my first book.

ALTERNATIVE ANCILLARY THERAPIES include aqua puncture, hypnosis, energy-field therapies, reiki and cranial manipulation. We have already reviewed all of the above. There is little evidence that any of them have a place in BD.

The Application of the Holistic Therapy Pathway to Bipolar Disorder

BD is a much more complex disorder to deal with than MDD and should be managed by a psychiatrist and family doctor, working with other mental-health services. The modern approach revolves around the use of mood stabilisers and major tranquillisers in different combinations to manage moods, with all other drug/talk/alternative therapies only relevant when mood control has been achieved. I deal with some specific details in the technical section, but include the following examples to illustrate how the condition operates in practice.

'I just can't sleep'

Peter comes to see his family doctor, complaining of low mood and difficulty in sleeping for the previous three months. He is a twenty-four-year-old postgraduate student struggling with bouts of low mood, fatigue, poor concentration and anxiety since his late teens, but had not looked for assistance. There were some occasions when his mood would briefly become elevated and his thoughts would race, but to his doctor he only reveals his low mood. His GP asks about suicidal thoughts. Peter admits to these, and says that he drinks heavily to help him sleep and has a stream of negative thoughts that he is worthless and the world would be better off without him. His mother had suffered from depression and, unknown to Peter, his uncle has suffered with bipolar disorder type 2. His present episode began with a period of prolonged stress, including a break-up with his girlfriend.

Together, Peter and his doctor draw up the following treatment plan, where Peter would:

- start exercising, improve his diet and take supplements;

- cease taking alcohol until his mood has improved;

- begin a course of antidepressants (SSRIs) to improve some of his physical symptoms and lift his mood;

- see his doctor weekly, in view of his suicidal thoughts;

- when feeling better, review stress triggers in his life;

- at a later stage, work with his doctor to help challenge his negative thoughts.

After six weeks, Peter notices no improvement, is still agitated and is unable to sleep. His doctor, concerned about his agitation, makes an appointment with the local psychiatrist, who reviews him two weeks later. The psychiatrist traces his history from childhood and notes his mother's history. He particularly inquires about periods of racing thoughts.

Peter admits to short periods of feeling 'high', where he would feel full of energy and nothing would be a problem. He also reveals that during such periods, he sometimes went on shopping sprees. He notes the presence of suicidal thoughts but the absence of specific plans to act on them. The psychiatrist concludes that Peter is going through a bout of bipolar disorder type 2 and explains what that means. Together, they draw up the following treatment plan, under which Peter will:

- reduce the dose of his antidepressant

- add a mood stabiliser (Lamictal), gradually increasing the dose over the following weeks

- stay off alcohol, improve his diet, and continue to take fish oils

- if experiencing serious suicidal thoughts, return to see him or his family doctor

- return for review at two-week intervals

- inquire about possible family history of BD.

Eight weeks later, Peter is feeling better and is sleeping. His mood has improved and he is calmer. His psychiatrist (now acquainted with Peter's family history of BD) lays out a plan where his antidepressant would be gradually reduced to a minimum dose, with a view to phasing it out. The specialist continues him on Lamictal. Six months later, on review by his family doctor, all is well. Peter is able to focus and concentrate on his studies, is off alcohol, is exercising and is eating well, and his mood has settled. He is still on his mood stabiliser, but he is off antidepressants. He has joined an Aware self-help group at college, and he finds that sharing his illness with others of his age group is of great assistance. He has worked with a CBT therapist on the advice of his psychiatrist and is also involved in a mindfulness program.

We can learn the following lessons from Peter's case:

- Severe sleep disturbance can be a presenting symptom of BD.

- In BD type 2, the presenting picture is almost identical in many cases to that of MDD.

- Racing thoughts are not a symptom of routine depression but can be a warning sign of bipolar disorder.

- It is important to mention any family history of BD.

- Most people will feel better after three to four weeks of drug therapy; if they are feeling worse, the possibility of BD should be considered.

- Mood stabilisers are the therapy of choice. Just as in MDD, stress and life events like relationship difficulties can trigger bouts of bipolar disorder.

- Antidepressants, although useful in MDD, require care with dosage in BD, as they can trigger bouts of racing thoughts or mania.

- This is best done under the supervision of a specialist.

- Most specialists, when the person is well, will gradually withdraw them.

- Suicidal thoughts are extremely common in the depression phase of BD, particularly in younger undiagnosed patients.

- Many people diagnosed with BD type 2 may have a previous history of anxiety as a child, previous experiences of depression, and short periods of racing thoughts.

'I feel so down'

Caroline, a thirty-year-old single insurance company executive, attends her family doctor on the advice of her sister, who is increasingly concerned about her mental health. Caroline explains how depressed she has felt for the previous three months, but becomes irritable when her sister comments in particular about her journey into the world of alternative therapy and the fortune she has spent on such treatments.

She admits to restlessness, insomnia, exhaustion, loss of interest in food and sex, suicidal ideation, and previous bouts of depression since her late teens. There were no obvious stress triggers, and there is no family history of depression. She was not coping at work and was also misusing alcohol. Her family doctor diagnoses depression but is uneasy about her irritability and suicidal thoughts, and also about her starting antidepressants without specialist review. Together, they draw up the following treatment plan, under which Caroline will:

- start exercising, improve her diet and take fish-oil supplements

- cease taking alcohol until her mood has improved

- take a short-acting sleeping tablet

- see a local psychiatrist for an urgent review of her case

- take a break from her job, in order to deal with her problems

- stay with her sister for a few weeks until she has improved

One week later, Caroline is assessed urgently by the local psychiatrist. She is now feeling terrible: her mood is deteriorating, she is extremely agitated and unable to sleep, and has increasing suicidal thoughts. Her detailed history reveals distressing, racing thoughts, which are driving her to distraction. The psychiatrist thinks that Caroline is suffering from a dysphoric bipolar episode, and agrees with her family doctor's decision to withhold antidepressants. He explains the diagnosis to Caroline and her sister and they draw up the following treatment plan, under which Caroline will:

- start a mood stabiliser (Epilim), gradually increasing the dose over the following weeks

- add in a major tranquilliser (Seroquel) at night to help her sleep, and reduce her racing thoughts

- stay off alcohol

- if experiencing any serious suicidal thoughts, return to see him or the family doctor

- return for regular reviews

- if not improving, possibly begin a period of inpatient care

- inquire as to any family history of BD

Eight weeks later, following a number of visits to the psychiatrist, Caroline is gradually improving: her racing thoughts are decreasing, her sleep is returning to normal, and her suicidal thoughts have gone. She is also less irritable with her sister.

We can learn from Caroline's case that in dysphoric bipolar disorder:

- racing thoughts are often extremely distressing

- the person may feel depressed, but is also suffering from a concomitant form of mania

- suicidal thoughts are very common in this situation

- antidepressants are best avoided in such cases

- mood stabilisers are the treatment of choice

- major tranquillisers can be extremely useful in such cases, to reduce racing thoughts

- extreme irritability with depression can sometimes be a warning symptom of BD

- alternative therapies in general are not useful in BD.

'I feel embarrassed'

Anne attends her doctor feeling embarrassed about her behaviour during a particularly difficult bout of elevated mood, when she had spent a fortune on a shopping spree and made sexual advance on her friend's partner. She had spent some time in hospital, had been diagnosed with bipolar type 1, was now well on Lithium and Seroquel and was attending the local psychiatrist regularly for blood tests and check-ups. He decides, with permission from the specialist, to send her to a senior CBT therapist for assistance.

The therapist over a period of time teaches Anne to deal with her elevated phases of mood (where she feels invincible) by introducing her to a 'stay safe' program devised by therapist Enda Murphy. This involves the person agreeing to liaise with three close friends where, if one of them notes that her mood is beginning to elevate, she checks with the other two as to whether either agrees that this is so. In such cases, Anne agrees to go for help and to become, with their help, more careful about her behaviour. After working with him for some time, Anne feels much more comfortable with what she needs to do at such times.

Her doctor carries out a full cardiac screen, discovers that she has elevated blood pressure and cholesterol and deals with these in the usual way. He also gives her advice on the risks of osteoporosis.

The lessons we can learn from Anne's case are:

- that bipolar type 1 can be associated with unusual behaviour

- many people with this condition are subsequently embarrassed about their behaviour at such times

- most people with BD type 1 are well controlled on Lithium plus a major tranquillisers like Seroquel; other possibilities include Epilim

- when the person is well, CBT can play a role in reducing the negative consequences of elevated mood

- everyone with BD should have a cardiac check-up and advice on osteoporosis

6

Our Journey Ends

It seems appropriate to finish our journey perched on the rocks overlooking the Atlantic Ocean in Fanore, County Clare, where mighty breakers crash against the grey limestone in a timeless struggle. Situated in the heart of the Burren, soul country to poet John O'Donohue, I find myself yet again seduced by its timeless, majestic and haunting landscape. Each rock, like ourselves, is unique and special, weathered by the relentless assault of the waves, as we are by life. They survive, as we do, by presenting a united front against the elements, or risk being eroded away in our journey through life.

At its core, our journey has been about connections and pathways in both the mind and the brain. Each of us emerges from the womb full of potential and possibilities. From that moment, we start to make the vital connections and lay down pathways that by early adult life determine the general route we will take for the rest of our lives. These pathways are, as we have seen, created through an intermingling of our genes and environment. They are hugely influenced by the social and cultural environment we are raised in: sometimes nourishing and healthy, sometimes not. At the heart of the former lies love, the key to it all.

But as we have learned on our journey, the story does not end there. Irrespective of how we arrive at a particular point in our lives, we have the power from that moment on to reshape both our brain and ourselves. We can reshape connections and, through them, crucial pathways in the brain, through a variety of interventions and therapies; in the process, we can change ourselves. I have seen countless people transform their lives in this manner, and the message of hope of this book is: 'So can you.'

On my own journey, I have learnt much from wonderful people like Enda Murphy (on the Raggy Doll Club) and Tony Bates (on mindfulness meditation), amongst others, but on reflection, I realised that my own approach to mental health had been shaped at the feet of a real master. I would like to share that experience.

In the late 1970s, I, together with my wife and our four-month-old baby, spent two years in Tanzania helping run a missionary hospital in the midst of appalling poverty. It was a life-altering period, where we learned much about ourselves and indeed about life itself. While we were there, I encountered Sr Kieran Saunders, MMM. This extraordinary woman was in her mid-seventies at the time, and was to be my rock for our two years there. She showed me what real love was all about. The most spiritual person I have ever met, she was always at my side, sharing her love and experience and teaching me to accept what could not be changed. She would be the last to leave at night, always present with the worst cases, especially the children and the most distressed.

One incident captured her, and it has stayed with me for life. Very late one night, I found her beside an old man who had been abandoned by his people and brought in to die. He was in an appalling state and would not survive till dawn. I found her picking maggots out of his body with her bare hands and dropping them into a bucket. I asked her a question I often feel ashamed about: why was she doing what she was, did she not know this man was dying? I will never forget her reply: 'We cannot let him go in front of his maker looking like this.' She finished, and he went in peace to a better place.

Six years later, we arrived in Drogheda, and to our joy this wonderful lady was 'retired' back to the home convent in the town. She explained to me that her role now was to be a more spiritual one, spending countless hours in meditation, and praying for those in active ministry, including her biggest challenge, namely one humble GP. She was a constant presence in our lives until her death, and I was lucky to spend time with her at her bedside before she died.

In all the time I knew Kieran, I never heard her criticising or rating another person. She would always see the fragile humanity at the heart of us all. It was not that she was naive in any way: she was one of the most perceptive people I have known. She had a constant smile, which radiated through the hardest of hearts, and a childlike appreciation of everything, from her meals to a walk in the forest. We had some wonderful mindfulness moments linked arm in arm with her, close to nature. When she died, we cried; to this day, she remains in our hearts, and hopefully she will be our guide through the pathways of the world to come. We can learn much from this special person.

It was Kieran who first introduced me to the knowledge that we are all special and unique and that we must learn to love and accept ourselves as well as others. When Enda introduced me many years later to the Raggy Doll Club, the seed fell on fertile ground: Kieran could have been a founder member of the club. At the heart of anxiety and depression is a tendency to rate ourselves as being of no worth. If we can learn to accept ourselves and others without condition, we have already started on a new pathway, one which will bring peace to our often tortured lives.

Next, she teaches us the importance of sharing ourselves with others. In giving of ourselves to others who need our help, we nourish and grow as human beings. I also realise that the inner peace and tranquillity that radiated from Kieran came not only from her selfless giving but also from the prayerful mindful meditation which acted as her power source. When you were with her, you were always in the present moment, and aware of everything around you. We can learn from her about applying mindfulness to our hectic lives. She also demonstrated the importance of searching for meaning in our lives; without this, so many of us Raggy Dolls will struggle.

Our journey has also taught us that there are many different routes back to mental health. I have always believed that we have to accept that foundations like empathy, lifestyle and placebo effects are integral to most successful therapy systems. After that, I feel that we have to try and be as scientific as possible when assessing the various drug, talk and alternative possibilities available. Many will argue that this is to exclude external forces and energy fields that they claim are extremely important. I have learnt my own lessons from Kieran, who, although immensely spiritual, embraced conventional medicine. She believed, like the Dalai Lama, whom we discussed earlier, that we should not be afraid to use our modern knowledge in any way possible to help deal with mental illness.

My final recipe for true mental health would be:

- Exercise from the cradle to the grave.

- Grasp the importance of nutrition, nutrition, nutrition.

- Take Omega 3 fish oils.

- Introduce mindfulness into our daily lives.

- Treat alcohol with respect; it is a bad enemy.

- Always accept our emotions; they are an integral part of who we are.

- Admitting our own emotional distress is a vital first step on the road to recovery.

- After that, share this emotional distress with at least one other person you know and trust, ideally a trained professional or therapist.

- Remember that many mental-health issues turn out to be simpler to solve than we might think, often calling for simple solutions.

- Use any therapy, but try to be as scientific as possible in assessing its effectiveness.

- Be aware that some therapies may be based on very shallow foundations.

- If unwell, the goal is not just to *feel* better, but to *get* better.

- There are many elements of alternative therapy systems that can be of assistance to those in distress, but ideally as a complementary adjunct to conventional therapies.

- There is a place for both drug and talk therapies; a combination of the two is often the answer.

- Perhaps we need to examine our search for meaning in life, as it may be more important than was previously thought.

- I have left the most important thing to last: we must learn to become true Raggy Dolls, learning to love and accept ourselves without conditions, as the wonderfully special human beings we truly are.

Technical Section

For Those Who Want To Know More

The technical section validates and fleshes out underlying biological mechanisms for those more scientifically orientated, anxious to access more information, or involved in the teaching/counselling areas or medical/nursing professions who may want to know more. I make no excuses for using exact biological and neurophysiological names and concepts in this chapter.

The Neuron

As neurons form the basis of brain pathways, we begin our journey by examining them in more detail. Neurons are brain cells which receive information, process it and pass it on. They are fluid-filled tiny units surrounded by a fine cell membrane to keep them distinct from other neurons. At their heart lies the nucleus, containing chromosomes and their genetic material which controls neuron functions.

Each cell has about twenty separate sections, each with different functions. Messages are being constantly passed from the nucleus/genes back and forth to these sections with instructions. All of the sections have their part to play. Some provide the energy; others are involved in making the proteins/enzymes necessary for the day-to-day running of the cell; others parcel the latter up into little bundles ready for transport; others get rid of unwanted material and so on. The nucleus is also in constant touch with the periphery of the cell, sensing and responding to its needs.

The structure of the basic neuron is shown in Figure 16. The main information collectors are the dendrites. The cell body contains the nucleus with our genes and all the basic internal machinery of the cell. The axon is a long tail-like structure that conveys information from the cell body to its terminal buttons. It is covered with myelin, which can be compared to the white protective structure surrounding electrical wires in our homes. The job of myelin is to speed up the conductivity of nerve cells. The terminal buttons are the end points of where axons divide into many branches. Each branch ends in a small knob-like structure, which in turn links up most often with dendrites to form the synapses we have dealt with in earlier chapters. The role of this terminal button is to release neurotransmitters like serotonin upon being activated by an electrical charge surging along the axon itself.

Information is passed from the axon of one cell to the dendrite of another through chemical messengers released into synapses. This information is then passed to the cell body, which in turn sends its own message along its axon to its terminal buttons, and so on. This is how neurons talk to each other. Although the cell body, through its genes, seems to be the boss, what happens at all the synapses at the level of the nerve cell membranes plays a huge role in how each cell behaves. So let's look at this in more detail.

Each terminal button is full of little balls or vesicles, full of chemical neurotransmitters. Many key neurotransmitters like serotonin, dopamine, and noradrenalin are stored in these vesicles. When the axon is fired, these little bags release their supply of messenger into the synapse between the terminal buttons of one cell and the dendrite end of the next.

THE CELL MEMBRANE forms the border of each neuron controlling movement of substances in and out of the cell. It is composed of two layers of lipid or fat molecules (phospholipids, in particular), with the water-repelling tails of these molecules directed toward the middle of the membrane and away from the fluid found outside and inside the cell. Protein molecules are embedded within this bi-lipid membrane.

Cholesterol and proteins are also found in the cell membrane. Cholesterol provides structural stability to the membrane, wedging between phospholipid molecules, which are in constant motion. Proteins take two forms. They either span the full width of the plasma membrane (integral proteins) or attach to only one side of the membrane (peripheral proteins). Integral proteins form the channels for movement of substances in and out of the cell. Some of the channels are controlled by the action of specific enzymes and are called 'gated'. The peripheral proteins act as carriers, helping molecules move through the membrane.

Within the cell membrane of the dendrite lie crucial protein molecules which we call POSTSYNAPTIC RECEPTORS. Chemical messengers link in very specifically with these receptors, e..g serotonin molecules link up with serotonin receptors, noradrenalin molecules with noradrenalin receptors and so on. Some of these receptors promote electrical firing of the cell. Others have the opposite effect and dampen down activity. Others, through more complicated reactions within the cell membrane, cause messengers to travel to the internal genes of our cells – so-called *second messengers.*

Neurotransmission begins when 'first messenger' neurotransmitters (such as serotonin, noradrenalin or dopamine) are released from the presynaptic terminal. The neurotransmitter in question binds to and activates postsynaptic receptors, which modify properties of the postsynaptic cell.

THE POSTSYNAPTIC RECEPTORS are large protein molecules embedded in the lipid neuronal membrane on the receiving neuron's surface. There are two types vital for normal brain functioning.

1.   IONOTROPIC RECEPTORS: These facilitate the movement of ions across the cell membrane. They are composed of two parts – a binding site for the neurotransmitter; and a channel or pore. When the neurotransmitter attaches itself to the relevant binding site, the receptor changes its shape to either open, allowing ions into the cell; or closed. This movement of ions in and out helps to determines whether or not the cell fires electrically.. One of our major neurotransmitters, glutamate, +activates two major ionotropic receptors called *NMDA* and *AMPA*, which are crucial players in long term synaptic memory.

2.   METABOTROPIC RECEPTORS are more complex receptors, which lack an ion channel. They are composed of a single protein with a binding site for the neurotransmitter; but are also attached to one of a family of *G proteins.* When the neurotransmitter binds to the binding site, a portion of the G proteins called an *alpha sub unit* is released and has two potential actions: (a) It can travel to a neighbouring ion channel and lead to it opening up to allow ions to pass through as above. (b) It can bind with an enzyme in the cell membrane to activate a second messenger, which in itself can either travel to other ion channels or lead to activation of our genes, as we will see later. Many routine

neurotransmitters like serotonin, dopamine and noradrenalin regularly activate these receptors.

SECOND MESSENGER SYSTEMS are worth examining in detail as malfunctions within them may underlie depression and bipolar mood disorder. When the first messenger, e.g. serotonin, latches on to the postsynaptic receptor, it sets in motion a cascade of chemical reactions, initially within the cell membrane and then in the cytoplasm of the neuron; finishing with information being passed to the genes in our nucleus. Metabotropic receptors in the cell membrane are coupled with particular second messenger systems. Second messenger signalling cascades exert a powerful control on almost all aspects of neuronal function – structure, gene expression, activity and survival. These cascades ultimately allow neuronal systems to adapt in response to environmental stimuli and particular therapies.

When a G protein receptor, for example, is occupied by its specific neurotransmitter, the second messenger produced activates enzymes in the neuronal cytoplasm, which add phosphate groups to a variety of further second messenger proteins within the receiving neuron. This sets in motion a complex molecular cascade that ultimately turns on genes and DNA in the receiving neuron. Phosphorylation is the key to second messenger system function altering many signalling pathway downstream effectors. Most of these effectors are enzymes that produce further intracellular second messengers.

It is the downstream intracellular signalling mediated by these neurotransmitter receptors that co-ordinates the behaviour of individual cells within the brain. A major intracellular signalling pathway implicated in synaptic and structural plasticity is AC-cAMP (adenylyl cyclase-cyclic adenosine monophosphate).

THE AC-CAMP SECOND MESSENGER SYSTEM: Activation of the G-protein receptor (by one of the above neurotransmitters) within the cell membrane leads to a release of the G protein alpha sub unit, which starts production of an important second messenger, cAMP and the phosphorylation enzyme PKA. As a result, cAMP is altered to form a key protein called CREB (cyclic AMP response element binding protein), which regulates many neuronally expressed genes, including BDNF (brain-derived neurotrophic factor), a key player in the functioning of our neurons as we will see later.

When activated, PKA is a crucial second messenger which also sets in motion a whole host of other second messenger cascades within the cell. But we are particularly interested in its ability to form CREB. All this is important, since the cAMP/CREB /BDNF cascade may represent the pathway by which antidepressants and indeed other therapies do their work.

The phosphoinositol (PIP2) second messenger system helps regulate the level of calcium in the cytoplasm of neurons (which is very low). Activation of a receptor coupled to the PIP2 cascade induces formation of two important second messengers: DAG and IP3. *DAG* activates *protein kinase C (PKC)*, involved in cellular processes including gene expression, modulation of ionic conduction, cellular proliferation and down-regulation of extracellular receptors. IP3 regulates release of intracellular calcium reserves.

THE GSK3 (GLYCOPROTEIN SYNTHASE KINASE 3) SECOND MESSENGER SYSTEM is being increasingly examined in relation to its importance in mood disorders as it is at the centre of a number of critical signalling cascades within the neuron. Levels of this messenger are strongly influenced by serotonin and dopamine. It is an important regulator of neuroplasticity, cell resilience/death and internal circadian rhythms.

Downstream effects of activated G proteins and other second messengers are relatively slow and prolonged and may take days to weeks to exert their full effect. There are many more similar second messenger systems to the above. For those interested see Dwivedi and Pandey's superb article on the subject and Goodwin and Jamison's excellent tome. Now that we have reviewed the flow of information from cell membrane to our genes, let's review what happens at DNA level – the world of epigenetics.

GENES AND EPIGENES: Before completion of the Human Genome Project, most biologists expected we would discover large numbers of active, protein-encoding genes. Many put the expected number near or above 100,000. The actual number is known to be fewer than 21,000 – a very surprising result. One reason for the lower number is the mechanisms that control and co-ordinate activation and repression of genes, collectively referred to as epigenetic functions.

Epigenetics traditionally studied heritable changes in gene expression not encoded in the DNA of the genome, but its use has widened to include the capacity of developmental and environmental influences to also alter gene expression.

These effects are mediated by attaching chemical groups to DNA and the histones around which it is wound. Types of modification include methylation, acetylating and phosphorylation (adding *methyl*, *acetyl* or *phosphor* groups). These modifications result in alteration of gene expression patterns, ultimately influencing the fate of the cell.

The DNA we inherit is contained in our chromosomes. Individual chunks of DNA are called genes. Most genes are actually switched off; much of it junk DNA from our evolutionary past. The 20,000 genes known to be in use have particular functions within each cell. These functions are mediated by the genes in question passing information to the cell machinery to make proteins each with specific functions. Genes not in use are switched off by the above epigenetic chemical proteins.

The mechanism for this involves strands of DNA opening up to allow genetic information required to make such proteins to be passed onto a cell messenger called RNA. This passes the information on to the manufacturing factory in the cell (ribosome) which makes the protein. Whether DNA opens up however is controlled by the epigenetic chemical groups activated. If a methyl group is added to the DNA, it switches off (DNA zipper). If an acetyl group attaches to the histone around which the DNA is wound, then it opens up (DNA unzipper). We now know that this process is strongly influenced by our upbringing and environment. So epigenetic mechanisms reduce or increase access to the cell's genes: controlling their expression.

NEUROTROPHINS are amongst epigenetic factors influencing the development and survival of neurons. These are a family of proteins in each neuron which determines its survival and synaptic plasticity (i.e. number of dendrites). They are unusual in that, when manufactured in the cell, they are actually secreted from the dendrite backwards into the presynaptic space. They almost become like a first messenger neurotransmitter like serotonin, producing long lasting changes to the dendrite.

BDNF is the most important and widely distributed neurotrophin in the brain. We have already seen how the AC-cAMP second messenger system produces CREB which, when phosphorylated, unlocks our DNA to give instructions to produce BDNF. This then travels to the dendrite cell membrane of the neuron it serves where it is secreted into the presynaptic area.

When BDNF arrives in the presynaptic space, it locks on to receptors in the cell membrane; setting off another second messenger cascade, mediated mainly through a trans-membrane receptor called TrkB. This cascade will activate our genes to organise the above functions; particularly neuroplasticity. One of the many second messengers TrkB activates is CREB. The circle is completed!

BDNF and other neurotrophins are vital for the survival and the function of neurons, and facilitate the release of key neurotransmitters like serotonin and dopamine. For the purposes of our discussion, BDNF has two key roles:

- NEUROPLASTICITY: the ability to increase or decrease the number of dendrites of a particular neuron. This is influenced by developmental and environmental circumstances, and particular therapies. Synaptic plasticity is increasingly being regarded as its primary role.

- NEUROPROTECTIVITY: the ability to nourish the neuron and keep it alive. This seems to be of lesser importance in terms of its functions than neuroplasticity.

These functions lie at the heart of our understanding of illnesses like anxiety and depression. Neuroplasticity is driven by dendrite increases and decreases,so at every stage of our lives different influences can alter these through BDNF levels. Many of the therapies discussed will work through BDNF. Neuroprotectivity is increasingly being scrutinised. We will review this later.

The Brain

To visualise the human brain, clench your left hand into a fist then cover it with your right hand. The left hand represents the ancient brain; the wrist being the brainstem; the clenched palm the limbic system. The right hand represents the modern brain; the cortex almost covering the other two.

Neuroscientists (see Kandel and Squires) over the past few decades have been concerned with two themes – the brain's 'hard wiring' and capacity for 'plasticity'. The former refers to how connections develop between cells, how cells function and communicate, and how inborn functions are organised. The brain's computational power is conferred by interactions among billions of nerve cells, assembled into networks or circuits that carry out specific operations in support of behaviour and cognition. In contrast, plasticity refers to the capacity of the nervous system to adapt or change as the result of experiences that occur during an individual's lifetime. Experience can modify the nervous system, and as a result we can learn and remember.

THE ANCIENT BRAIN: From an evolutionary viewpoint, the BRAINSTEM is the oldest part. It evolved over 500 million years ago and is a relic of the reptile era (e.g. dinosaurs). It is responsible for the reflexes involved in breathing, cardiac function and digestion amongst other life-sustaining functions. The LIMBIC SYSTEM is responsible for the expression of emotions, sleep, appetite, sex, controlling immune and stress systems, monitoring our hormones, and is a centre for sensory information travelling from the body to the cortex.

THE MODERN BRAIN is composed of the cortex; a mass of grey matter containing the neurons involved in cognition, sensory and motor functions, and the regulation of emotions. It controls vision, hearing, speech, and body movements; and is the attention, planning, creative, and logical part of the brain. As we will see later, the front part of the modern brain, the prefrontal cortex, is the real boss.

The brain is composed of grey and white matter.

WHITE MATTER indicates myelinated axons. Myelination is the result of oligodendrocytes (glial support cells) wrapping neuronal axons in a fatty sheath that speeds up transmission between neurons – up to a hundred times the speed of unmyelinated neurons. This facilitates cognitive processes and combining information from multiple sources. These help to connect different sections of the brain.

GREY MATTER indicates unmyelinated neurons and is mainly situated in the cortex and other areas of the brain which facilitate higher brain functions.

The total size of the brain is already approximately 90 percent of its adult size by age six; for those wishing to know more see Giedd's article on the developing adolescent brain.

The brain is composed of two hemispheres, one on the right and one on the left. Both are connected by a thick band of connecting neurons contained in a structure called the CORPUS CALLOSUM. This comprises of approximately 180 million myelinated axons, connecting similar parts of the left and right cerebral hemispheres. As both hemispheres give us differing views of the world, this structure is vital. It provides a particularly strong connection between the frontal lobes.

THE LEFT HEMISPHERE specialises in language, speech and intelligent behaviour – the 'logical' part of our brain. It assists us in being practical, analytical and capable of planning; good at mathematics; organised; factual; and looking at the small print. It is involved in processing and comprehending, language (both written/spoken); and positive thoughts/emotions. It seeks to provide a 'rational' explanation for our experiences, often in response to information emanating from the right brain. If there is no obvious explanation for an experience it will 'create' a story to explain it even if it is a fantasy. It will always try to create order from chaos.

THE RIGHT HEMISPHERE is more specialised in abstract thoughts, awareness, expression and modulation of emotion; and is the 'creative' part of our brain. It assists us to store visual information; comprehend the emotional significance of language; be imaginative, artistic and spatially aware of where we are; and to be intuitive. It enables us examine the bigger holistic picture and context of situations and processes negative thoughts and emotions. When we access memories, it provides us with a fuller more, comprehensive picture than the left brain.

Crucially, attention/awareness is a function of our right brain, so it struggles to compete with the practical left brain in our everyday lives. An established model of emotion associates the right hemisphere with emotional arousal. When we are anxious and 'imagining the worst', this part of the brain is overactive.

Both sides of the brain are in continuous communication, particularly the frontal lobes. This allows us the best of both worlds as we can fuse them together, forming a rich tapestry where creativity and practicality combine.

There are significant differences between male and female brains, which are important in anxiety and depression. These are firmly in place before we are born. When the brain is being formed in the womb, sex hormones are busy organising the future male/female brain. We will review the differences later.

The Mood System

THE FRONTAL MOOD DEPARTMENT relates to the prefrontal cortex, which makes up 29 percent of the modern brain and has extensive connections with every part of the brain. There are four main sections equating to the logic, emotional control, social behaviour and attention boxes.

DORSOLATERAL PREFRONTAL CORTEX (DLPFC) is the highest cortical area responsible for motor planning, organisation, and regulation. It plays a role in the integration of sensory and mnemonic information and regulation of intellectual function and action. It is also involved in everyday short-term working memory. It is the last part of the cortex to develop (myelination).

The DLPFC has been most commonly implicated in using, rather than maintaining, information no longer available in our environment. For example, although DLPFC is probably not involved in processes such as remembering a telephone number, it does seem to play a role in more difficult tasks, such as dialling the number in reverse order (rearranging the digits that we have just been told). DLPFC is involved in logically analysing situations, planning strategies, focusing conscious attention on thoughts, emotions, behaviour, deciding on options, meditating, problem solving and reasoning. The right DLPFC is associated with creativity/visual imagery; the left with concepts involving language and planning and making the logical practical decisions of everyday life.

It plays a key role in *working memory*, which integrates moment-to-moment perceptions across time, rehearses them, and combines them with stored information about past experience, actions, or knowledge. This memory mechanism is crucial for many simple aspects of everyday life: carrying on a conversation, adding a list of numbers or driving a car.

The DLPFC is our executive decision maker, particularly on the left side but with plenty of advice from the right. Executive functions are the high-level cognitive processes that facilitate new ways of behaving, and optimise one's approach to unfamiliar circumstances. As many situations in everyday life are not exactly the same as ones that we have encountered before, it follows that executive processes accompany a very wide range of behaviours.

VENTRAL PREFRONTAL CORTEX (VPFC) monitors emotions, deciding when, if, and how they should be 'modified'; and appropriate emotional behavioural responses. It is involved in comparatively simple tasks, such as short-term maintenance of information not perceived as 'working memory' (for example, memorising a phone number you have just been told, before keying the numbers into a telephone). It has also been suggested that parts of the VPFC are used to store different types of information (for example, the sound of a word versus its meaning). A portion of this section is in charge of our impulsive nature and is strongly supplied by our serotonin cable.

ORBITOFRONTAL CORTEX (OFC), situated above both eyes, is considered the most likely neural source of empathy. It is in constant communication with the amygdala (see below), dampening down its emotional surges and impulses and is a key player in our behaviour. It is now seen as the commander-in-chief of our social relationship pathway development, particularly in the first seven years of life. It assists us to:

- Defer immediate gratification; suppressing emotions for long term gain.

- Make sense of our social world.

- Make those lightening-fast assessments of people we encounter; deciding whether we face or withdraw from particular social situations.

- Control our unique capacity to 'read the mind' or 'sense' where people we meet are from an emotional point of view; the basis of empathy.

- Adapt our behaviour as situations change.

The OFC is ideally positioned to play a role in regulation of emotion-related responses in the context of a changing environment. It has both direct and indirect connections with areas important in the perception of emotionally significant cues and the expression of emotion. It is also being investigated for its role in impulsivity and addiction.

The OFC is implicated in a variety of higher-order executive functions. These include control and inhibition of inappropriate behavioural and emotional responses, decision making, maintaining behavioural flexibility to switch between different problem-solving strategies, and evaluation of contingencies between different stimuli to guide future behaviours to maximise reward and minimise punishment.

Some experts feel that OFC activity in the first two years of life has profound effects on how we will develop emotionally and behaviourally as adults. The OFC has a key role in expression of a range of psychopathologies. Examples include depression, OCD, PTSD, phobias, addictive behaviour, and attention deficit disorders. For those who would like to know more, there are some excellent articles by some world researchers, like Wayne Drevets, on the role of the OFC in the bibliography.

ANTERIOR CINGULATE CORTEX (ACC) is the 'meeting point' between the information emanating from our emotional limbic system and more rational logical areas of the PFC. Known functions, some central to intelligent behaviour, include information processing, attention, focused problem solving, error recognition, and the expression and modulation of emotion (emotional self control).

When well, the ACC makes sense of our inner emotional world, ensuring a healthy 'analysis' of how an emotion is affecting us; and that our rational mind 'assesses' whether such emotions are appropriate. The more activated it is, the calmer and more 'sensible' emotional responses will be. There is increased functioning in individuals with greater social insight and maturity, and higher levels of social awareness.

The ACC can be divided anatomically into *cognitive* (*dorsal*) and *emotional* (*ventral*) components. It is comprised of three parts, relating to Brodman's Areas 24, 25 and 32:

- AREA 32 (DORSAL ACC) assists awareness of our own emotional state and mental states of others. It is in constant communication with Area 24 below, both key players in psychotherapy.

- AREA 24 (ROSTRAL ACC) forms the main bulk of the ACC and works closely with DLPFC. It is involved in assessing and resolving emotional conflicts by focusing attention on such conflicts, helping us 'reason' them out.

- AREA 25 (SUB-GENUAL ACC) is still under scrutiny as to its exact role. We know from world experts, like Prof. Helen Mayberg, that it is highly activated when sad or depressed. It helps us become aware and attentive to emotional pain/sadness.

The four divisions of the frontal mood department are in regular communication. There is a hierarchical chain of command. The DLPFC is technically in charge, particularly the left side, but depends on information pouring in and out of the other departments to be effective. It works closely with the dorsal and rostral ACC in cognitively evaluating and reappraising emotions.

The Limbic Mood Department has four main sections equating to the stress/memory/pleasure/island boxes. Well covered in the main text, we will just summarise them here.

AMYGDALA: It plays a key role in activating stress pathways, and is involved in the creation, consolidation and expression of emotionally arousing – and usually negative – memories. It is the main processor of the primary emotions of fear, hate, love and anger.

HIPPOCAMPUS: Where memory is manufactured, filtered and retrieved. It also puts these recalled memories into context. This box becomes extremely active when dreaming, with memories consolidated at these times.

NUCLEUS ACCUMBENS is part of the pleasure/reward circuit.

INSULAR CORTEX is important in social emotions like pride, guilt, humiliation, lust, disgust and particularly empathy. It is involved in the anticipation and feeling of pain and ability to share in another person's pain. The right insular cortex is the major player, where we sense love/hate, resentment, embarrassment, trust/distrust, pride/humiliation, guilt; deception, etc. Neuroimaging studies of emotion in humans indicate conjoint activity in the anterior part of the right insular cortex and ACC during the experience of virtually all emotions. This is consistent with the idea that our emotions consist of both a feeling partly engendered in right insular cortex/ and a motivation engendered in ACC. For those who would like to know more see Craig and Damasio in bibliography.

MOOD CABLES: We have little to add to the information contained in the main text.

ADRENAL GLAND AND GLUCOCORTISOL: The mood system is completed by our adrenal gland and the stress hormone, glucocortisol, which it produces. We will be examining the role of the latter later in relation to our mood pathways.

THE AUTONOMIC NERVOUS SYSTEM (ANS) is the body's most critical life support system, regulating a wide range of cardiovascular, gastrointestinal, respiratory, and endocrine organs. Emotion and the ANS are intricately intertwined. It comprises two separate internal systems in the body that have opposite effects (activation of one may inactivate the other) but usually balance each other out.

SYMPATHETIC NERVOUS SYSTEM (SNS) is our primary survival network from an evolutionary point of view. This is our 'fight or flight' system. If one meets a leopard (as I have personal experience of) the SNS kicks in – one's heart and breathing rates goes up, pupils dilate, we go pale as blood is diverted away from our skin for more essential purposes; our mouth dries up and our digestive system temporarily switches off. We feel sweaty and our muscles tighten. The SNS is also a powerful stimulator of the adrenal gland, encouraging it to produce adrenaline which further activates all the above mechanisms. All of the above are activated in a panic attack.

PARASYMPATHETIC NERVOUS SYSTEM (PNS): This is our body's 'rest and digest' system. After a meal, while we are relaxing, the PNS kicks in – slowing our heart and breathing rate and increasing blood flow to our digestive system and skin.

Our emotions are intimately connected with activation of the ANS. If experiencing negative emotions like anxiety and anger, the SNS will usually be more active; if positive ones like happiness, the PNS will be more in charge.

Our Stress System is a key function of the mood system. The amygdala is commander-in-chief. When we come under stress, this system activates our hypothalamus and pituitary gland (HPA system) and brainstem. Through the ANS and bloodstream, our adrenal gland releases adrenalin, noradrenalin and glucocortisol. The first two are activated in acute stress; the latter in chronic stress. Both adrenaline/noradrenalin and glucocortisol feed back to the brain. When the stress or threat is removed, they encourage the amygdala to switch off. All returns to normal.

The Two 'Brain Mood Circuits' are two major circuits connecting key sections of our emotional and logical brain.

THE DORSAL SYSTEM (UPPER CIRCUIT) links together the DLPFC, Dorsal and Rostral ACC (Areas 32 and 24), and hippocampus. It is called dorsal because the structures it serves are on the upper side of the brain. This circuit controls:

- conscious rational decision making
- ability to consciously direct attention towards thoughts/events internally or externally

- future planning

- monitoring of our emotional/behavioural circuit

- 'reappraisal' of emotions and behaviour

THE VENTRAL SYSTEM (LOWER CIRCUIT) links together the VPFC; OFC; subgenual ACC (Area 25); amygdala and insula. It has strong connections with the brainstem including our serotonin, noradrenalin and dopamine control boxes. This circuit controls:

- social interaction and behaviour

- background thoughts

- stress responses

- generation, monitoring, and control of our emotions

- physical symptoms created in response to the emotions generated

- behavioural responses to the emotions generated

- creation and control of mood

Male versus Female Brains: There are key differences between both, which has been the subject of both fun and serious scientific research.

THE MALE BRAIN is larger, has more neurons or grey matter, but fewer connections between the various sections and most importantly between the two hemispheres. The amygdala is larger but the hippocampus is smaller. The serotonin system is twice as active as in the female brain. There is a smaller OFC/amygdala size ratio so men may be less capable of controlling emotional reactions. The size of the Corpus Callosum is smaller. The speech/language areas of the male brain are smaller than in women, so men are less communicative than women. Men tend to concentrate their emotions, particularly negative ones, in the right hemisphere; and their logical thoughts in the left. With poorer connections, they struggle to integrate both, tending to be either extremely logical or totally emotional.

THE FEMALE BRAIN is slightly smaller than the male, but make up for this with much greater interconnectivity between all parts of the brain. Females have a smaller amgydala; larger hippocampus and larger OFC/amygdala size ratio;

larger Corpus Callosum; larger speech/language areas and use both hemispheres when dealing with emotions. Women are better multitaskers. Their serotonin system is 50 percent less active than in the male. It has also been shown that oestrogen is a strong stimulator of dopamine; which is felt by some to explain why women progress more quickly from usage to addiction when using drugs like cocaine.

Brain Pathways

The world of brain pathways requires us to suspend preconceived ideas about the brain being a fixed organ incapable of change and enter the mind-boggling world of neuroplasticity. Neurons, like Dublin buses, run in packs. From the secure world of the womb to old age, pathways are constantly evolving and changing. Neurons and their supporting glial cells learn to link up and form local and systemic brain pathways. They do so via dendrite/axon connections. In some cases, they form local groups of cells with specific functions and in others longer connecting pathways between various parts of the brain.

Some brilliant research by scientists like Hebb, Merzenich, Kandel, Taub and Schwartz demonstrated an incredible fluidity and adaptability to such pathways. Genes are in charge but remain incredibly sensitive to environmental influences through epigenetic mechanisms, so pathways can be strengthened or weakened at will. There are three major rules that put order on what looks like chaos within the brain.

- Neurons that 'fire together, wire together'
- Neurons that 'fire apart, wire apart'
- Neurons ruthlessly obey the evolutionary rule – 'use it or lose it'

The first means that when two neurons close to one another consistently fire, synaptic connections between them strengthen through second messengers like PKA (discussed earlier) and BDNF/dendrite connections increase. This leads to the development of particular pathways and circuits, alterable by environmental factors. The second means that when neurons become more muted and inactive, the synaptic connections between them weaken, as do the pathways they serve. The third means an aggressive form of competitive neuroplasticity is at work in the brain; pathways not in use are quickly shut down and newer, more useful ones take over. At every stage of our life, these three rules are in operation. This extraordinary adaptability is what makes us so special. The main difficulty with the first concept is that when we learn and continue to use unhealthy patterns of thoughts/emotions/behaviour, we only strengthen them. If we do manage through therapy to make alternative ones, the brain has to work hard; in effect, restructuring new lines in favor of the old. Superficial attempts to change them won't last. It takes persistent effort to produce long term shifts in our pathways.

This explain clinical practice experience – how embedded, for example, negative and anxious thinking is in our emotional brain and the effort required to reshape it. This lies underneath the mantra – *do we want to feel better or get better?* But it is also the message of hope, for at no stage in our lives is it impossible to reverse some of these changes. To change brain pathways involves attention/awareness, and constant repetition – focused hard work.

Stress and Our Brain Pathways

Stress is the life-long enemy of both the mood system and brain pathways. This has been known clinically for eons, but we are beginning to understand the neurobiology. The crucial link is glucocortisol. This becomes apparent when we examine the effects of stress in the developing infant and child; and how it can lead to future illnesses like anxiety and depression.

Michael Meaney linked glucocortisol and epigenetics to give us an insight into how this works. He compared the stress response of rat pups whose mothers groomed them a lot in the first ten days of life versus those who did not. The former showed lower levels of glucocortisol and subsequently less anxiety and stress. The mechanisms involved were simple. Normally high glucocortisol levels feed back to glucocortisol receptors in the hypothalamus, reducing further production but, in the anxious rats, this feedback was ineffective. Further research showed that the receptor genes in the hypothalamus of the anxious rat pups showed many more methyl groups. These tended to switch off the genes in question, exaggerating the stress response, predisposing them to future anxiety.

Studies by Nemeroff and Plotsky found adverse early life experiences resulted in increased gene expression for corticotrophin-releasing factor (CRF) – the hormone released from the hypothalamus to initiate the HPA response, which in turn leads to excess glucocortisol being produced. Daily maternal separation during the first two weeks is associated in rats with profound and persistent increases in the expression of the messenger RNA for CRF, not only in the hypothalamus but also in limbic areas, including the amygdala. Nemeroff also found that, in depressed patients, secretion of CRF is markedly increased. This has suggested the interesting idea that in depression the neurons in the brain that secrete CRF are hyperactive. In view of this evidence, Nemeroff has suggested that adult vulnerability to stress and depression is probably mediated by the hypersecretion of CRF.

Current data supports the stress link in humans, where affection and nurturing seem to be protective epigenetic factor for future stress management. Another classic example linked bullying, BDNF and depression. This work by Eric Nestler linked bullying in mice with lower BDNF levels in the brain. In particular, he once again noted more methyl groups close to the BDNF gene histones in the hippocampus of these mice. High levels of glucocortisol are usually involved in such mechanisms. In humans, severe abuse has been shown to damage the left hippocampus in particular through such mechanisms, with increased levels of depression. We have already dealt with the resilience gene (the SERT gene) and its potential capacity to influence how stress is expressed in our lives.

Spiritual Pathways

These have been examined by Persinger, Davidson (meditation), Newberg and d'Acquili, and Beauregard, and summarised by Biello (see bibliography).

Persinger created a special brain helmet (called the 'God Machine' by the media) which delivered a magnetic stimulation to different parts of the brain to verify his theory that religious experiences occurred when the temporal lobe of the brain was stimulated. He was able to produce periods when those involved sensed a 'presence or spirit' and a feeling of 'bliss'. He maintained that those more right-brained were particularly susceptible to such activation. His work has, as could be expected, produced mixed responses.

Richard Davidson of Madison University has been at the forefront of assessing the effects of meditation in the brain. He showed a shift to the left PFC during it. He and others have examined the positive effects of meditation. They have demonstrated increased thickness of the PFC and right insular cortex, improvements in our ability to focus attention, immune function, and a possible reduction in depression relapses.

Andrew Newberg and Eugene d'Acquili (University of Pennsylvania) decided to perform experiments to assess what happened in the brain during mystical experiences, using different spiritual techniques like prayer and meditation; firstly in some Buddhist meditators and later in Franciscan sisters as they were praying. They found once again the PFC to be a major player in both.

Mario Beauregard of Montreal University also tried to find a 'God spot' in the brain when examining the brain activity of fifteen Carmelite sisters recalling mystical experiences. He demonstrated activation in six different parts of the brain. Whether one is a believer or not (the nuns were delighted), there is little doubt spiritual pathways are present in the brain; and that activation of these pathways leads to positive emotions, which may in turn improve mental health.

The Therapy Brain Pathways

We discussed earlier the three key secrets to neuroplasticity. Effective therapies have to strengthen healthy and weaken unhealthy pathways. This involves constant application of such therapies over a sustained period of time, which is why I am so wary of 'instant' solutions offered up by conventional or alternative therapists. The brain's plasticity is so powerful that there will often be immediate placebo effects, irrespective of the therapy involved. But unless the therapy is effective and sustained, such changes will be short lived. So significant changes in emotions, thinking patterns and particularly behaviour will be hard earned if very worthwhile. This explains why:

- Lifestyle changes like exercise and nutritional changes need to be constant.

- Drug therapies require longer periods to be effective

- Talk therapies require regular reinforcement.

- Many alternative therapies have short term benefits, but do not produce the long term effects so necessary for real improvements.

How synapses are strengthened and weakened – long term Potentiation/Depression (LTP/LTD) – is extraordinarily complex. The major mechanism for expression of LTP is an increase in the postsynaptic response to glutamate via the AMPA receptors. The increase in the synaptic response to glutamate is mediated by increased conductance of the AMPA receptor ion channels and accelerated insertion of these receptors into the postsynaptic membrane. The reverse occurs for LTD. Those interested should read the relevant sections in texts by Carlson, Kolb, and excellent review articles by Blitzer et al. Increasingly BDNF is being recognised as a key player in this process – see Bramham and Messaoudi.

We have dealt with brain pathways involved in empathy, exercise, nutrition and most alternative therapies in the main text. Let's examine in detail the brain pathways underlying drug and talk therapies.

Drug Therapy Pathways: When reviewing effects of drug therapy on brain pathways, we have to examine events at both neuron/synapse and mood system level. I often use the concept that drug therapy helps us to feel better so we can involve ourselves in talk therapy, which helps us to get better. Whilst this is often true, it disguises the fact that some drug therapies have a longer term action which can greatly contribute to overall healing. It's also true that most drugs work on the lower mood circuit with secondary effects on the upper. Let's examine some drug groups and how they work.

ANTIDEPRESSANTS: Modern groups include SSRIs and SRNIs which act on the serotonin and serotonin/noradrenalin systems respectively. Both take up to two weeks to kick in. Let's examine the synaptic mode of action of an SSRI like Escitalopram:

- Firstly the antidepressant blocks re-uptake of serotonin back into the neuron by attaching itself to the SERT receptor.

- The level of serotonin in the synapse tries to rise.

- However neurons have a healthy feedback system, where some serotonin receptors (such as 5 HT 1B and 5 HT 1D on the presynaptic neuron) act as 'auto receptors', sensing this sudden rise in levels of the neurotransmitter and preventing this cell releasing more serotonin into the synapse. The result is no major rise in serotonin.

- After two weeks, this inhibitory mechanism weakens and the level of serotonin begins to rise in the synapse.

- This leads to increased activation of serotonin G protein receptors in the postsynaptic cell membrane.

- These lead to activation of key second messenger signalling systems, particularly the AC-cAMP second messenger system and the phosphoinositol second messenger system, both transferring information to the nucleus and DNA.

- The former is of particular importance as it leads to elevated CREB levels and increased BDNF formation.

- This is transferred up to the cell membrane and eventually into the presynaptic space where it assists in restoration of critical circuit activity in the serotonin cable; improved synaptic plasticity and further neurotransmitter release.

When we use SSRIs in depression, there is an initial delay in onset of action of about two weeks: then we notice a gradual improvement in mood and physical and psychological symptoms. By eight weeks, many symptoms have greatly improved but, as clinical experience has demonstrated, if the drug is stopped, often return. If we continue for six to eight months this doesn't happen. It now seems that longer courses are needed because it takes that time to produce significant BDNF/dendrite changes in the PFC.

This explains difficulties in assessing SSRIs and indeed other antidepressants versus placebo therapies in trials at six and eight weeks, because these long term changes have not had a chance to take effect. We will examine their effects on the mood system later. Most side effects are caused by a total blockage of all serotonin receptors in the brain and gut. SRNIs like Venlaflaxine and Duloxetine work in a similar manner but on both serotonin and noradrenalin cables.

Mirtazapine is another modern antidepressant which is the first in a new class of antidepressants called the noradrenergic and selective serotonergic antidepressants (NaSSAs). Mirtazapine's primary mode of action is blockade of alpha2 receptors on the presynaptic noradrenergic and serotonergic neurons. This results in an increase in noradrenergic and serotonergic neurotransmission. Additional effects include antagonism of 5HT2 and 5HT3 receptors, thus potentially alleviating some of the effects of the SSRIs, such as impotence, sleep disturbances (5HT2 mediated) and nausea (5HT3). It also activates histamine H1 receptors which may result in sedation, so is usually given at night. Its main side effect is weight gain as it stimulates appetite centres in the brain. I find it a useful 'add in' drug in small doses.

A new drug called Agomelatine is about to be released. This acts by increasing the activity of melatonin receptors MT1 and MT2 and by blocking postsynaptic 5HT2C serotonin receptors, leading to a lift in mood, and improvements in sleep and circadian rhythms. The former effect may explain the sleep/circadian improvements; the latter may cause a release of dopamine and noradrenalin possibly explaining the lift in mood and may also explain reduced sexual side effects. What makes this new drug an interesting prospect is its effectiveness combined with apparently a very clean side effect profile (although some have had to cease it due to altered liver function tests). Time will tell.

Mood Stabilisers assist in treating bipolar disorder and, to a lesser extent, major depression. There is increasing evidence that mood stabiliser involvement in the regulation of intracellular signalling pathways is implicated in the processes of neuroplasticity and neuroprotection relevant to both. In fact, the clinical effects of mood stabilisers require long-term treatment consistent with the time needed for the cascade of intracellular events and subsequent modulation of gene expression.

Let's examine the three major mood stabilisers in use and suggested modes of action at cellular level.

LITHIUM is a naturally occurring salt. Studies have consistently shown that lithium increases cell survival in a variety of neurotoxicity models. We can summarise its main effects as follows:

- It binds itself to the NMDA receptor for glutamate, changing its structure to reduce the excitatory effects of this neurotransmitter. It also down-regulates AMPA receptors with similar consequences.

- It inhibits the actions of a key second messenger enzyme, GSK-3. This enzyme is a strong inhibitor of CREB in the cell nucleus and is a crucial player in cell death.

- CREB in turn boosts expression of BDNF and Bcl 2, crucial in protecting the cell and regeneration of damaged neurons.

- CREB also inhibits genes which mediate possible destructive effects of excess glutamate.

- Lithium also increases levels of BDNF itself, which through its second messenger system further increases CREB levels.

- It also has effects on the phosphoinositol second messenger system.

- Finally it has been shown to actually increase grey matter in the brain.

VALPROATE (EPILIM) is one of the anti-epilepsy drug group (AEDs) shown to be of help in treating bipolar mania/hypomania. It has many actions similar to lithium. We can summarise its main effects as follows:

- It seems to block synaptic responses to NMDA glutamate excitatory effects, and also down-regulates AMPA receptors with similar consequences.

- It inhibits the second messenger enzyme GSK-3. This enzyme is a strong inhibitor of CREB in the cell nucleus and is a crucial player in cell death.

- CREB in turn boosts the expression of BDNF and Bcl 2, which are crucial in synaptic plasticity, protecting the cell and regeneration of damaged neurons.

- Finally it has been shown to increase grey matter in the brain.

For those who would like to examine actions of lithium and valporate in more detail see Goodwin and Jamison, and Paulus' reviews on the subject.

LAMOTRIGINE (LAMICTAL): is another modern AED increasingly important in stabilising low mood in bipolar and major depression. It has a different mode of action to lithium and valproate which is poorly understood but may include:

- Preferentially inhibiting neuronal hyper-excitability.

- Modifying synaptic plasticity via inhibition of neuronal voltage-activated sodium channels and possibly calcium channels. As a consequence, it reduces excessive transmitter release in the brain.

- Lamotrigine, through inhibition of voltage-gated sodium channels, has been shown to particularly inhibit the excessive synaptic release of glutamate.Glutamate is the primary excitatory neurotransmitter for at least 60 percent of neurons in the brain.

- Because lamotrigine prevents excessive glutamate release at synapses, it stabilises neuronal membranes by preventing toxicity from too much glutamate, without interfering with glutamate's normal functions.

- May have neuroprotective effects although not felt to act on the BDNF system.

PREGBALIN (LYRICA): Pregbalin, a structural analog of the inhibitory neurotransmitter GABA is thought to exert its anxiolytic effects through binding to the alpha-2-delta sub-unit of calcium channels in 'over-excited' presynaptic neurons, reducing release of excitatory neurotransmitters such as glutamate.

Talk Therapy Pathways: I have for years been influenced by the research of Eric Kandel (see bibliography for seminal articles). He has been at the forefront of trying to link neurobiology and talk therapy at both molecular and systems levels. His vision is one I share. In a series of innovative experiments with the marine snail Aplysia he showed how synaptic connections could be altered and strengthened through the regulation of gene expression connected to environmental learning. In this organism the number of synapses doubles or trebles as a result of this learning. Kandel feels that psychotherapy causes similar synaptic changes in the human brain. It is intriguing to think that talk therapies successful in bringing about persistent changes in attitudes, habits, and conscious and unconscious behaviour may do so by alterations in gene expression that produces structural changes in the brain.

Synaptic plasticity has become the target of much neurobiological research into its role in memory formation, for learning and memory must form the basis of all talk therapies. We dealt earlier with the mechanisms of LTP/LTD and BDNF in strengthening and weakening synaptic memory connections.

We also discussed in the main text the importance of OFC/amygdala/spindle cell/mirror neuron systems in how the young infant/child develops its social, emotional and behavioural paths for the future. All of this occurs through the above mechanisms of synaptic plasticity. Life will from then on, through nurturing or toxic relationships, add or subtract from this learned memory bank through similar mechanisms. It is increasingly accepted that the empathic bond between therapist and client at the heart of talk therapy pathways almost certainly involves the same OFC pathway. This assists in the 'safe' expression of emotional difficulties encountered, allowing the cognitive apparatus in the brain – the DLPFC, Areas 24 and 32, and the hippocampus – to revaluate emotions and behaviours involved. This *psychotherapeutic reappraisal* will also involve reshaping local and systemic synaptic connections and pathways. Because of the latter, it is felt the primary focus of action of talk therapies is on the upper brain circuit; with secondary effects on the lower. See articles by Kandel, Fuchs, Gabbard, Liggan and Corrigan, and texts by Doidge and Goleman in bibliography.

Alternative Therapy Pathways: To examine such a wide range of therapies in relation to the brain pathways involved would be a massive task. But if one takes an overview of the therapies themselves, it becomes easier:

- All will involve empathy and placebo pathways already discussed.

- Most will produce short-term positive effects due mainly to the above.

- As we now know that the brain pathway changes that persist usually involve cognitive and behavioural hard work, such short-term effects will usually not bear long-term fruit.

- Hard evidence from trials reported in high quality journals is either not available or, in many cases where present, not particularly positive in relation to many alternative therapies.

- Many of the short-term effect therapies will involve a quietening down of the lower mood circuit, e.g. massage in all its forms; reflexology; aromatherapy; acupuncture; yoga; Tai Chi etc.

- In some of these therapies there is an, exercise dimension – such as yoga and Tai Chi, so the positive effects of exercise may partially explain their benefits.

- Some of the more effective ones like meditation/mindfulness, EMDR, St John's wort, are more long-term therapies and will often involve both upper and lower circuits.

The real problem with alternative therapies is trying to elucidate which ones stand up scientifically to close scrutiny. Increasingly they are coming under the microscope by researchers like Prof. Edzard Ernst and Karen Pilkington and we are building up a body of evidence to assist us. If one were to attempt to rate them it might look like this:

- PROBABLY ONLY PLACEBO/EMPATHY EFFECTS (LACKING ANY REAL SCIENTIFIC BACKING OTHERWISE): homeopathy; craniosacral therapy; reiki; thought field therapy.

- PROBABLY PLACEBO/EMPATHY COMBINED WITH SHORT TERM STRESS REDUCING EFFECTS: massage in all its forms; aromatherapy; reflexology; creative therapies like music and art.

- PROBABLY PLACEBO/EMPATHY COMBINED WITH EXERCISE BENEFITS: yoga; Tai Chi. dance;

- PROBABLY PLACEBO/EMPATHY COMBINED WITH MODEST SCIENTIFIC BASIS: acupuncture; hypnotherapy; EMDR.

- PROVEN SCIENTIFIC BASIS: Meditation; mindfulness; St John's Wort; light therapy.

Some may argue that this is devaluing particular therapies like homeopathy. But one must remember the power of the placebo/empathy effects of any therapy, which can be up to 25–30 percent, particularly in the short-term. More valuable approaches like talk therapies will include this effect but also lead to long-term restructuring of brain pathways.

Anxiety Pathways

NEUROBIOLOGY OF ANXIETY: The area of the brain responsible for the acquisition and expression of fear conditioning is the amygdala; comprised of thirteen nuclei, three of which, the basal amygdala (BA), lateral amygdala (LA), and central nuclei, are involved in the pathways of fear response. Sensory stimuli are transmitted to the LA, and then are transferred to the central nucleus (CA) ('short loop' pathway). The 'long loop' pathway sends signals from the sensory cortex, insula, and prefrontal cortex to the LA. From there, information projects to the brain stem and hypothalamus producing autonomic and behavioural manifestations of the acute fear response. The molecular mechanism by which fear acquisition occurs in the LA is based on LTP. Consolidation of fear memories are mediated by NMDA receptors and calcium-gated ion receptors. The latter is important as we will see later when discussing therapies. There are also connections between the hippocampus and the amygdala to create the contextual memory of fear. Both structures contain high BDNF levels. Anxiety is associated with reduction in BDNF in both.

The amygdala can consolidate (convert short term memories into long term ones)/reconsolidate (further strengthen) and extinguish fearful memories. Both involve NMDA receptor actions, so are quite capable of plasticity – the basis for most therapies. A person's inability to extinguish maladaptive fear responses due to a disruption in the process of extinction can result in persistent anxiety. There are important links between the ACC and OFC with the amygdala; which modulate the latter. See reviews by Cannistraro and Rauch; and Ressler and Mayberg in bibliography.

OBSESSIVE COMPULSIVE DISORDER is in terms of its neurobiology better understood than other anxiety disorders, mainly due to the brilliant research of Jeffrey Schwartz (see bibliography). It seems to be caused by a breakdown of information between the OFC, the ACC and a part of our basal ganglia (which is in charge of coordinating our movements) called the *Caudate Nucleus*. All three structures have been shown to be overactive on neuroimaging in OCD. Particularly exciting was the normalising of these structures and circuits following therapy – further evidence the brain is indeed extremely plastic and capable of change, even in the presence of such a disruptive disorder.

Overactivity of the OFC and ACC create all the distressing symptoms of this disorder. The former has the task of detecting errors. Because it is overactive, the obsessive thoughts that 'something is wrong' persist. The ACC is activated by the OFC and seems to trigger the anxiety symptoms.

Under normal circumstances, once a person has checked out if something is genuinely wrong, they can move on to more relevant matters. The Caudate Nucleus is responsible for allowing them to do just that. It is a processing centre or filtering station for complex messages coming from the logical PFC, functioning like an automatic transmission in a car. It takes in messages from parts of the brain controlling body movement, physical feelings, and the thinking and planning that involve those movements and feelings. This assists in the smooth transition from one form of behaviour to another. Typically, when anyone decides to perform an action, intruding movements and misdirected feelings are filtered out automatically so the desired movement can be performed rapidly and efficiently. There is a quick, smooth shifting of gears. During a normal day, we make many rapid shifts of behaviour, smoothly, easily and usually without thinking about them. It is the functioning of the caudate that makes this possible. In OCD, the problem seems to be that smooth, efficient filtering and the shifting of thoughts and behaviour, are disrupted by a glitch in the caudate nucleus. As a result, the OFC/ACC overactivity continues – giving rise to the distressing, persistent symptoms of OCD. The aims of the main therapies in use – the SSRIs (felt to normalise the OFC which is why they take up to eight weeks to take effect), CBT, and the combination of 'mindfulness and behaviour therapy changes' suggested by Schwartz – are to normalise these dysfunctions.

GENERALISED ANXIETY DISORDER: The brain pathways underlying this disorder are more poorly understood than OCD. The primary symptom in GAD is 'worry', versus 'fear' which is more prevalent in acute disorders like panic attacks. There are differing underlying neurobiological mechanisms and pathways involved in both worry and fear. In some senses worry is more cognitive and fear is more visceral. In practice fear and worry pathways are both involved in GAD as it is a lifelong disorder of background worry/tension with intermittent periods of acute anxiety.

The amygdala lies at the heart of the web. Information flows between it and various parts of the logical PFC (DLPFC, ACC, and OFC). It also has efferent links to the brainstem, hypothalamus, and serotonin and noradrenalin mood boxes and cables. We have already examined in the main text how this complex system gives rise to the range of psychological and physical symptoms of GAD.

POST TRAUMATIC STRESS DISORDER: The neurobiology of PTSD according to Nemeroff and Newport bears striking similarities to major depression. However, there are key differences. PTSD bears the noteworthy distinction of being associated with normal to low levels of glucocortisol despite hypersecretion of CRF. Low glucocortisol levels in PTSD may be a consequence of exaggerated HPA axis negative feedback. These findings are in stark contrast to the findings in patients with major depression.

The main parts of our mood system otherwise involved seem to include the amygdala, hippocampus, the ACC (Areas 24 and 32), and the OFC. The amygdala seems to be overactive; the hippocampus in some cases is reduced in size; Areas 24 and 32 are underactive (reducing capacity to reappraise and extinguish fear); and the normal inhibitory effects of OFC on the amygdala are absent. There is increased activity/sensitivity of the noradrenalin system. All of the above are similar in some respects to the neurobiology of depression. The major difference seems to be the low systemic glucocortisol levels.

PANIC DISORDER: Original concepts behind this disorder were based on the evolutionary 'fight or flight' reaction, which involves the amgydala triggering the brainstem to activate the SNS and production of adrenalin to produce the symptoms. It is now felt that this model is probably too simplistic. The more modern view is that panic originates in an abnormally sensitive fear network, which includes the prefrontal cortex, insula, thalamus, amgydala, and projections from the latter to the brainstem and hypothalamus.

The amygdala is still felt to be at the centre of this process. Although much remains to be elucidated regarding the amygdala's role in panic, it seems reasonable to speculate that there may be a deficit in the relay and coordination of 'upstream' (cortical) and 'downstream' (brainstem) sensory information, which results from heightened amygdala activity with resultant behavioural, autonomic, and neuroendocrine activation.

For those who would like to know more (including the suggested mode of action of SSRIs and CBT and the gene/environmental influences) see the superb article by Gorman et al.

SIMPLE PHOBIAS and how they respond, particularly to CBT, have been investigated by researchers like Paquette and Straube. In 2003, Paquette investigated the effects of exposing subjects to spider visual stimuli and also CBT. In relation to our mood system, he noted the right DLPFC and bilateral hippocampus and surrounding areas were hyperactive when exposed to stimuli and this activity decreased following therapy. He felt the former reflected the use of metacognitive strategies aimed at self-regulating the fear triggered by the spider. The latter activation might be related to an automatic reactivation of the contextual fear memory that led to the development of avoidance behaviour and the maintenance of spider phobia.

Absence of activation in the DLPFC and hippocampus/surrounding areas after CBT supported the view that it reduces phobic avoidance by deconditioning contextual learned fear and decreasing cognitive misattributions and catastrophic thinking at the level of the former. This prevents reactivation of traumatic memories by allowing the phobic subjects to modify their perception of the fear-evoking stimuli. Once this perception has been reframed, the phobic stimuli would not constitute a threat anymore. Such cognitive restructuring would render obsolete the activation of the brain regions previously associated with the phobic reaction.

Straube in a 2006 study revealed that the processing of phobic threats is associated with increased activation in the insula and ACC in subjects suffering from specific phobias. Most importantly, successful CBT led to a reduction of hyperactivity within these brain regions.

The role of the amygdala is interesting as one would assume that it would be actively involved in phobias, but this does not seem to be the case. Numerous functional imaging studies with patients failed to show amygdalar activation when exposed to phobia-relevant stimulation. Straube felt the amygdala was involved in the initial processing of phobia-related threat and induction of fear, while sustained processing of threat-related stimuli, such as confrontation with real, imagined, or filmed feared objects, did not seem to be based on amygdalar activity

SOCIAL PHOBIA (SOCIAL ANXIETY DISORDER): Neurobiological pathways of this disorder have yet to be fully elucidated. Recognising its role in the mediation of social behaviour, models of social phobia have focused on the amygdala. Neuroimaging studies have shown that the amygdala and hippocampus are more activated in those with SP when viewing neutral faces versus normal subjects. It seems as if the various departments of the PFC are unable to regulate the latter. Other findings include a reduction in the dopamine system, and unusually no evidence of high glucocortisol levels.

Depression Pathways

Research into neurobiological pathways underlying MDD has revealed deficits in key structural and functional processes occurring in the brain. Initially assumed to be a 'chemical imbalance' in the brain, MDD is now felt to be more complex, involving neuronal networks and plasticity. Depression is increasingly being viewed as a 'recurrent' illness, with some studies revealing a relapse rate of up to 80 percent. Recurrence of MDD appears to be driven in part by neurobiological vulnerabilities. As a result clinical and neurobiological attention has moved away from treating individual episodes to reducing this relapse rate. Increasing evidence suggests episodes of depression become increasingly triggered over time – the kindling hypothesis. As episodes increase, future ones are predicted more by the number of prior episodes than life stressors. Early adverse experiences may also contribute to long-term neurobiological alterations associated with depression – particularly in the genetically vulnerable.

New data is emerging on the role of glial cells; second messenger systems; neurotrophic factors like BDNF; inflammatory molecules (called cytokines); interactions between underlying genetic potential vulnerabilities and stress; and how all of these create the structural and functional difficulties within key mood circuits. Future therapies will depend on this understanding.

To cover this topic would take a book in itself, so I plan to pick out some key data and refer readers to the relevant articles in the bibliography. Let's examine firstly the two theories of the causes of MDD – the 'neurotransmitter theory' and the 'neurotrophic theory'.

THE NEUROTRANSMITTER THEORY: For decades, depression has been linked particularly to disturbances in serotonergic, dopaminergetic and noradrenergic neurotransmission. Dysfunction in these systems was felt to cause the widespread psychological and behavioural consequences of MDD. They were also felt to lead to the high glucocorticol levels which in turn affected a wide array of organ and immune changes. This became the basis of the 'chemical theory' of depression so often quoted by media. It failed to deal however with the complexity of this illness and led to a one dimensional approach – very much drug-led.

THE NEUROTROPHIN THEORY assumes that deficiency in neurotrophin signalling systems with effects on cellular plasticity and viability together with an enhancement of cell death (apoptotic) processes, caused by increased glucocorticol and proinflammatory cytokines levels, play an important role in MDD. In the past decade, research has revealed more widespread structural and functional changes than hitherto thought. This has led to interest in second messenger signalling systems and the primary neurotrophin BDNF.

In this theory, stress and genetic vulnerability elevate glucocorticol levels and alter cellular plasticity via down-regulation of growth factors and receptor sensitivity. Reduction in growth factors like BDNF impacts negatively on structural and functional processes within the PFC and limbic system (especially the hippocampus). Chronic and recurrent MDD may result in subsequent atrophy and further disruptions in this neurocircuitry. Recovery and remission of MDD would therefore depend upon a reversal of these processes, such as an increase in BDNF levels.

Although there are still unanswered questions, this hypothesis seems to hold the best chance of an integrated solution to both the mystery of depression and its solution. See articles by Maletic et al, Manji and Drevets, Martinowich and Manji, Pav et al and Charney and Manji.

LINKS BETWEEN GENETIC VULNERABILITY AND STRESS: Attention has shifted from just focusing on genes involved in MDD to how genes create a potential vulnerability to stress in the entire serotonin system by modulating reuptake of serotonin released into the synaptic cleft. It is encoded by a single gene (SLC6A4). This gene is influenced in its expression by a neighbouring genetic promoter (5-HTTLPR) with short and long allele versions, resulting in differential serotonin expression and function (see Pezawas et al, Murphy et al and Hamann). Serotonin appears to be critical for the development of emotional circuitry in the brain. Even transient alterations during early development modify neural connections implicated in mood disorders. Evidence (see Canli and Lesch) suggests that 5-HTTLPR genotype moderates the effect of environmental variables, particularly developmental and life experience stressors, on later emotional and social behaviour.

The short allele version is associated with increased serotonin availability. It has been shown that those with the short version have greater activity in the amygdala when at rest (suggesting it is in a higher state of alert) are more at risk of anxiety and MDD; and more likely to suffer a bout of depression following environmental adversity.

One fascinating experiment by Pezawas involved scanning of individuals who were short version carriers but did not have a history of depression. Quite incredibly there was a *25 percent reduction in grey matter in rostral and dorsal ACC and a 15 percent reduction in the amygdala* discovered in such cases. There was also evidence of poorer connections between the ACC and amgydala. This was one of the first signs that a genetic vulnerability to stress may lead to a neurobiological vulnerability to depression. There are most likely many other similar genes, but the SERT data is opening up a new understanding of MDD.

Of note: expression of this gene probably requires environmental stressors both in childhood and later in the teen/young adult phases to activate such changes. There are also many who have this short version but do not develop depression; so we have still much to discover. Recently it has been shown that gene to gene interactions can influence expression of the short version. It has been recently shown that a version of the BDNF gene can protectively modulate the latter (see Pezawas et al).

BDNF plays an important role in synaptic plasticity and LTP/LTD – the mechanism by which synaptic connections are strengthened or weakened. It is widely accepted that MDD is associated with reduction in BDNF levels in the brain. Neurotrophic factors such as BDNF enhance cell survival by activating two distinct signalling pathways: the PI-3-kinase pathway, and the ERK–MAP-kinase pathway. One of the major mechanisms by which BDNF promotes cell survival is by increasing the expression of the major cytoprotective protein, Bcl-2, which prevents cell death via a variety of mechanisms reviewed later.

BDNF is first synthesised as a precursor *proBDNF,* which is altered, in the synapse itself, to generate mature BDNF (*mBDNF*). Recent studies demonstrated that proBDNF and mBDNF facilitate LTD/LTP respectively, implying opposing cellular functions – the so called yin-yang paradox. This may turn out to be how the brain strengthens and weakens critical circuits (see articles by Bramham and Messaoudi; Maletic et al, and Martinowich and Manji). Most effective therapies for depression will end up increasing mBDNF in key parts of our mood system.

THE ROLE OF GLIAL CELLS: Glial cells are involved in an intricate interaction with neurons in which astrocytes and microglia maintain homeostasis of the neuronal environment by modulating electrolytes, neurotransmitters, cytokines and neurotrophic factors. Neurons reciprocate support of glial function via neurotrophin signalling.

Astrocytes, the prevailing glial cell population in the CNS, are an essential component of the blood-brain barrier, and provide an important nutrient supply to neurons. Astrocytes participate in the neurotransmitter uptake from synapses, their synthesis from precursors, supply of neurotransmitter precursors to neurons and disposal of neurotransmitter excess. They are important regulators of synapse numbers during development and in adulthood and are necessary for synapse maturation, proper receptor density and composition. Reduced neuron supportive functions due to compromised astrocyte numbers or function can cause neurons to become more vulnerable to excessive glucocortisol-mediated glutamate levels. In MDD, the functions of astrocytes are under increasing scrutiny as being a key part of the whole picture. An integral part of maintaining the health of these glial–neuron interactions may be mediated by BDNF. All of these functions and their role in MDD are dealt with by Pav et al, Maletic et al and McNally et al.

THE ROLE OF OUR IMMUNE SYSTEM in causation and consequences of MDD is under scrutiny. Depression and stress are associated with a rise in key inflammatory markers in the blood called cytokines. This occurs because involvement of the SNS in both activates macrophages (important immune cells) to release proinflammatory cytokines. These in turn may diminish neurotrophic support and can lead to neuronal and glial damage. Disruptions as a result of cytokines overactivity may be experienced as fatigue, loss of appetite and libido, further worsening the physical symptoms of depression.

There have been numerous links between heart disease, our immune system and depression. Increased levels of *IL-6*, a proinflammatory cytokine involved in fat metabolism, are observed in major depression. *IL-6* levels are one of the features of *metabolic syndrome* (a mix of obesity, high cholesterol and elevated blood sugars predisposing the sufferer to heart disease). This suggests cytokines such as IL-6 may be a shared element in the biology of both coronary heart disease and MDD.

Successful treatment with drug therapy has been shown to normalise cytokine levels. (See Prof Ted Dinan of UCC, also Maletic et al; Pav et al; Bornstein et al; and an excellent recent review by McNally et al.)

THE ROLE OF THE SECOND MESSENGER SIGNALLING SYSTEM in MDD is under intense scrutiny. I reviewed earlier this incredibly complex intracellular system. We are slowly mapping out the different signalling cascades. Much of the interest has been in MDD in identifying which ones are underlying the various neurotrophic molecules like BDNF and Bcl-2. Some of the main ones involved are the AC-cAMP – Creb; phosphoinositol, GSK 3, BDNF – Creb pathways. How they are involved in the neurobiology and treatment of MDD is almost beyond the scope of this book, but we will be examining some of these systems in bipolar further on. I direct readers interested in their role in MDD to articles – Coyle and Duman, Dwivedi and Pandey, and text by Goodwin and Jamison.

THE ROLE OF OUR MOOD SYSTEM: If we examine the structural and functional consequences of all of the above on our mood system, they can be summarised as follows:

- Reductions in neuronal/glial cells in the DLPFC, ACC (areas 24 and 32), OFC and VLPFC

- Reductions in neuronal/glial cells in the amygdala and hippocampus

- Overactivity of the amygdala, OFC, ACC (area 25), VLPFC

- Underactivity of the hippocampus, DLPFC (particularly on left side), the ACC (areas 24 and 32) and the Nucleus Accumbens

- Underactivity of the three main mood systems – serotonin, noradrenalin and dopamine cables

- Overactivity of the stress system – particularly stress peptide CRH; adrenal gland and glucocortisol

- Underactivity functionally of the dorsal or upper mood circuit

- Overactivity functionally of the ventral or lower mood circuit

THE NEUROBIOLOGY OF DEPRESSION RELAPSE AND PREVENTION is a critical area in mental health. As stated earlier, the more we experience bouts of MDD, the more likely we will relapse. The neurotrophin theory together with changes in our mood system, explain why. For reasons already outlined, there is loss of glial cell/neuron/dendrite tissue in key areas of the mood system like the ACC, DLPFC, OFC, amygdala and hippocampus. This ends up with increasing dysfunction of key pathways between the emotional and logical brain. Initially significant activation of the stress system is necessary to set off a particular bout of depression. However each time a bout occurs, further barrages of stress peptides, glucocortisol and inflammatory cytokines bombard both glial cells and neurons in the above structures. This increases the damage to the crucial mood pathways. In particular the links between the ACC and amygdala become weakened, so the capacity of the latter to reappraise becomes weakened. So too is the ability of the left DLPFC to exert any influence inhibited.

With each subsequent bout, further structural and functional changes occur, increasingly weakening the capacity of the upper logical circuit to switch off the negative barrage from the amygdala. Eventually it takes insignificant stress to kickstart episodes. So simple negative thinking, for example, may itself become the neurobiological trigger for a bout.

For many this suggests a hopeless situation as it seems out of their control. But that overlooks the incredible neuroplasticity of the brain. Its ability to reshape and reorganise is quite extraordinary. The depression relapse process involves the neurotrophin system. Incredibly the same system, if activated by the relevant therapies discussed, can produce major improvements in the *functioning* of mood system pathways. For example, mood stabilisers and drug therapies can play important roles in prevention of relapses. Exercise and nutrition must play a part. CBT and mindfulness strengthen up the logical pathway's capacity to exert control over our disobedient emotional brain. This is the basis of my belief that understanding the neurobiological basis of relapses may assist us in prevention. We can change our pathways but it takes time and effort to do so!

THE PLACE OF MBCT IN DEPRESSION RELAPSES: It is worth examining the potential of this therapy in depression relapse. It has been estimated that the risk of repeated episodes in their lifetime, each exceeds 80 percent. Some patients will experience an average of four major depressive episodes lasting at least five to six months. MBCT differs from routine CBT. There is little emphasis in MBCT on changing the content of thoughts; rather on changing our awareness of and relationship to thoughts. One study by Teasdale et al showed that in those who had a history of three or more episodes of MDD, risk of relapse was halved. Research involving Dr Tony Bates and Prof Kevin Malone supported these findings.

ALTERNATIVE/COMPLEMENTARY MEDICINE IN DEPRESSION: Let's now examine evidence for a few alternative therapies felt to be of use in MDD. In general, the evidence for effectiveness is limited to a few therapies. See articles by van der Watt, Jorm et al, Thachil et al, Pilkington et al, and text by Singh and Ernst.

ST JOHN'S WORT There does seem to sufficient evidence to support the use of this herb in depression. Pilkington has done a good review of all the trials. But it has to be balanced against possible side effects. These are well reviewed by Hammerness et al, and Singh and Ernst.

YOGA: has been once again one of the alternative therapies felt to be of assistance in MDD. Pilkington et al have once again done an excellent review. They examine Hatha yoga, the system on which much of Western yoga is based with its three basic components, asanas (postures), pranayama (breathing exercises) and dhyana (meditation). The overall impression was positive but reviews comparing it with exercise regimes were suggested to clarify its role.

THE NEUROBIOLOGY OF BIPOLAR MOOD DISORDER (BD) is extraordinarily complex – in harmony with the range and diversity of the illness itself. There are many similarities with MDD but some key differences. BD is associated with alterations in intracellular signalling cascades involved in the regulation of neurotransmitters, synaptic plasticity, gene expression, neuronal survival and neuronal death. It is also associated with areas of neuronal/glial cell/dendrite loss in various parts of our mood system and resulting breakdown in mood systems and circuits.

BD must address its neurobiology at different physiological levels, i.e. molecular, cellular, systems, and behavioural. Abnormalities in gene expression underlie the neurobiology of the disorder at the molecular level. This will become evident as we identify susceptibility and protective genes for BD. Once accomplished however we will have to examine the impact of the faulty expression of these gene-products (proteins) on integrated cell function. It is at these levels that some protein candidates have been identified as targets for the actions of mood-stabilising agents. The precise manner in which these candidate molecular and cellular targets may or may not relate to the faulty expression of susceptibility gene products is yet to be determined. The task becomes more daunting when one considers that a major component of BD may stem from discordant biological rhythms that drive the periodic recurrent nature of the disorder in parentheses. At the heart of it all, lies the second messenger system.

The second messenger signalling cascades in bipolar disorder

have been examined as potential culprits. Multicomponent, cellular signalling pathways interact at various levels, forming complex signalling networks which allow the cell to receive, process, and respond to information. These pathways are thus undoubtedly involved in regulating such diverse vegetative functions as mood, appetite and wakefulness so it is no surprise that they are under close scrutiny in this illness.

THE AC-cAMP SECOND MESSENGER SYSTEM: We previously discussed how activation of G proteins can lead to the production of second messenger cAMP which in turn activates the enzyme PKA. Most of the effects of cAMP are mediated by PKA so studying its status provides direct evidence of altered cAMP signalling. In addition, PKA by phosphorylating components of other signalling cascades provides the means for cross-talk between the AC-cAMP and other signalling systems. One of the transcription factors phosphorylated and modulated by PKA is CREB, which as we have seen, regulates a number of neuronal processes, including neuron development, apoptosis, and synaptic plasticity. Therefore recent studies have focused on the role of PKA in mood disorders.

At the functional level, PKA is involved in many physiological functions in the brain, including neurotransmitter synthesis and release, gene expression, synaptic plasticity, memory, and cell survival. Through its involvement in the cross-talk between different signalling mechanisms it profoundly affects physiological functions mediated by other signalling pathways. Post-mortem studies and studies of peripheral cells have consistently shown an increase in cAMP and PKA activity in patients with BD. Studies have shown that lithium and valproic acid (Epilim) have a regulatory action on this signalling pathway, so it is felt to be at the centre of the pathogenesis of BD. See Dwivedi's excellent recent article, Kapczinski et al, and Goodwin and Jamison for more information.

THE PHOSPHOINOSITOL SECOND MESSENGER SYSTEM is important in BD. As we have seen activation of a receptor coupled to the phosphatidylinositol (PIP2) cascade induces the formation of two important second messengers: DAG and IP3. DAG activates PKC, involved in cellular processes including secretion, exocytosis, and gene expression, modulation of ionic conduction, cellular proliferation and down-regulation of extracellular receptors. IP3 regulates the release of intracellular reserves of calcium. Both seem to play a part in BD.

Increased levels of PIP2 has been found in the platelets of manic and depressed bipolar patients. Post-mortem studies and studies of peripheral cells have shown that, in BD, PKC levels are increased and lithium treatment reduces those levels.

THE PROTEIN KINASE C SIGNALLING PATHWAY: PKC is one of the major intracellular mediators of signals generated upon external stimulation of cells via a variety of neurotransmitter receptors. In view of the pivotal role of the PKC signalling pathway in the regulation of neuronal excitability, neurotransmitter release, and long-term synaptic events, PKC activity may play a role in the anti-manic effects of lithium and Epilim.

ABNORMALITIES OF CALCIUM SIGNALLING SYSTEMS play a critical role in regulating the synthesis and release of neurotransmitters, neuronal excitability, and long-term neuroplastic events. A number of studies have investigated intracellular Ca2+ in peripheral cells in BD. These have consistently revealed elevations in both resting and stimulated intracellular Ca2+ levels in platelets, lymphocytes and neutrophils of patients with BD. The regulation of free intracellular Ca2+ is a complex, multi-faceted process, and the abnormalities observed in BD could arise from abnormalities at a variety of levels. There is increasing evidence of the toxic effects of intracellular Ca in both neurons and glial cells.

THE GSK 3 (GLYCOPROTEIN SYNTHASE KINASE 3) SECOND MESSENGER SYSTEM is also crucial in BD. GSK 3 has an important influence on neuronal function, affecting structure, remodelling, gene expression, survival, and many other aspects of cellular operations. It is activated and in particular inhibited by a multitude of internal signalling cascades.

GSK3 is detrimental to neural plasticity. One of the most replicated actions of GSK3 is impeding neuron survival following exposure to many insults capable of causing apoptosis and eventual cell death. Since BD, like MDD, is associated with loss of neurons/glial cells, this process is felt to be increasingly important.

In mood disorders like BD, impaired inhibitory control of GSK3 may reduce CREB activity contributing to deficient BDNF actions. The inhibitory effects of therapeutic treatments on GSK3 (like lithium and Epilim) may contribute to facilitated CREB activity and BDNF expression and activation of intracellular signalling pathways. See excellent articles by Jope et al, and Manji et al.

THE BDNF SYSTEM is almost certainly involved in BD. Genetic studies in humans indicate a linkage of BDNF to bipolar disorder. Chromosome 11p13-14 is one possible locus for the genes responsible for the development of bipolar disorder. The BDNF gene is located in this region of the chromosome. Some experts recently suggested the possibility that BDNF overactivity may be associated with the manic state. Studies showed there is a positive association between genetic polymorphism of BDNF and bipolar disorder, agents that induce mania increase BDNF; atypical antipsychotics, often used for the treatment of mania, decrease the level of BDNF in PFC and hippocampus. See Dwivedi et al.

MAP KINASE/ BCL-2 SIGNALLING CASCADE: Increasing evidence suggests neurotrophic factors inhibit cell death cascades by (in large part) activating the MAP kinase signalling cascade, and up-regulating major cell survival proteins such as bcl-2. Bcl-2 is now recognised as a major neuroprotective protein, since over-expression protects neurons against diverse insults, including ischemia and excessive glutamate. Accumulating data suggests that Bcl-2 is not only neuroprotective, but also exerts neurotrophic effects and promotes dendrite sprouting and axonal regeneration. Overall, it is clear that the neurotrophic factors/MAP kinase/Bcl-2 signalling cascade plays a critical role in cell survival in the CNS, and that there is a fine balance maintained between the levels and activities of cell survival and cell death. Modest changes in this signalling cascade or in the levels of the Bcl-2 family of proteins (potentially due to genetic, illness or insult-related factors) may therefore profoundly affect cellular viability and the pathogenesis of BD (see Manjiet al).

THE ROLE OF OUR MOOD SYSTEM: If we examine the structural and functional consequences of the above on our mood system, they can be summarised as follows:

- Reductions in neuronal/glial cells in the DLPFC, ACC (areas 24 and 32), OFC and VLPFC

- Reductions in neuronal/glial cells in the amygdala and hippocampus

- Overactivity functionally of the amygdala, OFC, ACC (area 25), VLPFC

- Increased size structurally of amygdala

- Reduced size in left nucleus Accumbens

- Underactivity functionally of the hippocampus, DLPFC (particularly on left side), the ACC (areas 24 and 32)

- Underactivity of the serotonin cable in both manic and depressive phases of BD

- Overactivity of the dopamine cable in manic and reduced in depressed phases of BD

- Overactivity of noradrenalin cable in mania

- Overactivity of the stress system – particularly stress peptide CRH, adrenal gland and glucocortisol

Drugs and Therapies Commonly Used for Depression and Anxiety

Common Antidepressant Drugs in Use

DRUGS WHICH AFFECT THE SEROTONIN CABLE

- Fluoxetine (Prozac, Prozamel, Gerozac)
- Citalopram (Cipramil, Citrol, Ciprager)
- Escitalopram (Lexapro)
- Paroxetine (Seroxat, Meloxat, Parox)
- Sertraline (Lustral) – this has minor effects on the dopamine cable as well

Possible main side effects of these drugs

- Initial nausea in first week in some cases
- Reduced libido and delayed orgasm in some cases
- Slightly heavier periods in some women
- Occasional mild tremors
- Initial fatigue and anxiety in certain cases

DRUGS WHICH AFFECT THE NORADRENALIN CABLE
Reboxetine (Edronax)

- Possible main side effects of this drug
- Sweating, headaches and nausea
- Sleep difficulties
- Dry mouth
- Impotence in some cases

DRUGS WHICH AFFECT THE SEROTONIN AND NORADRENALIN CABLE

- Venlafaxine (Effexor XL)
- Cymbalta (Duloxetine)
- Zispin (Mirtazapine)

Possible main side effects of these drugs

- A mixture of both of the above groups of symptoms
- In the case of Mirtazapine: weight gain

OLDER ANTIDEPRESSANTS IN USE

- Amitriptyline
- Trazodone (Molipaxin)
- Tofranil (Imipramine)
- Trimipramine (Surmontil)
- Lofepramine (Gamanil)
- Dothiepin (Prothiaden)

Main side effects of these drugs

- Drowsiness (apart from Imipramine)
- Higher risk of serious consequences if taken in overdose
- Dry mouth, constipation and blurred vision are quite common

The mood stabilisers

- Lithium (Priadel or Camcolit)
- Lamotrigine (Lamictal)
- Sodium Valproate (Epilim)
- Carbamazepine (Tegretol)

Main side effects of these drugs

- Weight gain (particularly Lithium and sodium Valproate)
- Skin rashes (particularly Lamotrigine)

- Teratogenic (all bar Lamotrigine)
- Dangerous in overdose (particularly Lithium)

DRUGS WHICH AFFECT THE MELATONIN SYSTEM
- Agomelatine (Valdoxan)

Possible side effects of this drug
- No major side effects but liver function tests are advised

MAJOR TRANQUILLISERS (ALSO KNOWN AS ATYPICAL ANTIPSYCHOTICS)

- Olanzapine (Zyprexa)
- Quetiapine (Seroquel)
- Risperdal (Risperidone)
- Aripiprazole (Abilify)

Possible main side effects of these drugs

- Weight gain (particularly Olanzapine)
- Increased risks of Insulin Resistance and Diabetes
- Potential risks of Metabolic Syndrome and Coronary Heart Disease

Common Anti-anxiety Drugs in Use

THE BENZODIAZEPINES: LONG-ACTING

- Diazepam (Valium)
- Chlordiazepoxide (Librium)
- Clonazepam (Rivotril)

THE BENZODIAZEPINES: SHORT- TO MEDIUM-ACTING

- Bromazepam (Lexotane)
- Alprazolam (Xanax, Gerax)

Possible main side effects of Benzodiazepines

- Drowsiness
- Impairment of concentration

- High risk of becoming dependent if used for long periods

- High risk of developing tolerance to these drugs

PREGBALIN (LYRICA)
Possible side effects of this drug

- Dizziness and coordination difficulties

- Drowsiness

- Weight gain

- Dry mouth

- Headaches

Antidepressants in Pregnancy

- Should be used only if significant depression is present and other therapies are not sufficient

- There is no evidence that modern SSRIs (apart from Paroxetine) are teratogenic

- I recommend using the minimal dose necessary and withdrawing it at thirty-eight weeks (to restart after baby is born if required) to reduce any withdrawal symptoms in the newborn baby

- There must be full consultation with and information given to mother (and father) before any course is started – the mother must be happy to proceed

- There is evidence of greater incidence of low birth weight and prematurity in babies born to both those treated with antidepressants and those born to mothers with untreated depression

- Treating the mother may reduce the risks of potential suicide and possibility of serious postnatal depression affecting both mother and newborn baby

- Using an antidepressant in pregnancy does not mean you are somehow inferior or 'putting your baby at risk', it may at times be more damaging in some situations not to use them

- If in doubt, have a chat with your family doctor and if necessary seek a specialist psychiatric opinion

Antidepressants in Breastfeeding

- Amounts of modern SSRIs found in breast milk are quite small

- Postnatal depression if severe may require use of an antidepressant if other therapies not sufficient

- There is no evidence that usage of these drugs in the postnatal period has any adverse effects on babies

- I personally am quite comfortable with using them 'if required'

- Treatment of postnatal depression may reduce risk of suicide

Light Therapies for SAD

- Light box/lamp of at least 10,000 lux is considered standard

- Some feel the blue wavelength part of the light spectrum is the most effective

- It requires thirty minutes of therapy per day at 10,000 lux

- Morning is much better than evening

- Ideally combined with use of a dawn simulator set to come on an hour before rising in the winter months

- Some do well with simple dawn simulator (250 – 400 lux)

- Dawn simulators are also ideal for many who get simple winter blues but do not suffer from depression or SAD

Two useful contact details of suppliers
- www.brighterday.ie

- www.sad.co.uk

Help Groups and Contact Details

AWARE

Aware is a voluntary organisation established in 1985 to support those experiencing depression and their families. Aware endeavours to create a society where people with mood disorders and their families are understood and supported, and obtain the resources to enable them to defeat depression. Weekly support group meetings at approximately fifty locations nationwide, including Northern Ireland, offer peer support and provide factual information, and enable people to gain the skills they need to help them cope with depression, and the 'Beat the Blues' educational programme is run in secondary schools.

> 72 Lower Leeson Street, Dublin 2 | (01) 661 7211 | info@aware.ie | www.aware.ie | Helpline: 1890 303 302

SAMARITANS

Samaritans was started in 1953 in London by a young vicar called Chad Varah; the first branch to be opened in the Republic of Ireland was opened in 1970, in Dublin. Samaritans is available twenty-four hours a day to provide confidential emotional support for people who are experiencing feelings of distress or despair, including thosewhich may lead to suicide.

> jo@samaritans.org | www.samaritans.org | Texts: 0872 60 90 90 | Helpline: 1850 60 90 90

GROW

Established in Ireland in 1969, GROW is Ireland's largest mutual help organisation in the area of mental health. It is anonymous, non-denominational, confidential and free. No referrals are necessary. Grow aims to achieve self-activation through mutual help. Its members are enabled, over time, to craft a step by step recovery or personal growth plan and along the way to develop leadership skills that will help others.

> Barrack Street, Kilkenny | 056 61624 | grownational@grow.ie | www.grow.ie Helpline: 1890 474 474

IRISH SUICIDOLOGY ASSOCIATION

The Irish Association of Suicidology, an all-Ireland association, was established in 1996 in response to the tragedy of suicide in Ireland at a time when suicide rates were increasing rapidly. The aims and objectives of the IAS are to facilitate communication between clinicians, volunteers, survivors and researchers in all matters relating to suicide and suicidal behaviour; to promote awareness of the problems of suicide and suicidal behaviour in the general public by holding conferences and workshops and by communication of relevant materials through the media; to ensure that the public is better informed about suicide prevention; to support and encourage relevant research; and to encourage and support the formation of groups to help those bereaved by suicide.

16 New Antrim Street, Castlebar, County Mayo | 094 925 0858 | office@ias.ie | www.ias.ie

CONSOLE
Console is a registered charity supporting and helping people bereaved through suicide. They respect each individual's unique journey through the grieving process following their tragic loss. Console promotes positive mental health within the community in an effort to reduce the high number of attempted suicides and deaths through suicide.

Console Dublin: All Hallows College, Gracepark Rd, Drumcondra, Dublin 9
01 857 4300| info@console.ie | www.console.ie | Helpline: 1800 201 890

RAINBOWS IRELAND
Rainbows was founded in America by Suzy Yehl Marta to help children and adults who have been bereaved through parental death, separation or divorce to work through the grieving process which follows any significant loss. The charity provides a safe setting in which children can talk through their feelings with other children who are experiencing similar situations.

Loreto Centre, Crumlin Road, Dublin 12 | 01 473 4175

CHILDLINE
Childline, a service run by the ISPCC, seeks to empower and support children using the medium of telecommunications and information technology. The service is designed for all children and young people up to the age of eighteen years in Ireland.

Helpline: 1890 66 66 66

Cuan Mhuire

This is a charitable organisation founded by Sister Consilio Fitzgerald in 1965. It provides a comprehensive structured, abstinence-based residential program dealing with alcohol, gambling and drug addiction in the north and south of Ireland, with centres in Athy, Athenry, Newry, Limerick and Cork.

063 00555 | cuanmhuire@gmail.com

Gamblers Anonymous Ireland and Gam-Anon

Self-help meetings for gamblers and those close to them.

Dublin 01 872 1133 | Cork 087 349 4450 | Galway 087 349 4450 info@gamblersanonymous.ie

Ál-Anon/Alateen

Self-help meetings for spouses and teenagers (aged twelve to seventeen) affected by those addicted to alcohol.

5 Capel Street, Dublin 1 | 01 873 2699 | info@al-anon-ireland.org | Peace House, 224 Lisburn Road, Belfast | 028 9068 2368

Narcotics Anonymous

Self help groups for those addicted to drugs.

4–5 Eustace Street, Dublin 2 | 01 672 8000 | na@ireland.org

The Irish Council for Psychotherapy

Offer a guide to and directory of psychotherapists who work in Ireland.

73 Quinns Road, Shankhill, County Dublin | 01 272 2105 | info@icpty.ie

Schizophrenia Ireland

Schizophrenia Ireland is the national organisation dedicated to upholding the rights and addressing the needs of all those affected by enduring mental illness, including, but not exclusively, schizophrenia, schizo-affective disorder and bipolar disorder, through the promotion and provision of high-quality services and working to ensure the continual enhancement of the quality of life of the people it serves.

38 Blessington Street, Dublin 7 | 01 860 1620 | info@sirl.ie

The Irish Association of Cognitive Behavioural Therapy

This was founded in 2003 by its co-founders Enda Murphy and Brian Kelly. Its primary aim is the provision of low intensity CBT/CBM training and support to health professionals and organisations for use in their clinical practice.

cbtireland@eircom.net

NO PANIC

No Panic is a totally voluntary charity, whose aims are to aid the relief and rehabilitation of those people suffering from panic attacks, phobias, obsessive compulsive disorders, other related anxiety disorders, including tranquilliser withdrawal, and/or to provide support to sufferers and their families and or carers. Founded by Colin M. Hammond in the UK, this group has extended its successful activities to Ireland; where it is organised by therapist Caroline McGuigan.

UK head office: TEL: +44 (0) 1952 590005 | FAX: +44 (0) 1952 270962
Helpline: (UK Free-Phone) 0808 808 0545 | Non-UK: 0044 1 952 590545
Ireland office: 01 272 1872
Helpline Ireland: 01 272 1897

HEADSTRONG

Headstrong is a new initiative spearheaded by well known psychologist Dr Tony Bates working with communities in Ireland to ensure that young people aged twelve to twenty-five are better supported to achieve mental health and wellbeing. Headstrong was set up in response to an identified need to address the issue of youth mental health in Ireland.

It is an independent, non-profit, NGO. It does not provide direct services to young people, rather it works with those who do, acting as an expert partner to the Health Services Executive and other people and services concerned with providing mental health and well-being support to young people in Ireland. Headstrong views mental health as being much more than the absence of mental illness, rather it sees mental health as existing along a continuum spanning from general well-being to distress to mental health disorders requiring specialised care. Headstrong's Jigsaw Programme aims to change the way communities in Ireland think about mental health and support young people in the process.

36 Waterloo Road, Ballsbridge, Dublin 4 | 01 6607343 |
www.headstrong.ie | info@headstrong.ie

Bibliography

Akil, H. (2005), 'Stressed and depressed', *Nature Medicine*, 11, 116-8

Alexopolous, G. S. (2003), 'Role of executive function in late-life depression', *Journal of Clinical Psychiatry*, 64 (14), 18-23

Allman, J. M., A. Hakeem, J. M. Erwin, E. Nimchinsky and P. Hof (2001), 'The anterior cingulate cortex. The evolution of an interface between emotion and cognition', *Annals of the New York Academy of Sciences*, 935 (1), 107-17

Ananth, J., K. S. Burgoyne, R. Gadasalli and S. Aquino (2001), 'How do the atypical antipsychotics work?', *Journal of Psychiatry and Neuroscience*, 25 (5), 385-94

Anderson, M. C., K. N. Ochsner, B. Kuhl, J. Cooper, E. Robertson, S. W. Gabrieli, G. H. Glover, J. D. E. Gabrieli (2004), 'Neural systems underlying the suppression of unwanted memories', *Science*, 303, 232-35

Anderson, C. M. and R. A. Swanson (2000), 'Astrocyte glutamate transport: Review of properties, regulation, and physiological functions', Glia, 32, 1-14

Andrews, G. (2001), 'Placebo response in depression: bane of research, boon to therapy', *The British Journal of Psychiatry*, 178, 192-94

Arango, V., M. D. Underwood and J. J. Mann (2002), 'Serotonin brain circuits in major depression'. *Progress in Brain Research*, 136, 443-53

Arnsten, F. T. and R. M. Shansky (2004), 'Adolescence: Vulnerable period for stress-induced prefrontal cortical function?', *Annals of the New York Academy of Sciences*, 1021 (1), 143-47

Asbahr, F. R. (2004), 'Anxiety disorders in childhood and adolescence: clinical and neurobiological aspects', *Jornal de Pediatria*, 80 (2), 28-34

Bates, T. (2004), 'Conversations that keep us alive', *3TS Conference*, Dublin (1999), Depression: *The Commonsense Approach*, Dublin: Newleaf

Ballamier, M., A. W. Toga, R. E. Blanton, E. R. Sowell, H. Lavretsky, J. Peterson, D. Pham and A. Kumar (2004), 'Anterior cingulate, gyrus rectus, and orbitofrontal abnormalities in elderly depressed patients: an

MRI based parcellation of the pre frontal cortex', *American Journal of Psychiatry*, 161, 99-108

Bandelow, B., D. Wedekind and T. Leon (2007), 'Pregabalin for the treatment of generalised anxiety disorder: A novel pharmacologic intervention', *Expert Review of Neurotherapeutics*, 7 (7), 769-81

Bender, E. (2004), 'Brain data reveal why psychotherapy works', *Psychiatric News*, 39 (9), 34-76

Benedetti, F., H. S. Mayberg, T. D. Wager, C. S. Stohler and J. Zubieta (2005), 'Neurobiological mechanisms of the placebo effect', *The Journal of Neuroscience*, 25 (45), 10390-402

Bergmann, U. (1998), 'Speculations on the neurobiology of EMDR', *Traumatology*, 4 (1), 4-16

Biello, D. (2007), 'Searching for God in the brain', *Scientific American*

Bjorklund, A. and O. Lindvall (2000), 'Self-repair in the brain', *Nature*, 405, 892-95

Bjornebekk, A., A. A. Mathe and S. Brene (2005), 'The antidepressant effect of running is associated with increased hippocampal cell proliferation', *The International Journal of Neuropsychopharmacology*, 8, 357-68

Blitzer, R. D., R. Iyengar and E. M. Landau (2005), 'Postsynaptic signalling networks: Cellular cogwheels underlying long-term plasticity', *Biological Psychiatry*, 57 (2), 113-9

Blumenthal, J. A., M. A. Babyak, K. A. Moore, W. E. Craighead, S. Herman, P. Khatri, R. Waugh, M. A. Napolitano, L. M. Forman, M. Appelbaum, P. M. Doraiswamy and K. R. Krishnan (1999), 'Effects of exercise training on older patients with major depression', *Archives of Internal Medicine*, 159, 2349-56

Bodian, S. (2006), *Meditation for Dummies*, Hoboken: Wiley

Boyne, E. (2003), *Psychotherapy in Ireland*, Dublin: The Columba Press

Brody, A. L., S. Saxena, M. A. Mandelkern, L. A. Fairbanks, M. L. Ho and L. R. Baxter (2001), 'Brain metabolic changes associated with symptom factor improvement in major depressive disorder', *Biological Psychiatry*, 50 (3), 171-8

Brown, S. and L. M. Parsons (2008), 'The neuroscience of dance', *Scientific American*

Bunge, S. A. and P. D. Zelazo (2006), 'A brain-based account of the development of rule use in childhood', *Current Directions in Psychological Science*, 15 (3), 118-21

Butcher, J. N., S. Mineka, J. M. Hooley, R. C. Carson (2004), *Abnormal Psychology,* Boston: Pearson Education

Butterweck, V., H. Winterhoff and M. Herkenham (2003), 'Hyperforin-containing extracts of St John's wort fail to alter gene transcription in brain areas involved in HPA axis control in a long-term treatment regimen in rats', *Neuropsychopharmacology,* 28, 2160-68

Cahill, L. (2005), 'His brain, her brain', *Scientific American*

Canli, T. and K. P. Lesch (2007), 'Long story short: the serotonin transporter in emotion regulation and social cognition', *Nature Neuroscience,* 10 (9), 1103-9

Canli, T., M. Qui, K. Omura, E. Congdon, B. W. Haas, Z. Amin, M. J. Herrman, R. T. Constable and K. P. Lesch (2006), 'Neural correlates of epigenesis', *Proceedings of the National Academy of Sciences of the USA,* 103 (43), 16033-38

Cameron, J. L. (2004), 'Interrelationships between hormones, behaviour, and affect during adolescence: Complex relationships exist between reproductive hormones, stress-related hormones, and the activity of neural systems that regulate behavioural affect', *Annals of the New York Academy of Sciences,* 1021 (1), 134-42

Canli, T. (2008), 'The character code', *Scientific American*

Capuron, L and A. H. Miller (2004), 'Cytokines and psychopathology: Lessons from interferon', *Biological Psychiatry,* 56, 819-24

Carlson, N. R. (2004), *Physiology of Behaviour,* Boston: Pearson Education

Charney, D. S. and H. K. Manji (2004), 'Life stress, genes, and depression: Multiple pathways lead to increased risk and new opportunities for intervention', *Science Signalling,* 225 (5)

Cheung, Y., K. H. Chou, J. Decety, I. Y. Chen, D. Hung, O. J. L. Tzeng and C. P. Lin (2009), 'Sex differences in the neuroanatomy of human mirror-neuron system: A voxel-based morphometric investigation', *Neuroscience,* 158 (2), 713-20

Coppen, A. (2005), 'Treatment of depression: time to consider folic acid and vitamin B12', *Journal of Psychopharmacology,* 19 (1), 59-65

Corrigan, F. M. (2004), 'Psychotherapy as assisted homeostasis: Activation of emotional processing mediated by the anterior cingulate cortex', *Medical Hypotheses,* 63, 968-73

Cotter, D., D. McKay, S. Landau, R. Kerwin and I. Everall (2001), 'Reduced glial cell density and neuronal size in the anterior cingulate cortex in major depressive disorder, *Archives of General Psychiatry*, 58, 545-53

Cowen, P. (2008), 'Treatment of major depression: Beyond generalised serotonin potentiation', *Advances in Clinical Neuroscience and Rehabilitation*, 7 (6), 8-10

Coyle, J. T. and R. Schwarcz (2000), 'Mind glue-Implications of glial cell biology for psychiatry', *Archives of General Psychiatry*, 59, 90-3

Coyle, J. T. and R. S. Duman (2003), 'Finding the intracellular signalling pathways affected by mood disorder treatments', *Neuron*, 38, 157-60

Craig, A. D. (2005), 'Forebrain emotional asymmetry: A neuroanatomical basis?', *Trends in Cognitive Sciences*, 9 (12), 566-71

Craig, A. D. (2004), 'Human feelings: Why are some more aware than others?', *Trends in Cognitive Sciences*, 8 (6), 239-41

Crane, R. and D. Elias (2006), 'Being with what is-Mindfulness practice for counsellors and psychotherapists', *Therapy Today*, 17 (10), 31

David, L. (2006), *Using CBT in General Practice*, Bloxham: Scion

Davidson, R. J. (2004), 'What does the prefrontal cortex "do" in affect: Perspectives on frontal EEG asymmetry research', *Biological Psychology*, 67, 219-233

Davidson, J. R. T., K. M. Gadde, J. A. Fairbank, K. R. R. Krishnan, R. M. Califf, C. Binanay, C. B. Parker, N. Pugh, T. D. Hartwell, B. Vitiello, L. Ritz, J. Severe, J. O. Cole, C. de Battista, P. M. Doraiswamy, J. P. Feighner, P. Keck, J. Kelsey, K. Lin, P. D. Londborg, C. B. Nemeroff, A. F. Schatzberg, D. V. Sheehan, R. K. Srivastava, L. Taylor, M. H. Trivedi and R. H. Weisler (2002), 'Effect of hypericum perforatum (St John's wort) in major depressive disorder: A randomised controlled trial', *Journal of the American Medical Association*, 287 (14), 1807-14

Davidson, R. J. (2001), 'Toward a biology of personality and emotion', *Annals of the New York Academy of Sciences*, 935 (1), 191-207

Davison, G. C., J. M. Neale and A. M. Kring (2004), *Abnormal Psychology*, Hoboken: John Wiley and Sons

DePaulo, J. R. and L. A. Horvitz (2002). *Understanding Depression*, Hoboken: John Wiley & Sons

Diego, C., A. Siracusano, P. Calabresi and G. Bernardi (2005), 'Removing pathogenic memories: A neurobiology of psychotherapy', *Molecular Neurobiology*, 32 (2), 123-32

Dinan, T. G. (2008), 'Inflammatory markers in depression', *Current Opinion in Psychiatry*, 21, 1-5

Dinan, T. G. (1999), 'Psychiatry-physical consequences of depressive illness', *Irish Medical Times*

Dinan, T. G. (1994), 'Glucocorticoids and the genesis of depressive illness. A psychobiological model', *The British Journal of Psychiatry*, 164, 365-71

Dishman, R. K., H. Berthoud, F. W. Booth, C. W. Cotman, V. R. Edgerton, M. R. Fleshner, S. C. Gandevia, F. Gomez-Pinilla, B. N. Greenwood, C. H. Hillman, A. F. Kramer, B. E. Levin, T. H. Moran, A. A. Russo-Neustadt, J. D. Salamone, J. D. van Hoomissen, C. E. Wade, D. A. York and M. J. Zigmond (2006), 'Neurobiology of exercise', *Obesity*, 14, 345-56

Dobbs, D. (2006), 'A revealing reflection', *Scientific American*

———. (2006), 'Mastery of emotions', *Scientific American*

———. (2006), 'Turning off depression', *Scientific American*

Doidge, N. (2008), *The Brain that Changes Itself*, London: Penguin Books

Drevets, W. C. (2007), 'Orbitofrontal cortex function and structure in depression', *Annals of the New York Academy of Sciences*, 1121 (1), 499-527

———. (2001), 'Neuroimaging and neuropathological studies of depression: Implications for the cognitive-emotional features of mood disorders', *Current Opinion in Neurobiology*, 11, 240-49

———. (2000), 'Neuroimaging of mood disorders', *Biological Psychiatry*, 48, 813-29

———. (1999), 'Prefrontal cortical-amygdalar metabolism in major depression', *Annals of the New York Academy of Sciences*, 877, 614-37

Dryden, W. (2003), *Handbook of Individual Therapy*, London: Sage

Duman, R. S. and L. M. Monteggia (2006), 'A neurotrophic model for stress-related mood disorders', *Biological Psychiatry*, 59 (12), 1116-27

Duman, R. S., G. R. Heniger and E. J. Nestler (1997), 'A molecular and cellular theory of depression', *Archives of General Psychiatry*, 54 (7), 607-8

Dwivedi, Y. and G. N. Pandey (2008), 'Adenylyl cyclase-cyclicAMP signaling in mood disorders: Role of the crucial phosphorylating enzyme protein kinase A', *Neuropsychiatric Disease and Treatment*, 4 (1), 161-76

Engelman, D. M. (2005), 'Membranes are more mosaic than fluid', *Nature*, 438, 578-80

Ernst, E., J. I. Rand and C. Stevinson (1998), 'Complementary therapies for depression: An overview', *Archives of General Psychiatry*, 55 (11), 1026-32

Esch, T. and G. B. Stefano (2005), 'The neurobiology of love', *Neuroendocrinology Letters*, 3 (26), 175-92

Etkin, A. and T. D. Wager (2007), 'Functional neuroimaging of anxiety: A meta-analysis of emotional processing in PTSD, social anxiety disorder, and specific phobia', *American Journal of Psychiatry*, 164, 1476-88

Etkin, A., C. Pittenger, J. Polan and R. Kandal (2005), 'Towards a neurobiology of psychotherapy: Basic science and clinical applications', *Journal of Neuropsychiatry- Clinical Neuroscience*, 17, 145-58

Evans, D. L., D. S. Charney, L. Lewis, R. N. Golden, J. M. Gorman, K. R. Krishnan, C. B. Nemeroff, J. D. Bremner, R. M. Carney, J. C. Coyne, M. R. Delong, N. Frasure-Smith, A. H. Glassman, P. W. Gold, I. Grant, L. Gwyther, G. Ironson, R. L. Johnson, A. M. Kanner, W. J. Katon, P. G. Kaufmann, F. J. Keefe, T. Ketter, T. P. Laughren, J. Leserman, C. G. Lyketsos, W. M. McDonald, B. S. McEwen, A. H. Miller, D. Musselman, C. O'Connor, J. M. Petitto, B. G. Pollock, R. G. Robinson, S. P. Roose, J. Rowland, Y. Sheline, D. S. Sheps, G. Simon, D. Spiegel, A. Stunkard, T. Sunderland, P. Tibbits and W. J. Valvo (2005), 'Mood disorders in the medically ill: Scientific review and recommendations', *Biological Psychiatry*, 58, 175-189

Fales, C. L., D. M. Barch, M. M. Rundle, M. A. Mintun, A. Z. Snyder, J. D. Cohen, J. Mathews and Y. I. Sheline (2008), 'Altered emotional interference processing in affective and cognitive-control brain circuitry in major depression', *Biological Psychiatry*, 63, 377-84

Farb, N. A. S., Z. V. Segal, H. Mayberg, J. Bean, D. McKeon, Z. Fatima and A. K. Anderson (2007), 'Attending to the present: mindfulness meditation reveals distinct neural modes of self-reference', *Social, Cognitive and Affective Neuroscience*, 2 (4), 313-22

Fava, G. A., C. Ruini, C. Rafanelli, L. Finos, S. Conti and S. Grandi (2004), 'Six-year outcome of cognitive behaviour therapy for prevention of recurrent depression', *American Journal of Psychiatry*, 161, 1872-6

Fields, R. D. (2005), 'Making memories stick', *Scientific American*

Frangou, S. (2005), 'Advancing the pharmacological treatment of bipolar depression', *Advances in Psychiatric Treatment*, 11, 28–37

Fuchs, T. (2004), 'Neurobiology and psychotherapy: An emerging dialogue', *Current Opinion in Psychiatry*, 17, 479-485

Fyer, A. J. (1998), 'Current approaches to etiology and pathophysiology of specific phobia', *Biological Psychiatry*, 44 (12), 1295-1304

Gabbard, G. (2000), 'A neurobiologically informed perspective on psychotherapy', *British Journal of Psychiatry*, 177, 117-122

Gage, F. H. (2003), 'Brain repair yourself', *Scientific American*

George, M. S. (2003), 'Stimulating the brain', *Scientific American*

Gershon, A. A., T. Vishne and L. Grunhaus (2007), 'Dopamine D2-like receptors and the antidepressant response', *Biological Psychiatry*, 61, 145-53

Goldapple, K. (2004), 'Modulation of cortical-limbic pathways in major depression: Treatment-specific effects of cognitive behaviour therapy', *Archives of General Psychiatry*, 61, 34-41.

Goldberg, E. (2001), *The Executive Brain*, New York: Oxford University Press.

———— (2004), *Destructive Emotions*, London: Bloomsbury

Goleman, D. (2006), *Social Intelligence*, London: Arrow Books

Goodwin, F. K. and K. R. Jamison (2007), *Manic-Depressive Illness*, New York: Oxford University Press.

Goossens, L., S. Sunaert, R. Peeters, E. J. L. Griez and K. R. J. Schruers (2007), 'Amygdala hyperfunction in phobic fear normalises after exposure', *Biological Psychiatry*, 62, 1119-25

Gould, T. D. and H. K. Manji (2002), 'Signaling networks in the pathophysiology and treatment of mood disorders', *Journal of Psychosomatic Research*, 53, 687-97

Graeff, F. G. and C. M. Del-Ben (2008), 'Neurobiology of panic disorder: From animal models to brain neuroimaging', *Neuroscience and Behavioural Reviews*, 32 (7), 1326-35

Graybiel, A. M. and S. L. Rauch (2000), 'Toward a neurobiology review of obsessive-compulsive disorder', *Neuron*, 28, 343-7

Greenwald, B. S., E. K. Ginsberg, K. R. R. Krishnan, M. Ashtari, C. Auerbacch and M. Patel (1998), 'Neuroanatomic localization of MRI signal hyperintensities in geriatric depression', *Stroke*, 29, 613-17

Gross, R. (2001), *Psychology. The Science behind Mind and Behaviour*, London: Hodder and Staughton.

Groves, J. O. (2007), 'Is it time to reassess the BDNF hypothesis of depression?', *Molecular Psychiatry*, 12, 1079-88

Hamann, S. (2005), 'Blue genes: Wiring the brain for depression', Nature *Neuroscience*, 8 (6), 701-3

Hammerness, P., E. Basch, C. Ulbricht, E. P. Barrette I. Foppa, S. Basch, S. Bent, H. Boon and E. Ernst (2003), 'St John's wort: A systematic review of adverse effects and drug interactions for the consultation psychiatrist', *Psychosomatics*, 44 (4), 271-82

Harrison, E. (2003), *The 5-Minute Meditator*, London: Piatkus Books

Harrison, P. J. (2002), 'The neuropathology of primary mood disorder', *Brain*, 125 (7), 1428-49

Hilty, D. M., K. T. Brady and R. E. Hales (1999), 'A review of bipolar disorder among adults', *Psychiatric Services*, 50, 201-3

Hayley, S., M. O. Poulter, Z. Merali and H. Anisman (2005), 'The pathogenesis of clinical depression: Stressor- and cytokine-induced alterations of neuroplasticity', *Neuroscience*, 135 (3), 659-78

Holford, P. (2003), *Optimum Nutrition for the Mind*, London: Judy Piaktus Ltd

Hollaway, M. (2003), The Mutable Brain, *Scientific American*

Jamieson, K. and T. G. Dinan (2001), 'Glucocorticoids and cognitive function: from physiology to pathophysiology', *Human Psychopharmacology: Clinical and Experimental*, 16 (4), 293-302

Jha, A. P., J. Krompinger and M. J. Baime (2007), 'Mindfulness training modifies subsystems', Cognitive, Affective and Behavioural Neuroscience, 7 (2), 109-19

Jope, R. S. and M. Roh (2006), 'Glycogen synthase kinase-3 (GSK3) in psychiatric diseases and therapeutic interventions', *Current Drug Targets*, 7 (11), 1421-1434

Jorm, A. F., H. Christensen, K. M. Griffiths and B. Rodgers (2002), 'Effectiveness of complementary and self-help treatments for depression', *Medical Journal of Australia*, 176, 84-96

Julian, R. M. (2001), *A Primer of Drug Action*, New York: Henry Holt and Company, LLC

Kabat-Zinn, Jon (2008), *Wherever You Go*, There You Are, London: Piatkus
———. (2008), *Full Catastrophe Living*, London: Piatkus

Kandel, E. R. and L. R. Squire (2001), 'Neuroscience: Breaking down scientific barriers to the study of brain and mind', Annals of the New York *Academy of Sciences*, 935 (1), 118-35

Kandel, E. R. (1999), 'Biology and the future of psychoanalysis: A new intellectual framework for psychiatry revisited', *American Journal of Psychiatry*, 156, 505-24

Kapczinski, F., B. N. Frey and V. Zannato (2004), 'Physiopathology of bipolar disorders: What has changed in the last 10 years?', *Revista Braileira de Psiquiatria*, 26 (3), 17-21

Kemmer, S. (2007), 'Sticking point', *Scientific American*

Kennedy, S. H., M. Javanmard and F. J. Vaccarino (1997), 'A review of functional neuroimaging in mood disorders: Positron emission tomography and depression', *Canadian Journal of Psychiatry*, 42, 467-75

Khan, A., H. A. Warner and W. A. Browne (2000), 'Symptom reduction and suicide risk in patients treated with placebo in antidepressant clinical trials- An analysis of the FDA database', *Archives of General Psychiatry*, 57, 311-17

Kim, S. H. and S. Hamann (2007), 'Neural correlates of positive and negative emotion regulation', *Journal of Cognitive Neuroscience*, 19 (5), 776-98

Kingston, T., B. Dooley, A. Bates, E. Lawlor and K. Malone (2007), 'Mindfulness-based cognitive therapy for residual depressive symptoms', *Psychology and Psychotherapy: Theory, Research and Practice*, 80, 193-203

Kolb, B. and I. Q. Whishaw (2002), *An Introduction to Brain and Behaviour*, New York: Worth.

Kramer, P. D. (1994), *Listening to Prozac*, London: Fourth Estate

Kraft, U. (2005), 'Lighten up', *Scientific American*

Kronmuller, K., J. Pantel, B. Gotz, S. Kohler, D. Victor, C. Mundt, V. A. Magnotta, F. Giesel, M. Essig and J. Schroder (2008), 'Life events and hippocampal volume in first-episode major depression', *Journal of Affective Disorders*, 110, 241–7

Krystal, J. H. (2007), 'Neuroplasticity as a target for the pharmacotherapy of psychiatric disorders: New opportunities for synergy with psychotherapy', *Biological Psychiatry*, 62, 833-4

Kumari, V. (2006), 'Do psychotherapies produce neurobiological effects?', Acta *Neuropsychiatrica*, 18, 61-70

Kuyken, W., T. Dalgleish and E. R. Holden (2007), 'Advances in cognitive-behavioural therapy for unipolar depression', *The Canadian Journal of Psychiatry*, 52 (1), 5-13

Lam, R. W. and R. D. Levitan (2002), 'Pathophysiology of seasonal affective disorder: A review', *Journal of Psychiatry and Neuroscience*, 25 (5), 469-80

LeDoux, J. E. (2002), 'Emotion, memory and the brain', *Scientific American*

Leonard, B. E. (2007), 'Melatonin receptors and antidepressant strategies', *Irish Psychiatrist*, 8 (1), 37-40

Li, D., P. Chokka and P. Tibbo (2001), 'Towards an integrative understanding of social phobia', *Journal of Psychiatry and Neuroscience*, 26 (3), 190-202

Liggan, D. Y. and J. Jay (1999), 'Some neurobiological aspects of psychotherapy: A review', *Journal of Psychotherapy Practice and Research*, 8 (2), 103-14

Liotti, M. and H. S. Mayberg (2001), 'The role of functional neuroimaging in the neuropsychology of depression', *Journal of Clinical and Experimental Neuropsychology*, 23 (1), 121-36

Logan, A. C. (2004), 'Omega-3 fatty acids and major depression: A primer for the mental health professional', *Lipids in Health and Disease*, 3(1), 25

———(2003), 'Neurobehavioral aspects of Omega-3 fatty acids: possible mechanisms and therapeutic value in major depression', *Alternative Medical Review*, 8 (4), 410-425

Lucey, J. V. (1999), 'Obsessive compulsive disorder', *Irish Medical Times*

———. (2004), 'Generalised anxiety disorder', *Forum*

Lynch, T. (2001), *Beyond Prozac*, Dublin: Marino Books

Maletic, V., M. Robinson, T. Oakes, S. Lyengar, S. G. Ball and J. Russell (2007), 'Neurobiology of depression: An integrated view of key findings', *International Journal of Clinical Practice*, 61 (12), 2030-40

Manji, H. K., W. C. Drevets and D. S. Charney (2001), 'The cellular neurobiology of depression', *Nature Medicine*, 7 (5), 541-7

———. (2001), 'The cellular neurobiology of depression', *Nature Medicine*, 7 (5), 541-7

Manji, H. K., J. A. Quiroz, J. L. Payne, J. Singh, B. P. Lopes, J. L. Viegas and C. A. Zarate (2003), 'The underlying neurobiology of bipolar disorder', *World Psychiatry*, 2 (3), 136-46

Mann, J. J. (2003), 'Neurobiology of suicidal behaviour', *Nature Reviews Neuroscience*, 4, 819-28

Marano, H. E. (1999), 'Depression beyond serotonin', *Psychology Today*

———. (2002), 'The many faces of depression', *Psychology Today*

Marchand, W. R., V. Dilda and C. R. Jensen (2005), 'Neurobiology of mood disorders', *Hospital Physician*, September, 43, 17-26

Maron, E. and J. Shlik (2006), 'Serotonin function in panic disorder: Important, but why?', *Neuropsychopharmacology*, 31, 1-11

Martinowich, K., H. Manji and B. Lu (2007), 'New insights into BDNF function in depression and anxiety', *Nature Neuroscience*, 10, 1089-93

Mathew, S. J., R. B. Price and D. S. Charney (2008), 'Recent advances in the neurobiology of anxiety disorders: Implications for novel therapeutics', *American Journal of Medical Genetics*, 148, 89-98

Mayberg, H. S., J. A. Silva, S. K. Brannan, J. L. Tekell, R. K. Malhurin, S.

Mayberg, H. S. (2003), 'Modulating dysfunctional limbic-cortical circuits in depression: Towards development of brain-based algorithms for diagnosis and optimised treatment', *British Medical Bulletin*, 65, 193-207

————. (2005), 'Deep brain stimulation for treatment resistant depression', *Neuron*, 45 (5), 651-60

McGinnis and P. A. Jerabek (2002), 'The functional neuroanatomy of the placebo effect', *American Journal of Psychiatry*, 159, 728-37

McEwen, B. S. and J. P. Olie (2005), 'Neurobiology of mood, anxiety, and emotions as revealed by studies of a unique antidepressant: Tianeptine', *Molecular Psychiatry*, 10, 525-37

McGaugh, J. L. (2002), 'Memory consolidation and the amygdala: A systems perspective', *Trends in Neurosciences*, 25 (9), 456-80

McKeown P., J. Healy, G. Bailey and G. Ward (2000), *Depression – Keeping Hope Alive*, Dublin: Aware

McKeon, P. (1999), *'Depression and suicide'*, Forum

————. (1995), *Coping with Depression and Elation*, London: Sheldon Press

McNally, L., Z. Bhagwagar and J. Hannestad (2008), 'Inflammation, glutamate, and glia in depression: A literature review', *CNS Spectrums*, 13 (6), 501-10

Meyer, J. H., N. Ginovart, A. Boovariwala, S. Sagrati, D. Hussey, A. Garcia, T. Young, N. Praschak-Rieder, A. A. Wilson and S. Houle (2006), 'Elevated monoamine oxidase A levels in the brain', *Archives of General Psychiatry*, 63, 1209-16

Milad, R. and S. L. Raunch (2007), 'The role of the orbitofrontal cortex in anxiety disorders', *Annals of the New York Academy of Sciences*, 1121 (1), 546-61

Moffitt, T. E., H. Harrington, A. Caspi, J. Kim-Cohen, D. Goldberg, A. M. Gregory and R. Poulton (2007), 'Depression and generalised anxiety disorder', *Archives of General Psychiatry*, 64 (6), 651-60

Mohandas, E. (2008), 'Neurobiology of spirituality', *Mens Sana Monographs*, 6 (1), 63-80

Molnar-Szakacs, I. and K. Overy (2006), 'Music and mirror neurons: From motion to emotion', *Scan*, 1, 235-41

Montgomery, S. A. (2006), 'Pregabalin for the treatment of generalised anxiety disorder', *Expert Opinion on Pharmacotherapy*, 7 (15), 2139-54

Morgane, P. J., J. R. Galler and D. J. Mokler (2005), 'A review of systems and networks of the limbic forebrain/limbic midbrain', *Progress in Neurobiology*, 75, 143-60

Moss, H. and A. R. Damasio (2001), 'Emotion, cognition, and the human brain', *New York Academy of Sciences*, 935, 98-100

Mundo, E. M. (2006), 'Neurobiology of dynamic psychotherapy: An integration possible?', *The Journal of the American Academy of Psychoanalysis and Dynamic Psychiatry*, 34 (4), 679-91

Murck, H. (2003), 'Atypical depression spectrum disorder-neurobiology and treatment', *Acta Neuropsychiatrica*, 15 (4), 227-41

Murphy, D. L., A. Lerner, G. Rudnick and K. Lesch (2004), 'Serotonin transporter: Gene, genetic disorders, and pharmacogenetics', *Molecular Interventions*, 4, 109-23

Murphy, E. (2009), 'The raggy doll club', *Forum*

Nash, M. R. and G. Benham (2005), 'The truth and the hype of hypnosis', *Scientific American*

Nataraja, S. (2008), *The Blissful Brain*, London: Octopus Publishing Group Ltd

Nemeroff C. B and W. W. Vale (2005), 'The neurobiology of depression: Inroads to treatments and new drug discovery', *Journal of Clinical Psychology*, 7, 5-13

Newport, D. J. and C. B. Nemeroff (2003), 'Neurobiology of posttraumatic stress disorder', *Focus*, 1 (3), 313-21

Ninan, P. T., M. Fava and K. J. Ressler (2004), 'Enhancement of treatment response in depression in the primary care setting', *Journal of Clinical Psychiatry*, 6 (6), 253-61

Nutt, D. J. (2001), 'Neurobiological mechanisms in generalised anxiety disorder', *Journal of Clinical Psychiatry*, 62, 22-7

O'Brien, S. M., L. V. Scott and T. G. Dinan (2004), 'Cytokines: Abnormalities in major depression and implications for pharmacological treatment', *Human Psychopharmacology: Clinical and Experimental*, 19 (6), 397-403

Ochsner, K. N. and J. J. Gross (2005), 'The cognitive control of emotion', *Trends in Cognitive Sciences*, 9 (5), 242-9

Ochsner, K. N., R. D. Ray, J. C. Cooper, E. R. Robertson, S. Chopra, J. D. Gabrieli and J. J. Gross (2004), 'For better or for worse: neural systems supporting the cognitive down- and up-regulation of negative emotion', *Neuroimage*, 23 (2), 483-99

Ochsner, K. N., S. A. Bunge, J. J. Gross and J. D. Gabrieli (2002), 'Rethinking feelings: an fMRI study of the cognitive regulation of emotion', *Journal of Cognitive Neuroscience*, 14, 1215-29

Ó Mathúna, D. and W. Larimore (2006), *Alternative Medicine*, Michigan: Zondervan

Ongur, D., W. C. Drevets, and J. L. Price (1998), 'Glial reduction in the subgenual prefrontal cortex in mood disorders', *Proclamation of the National Academy of Sciences*, 95 (22), 13290-5

O'Reardon, J. P., H. B. Solvason, P. G. Janicak, S. Sampson, K. E. Isenberg, Z. Nahas, W. M. McDonald, D. Avery, P. B. Fitzgerald, C. Loo, M. A. Demitrack, M. S. George and H. A. Sackeim (2007), 'Efficacy and safety of transcranial magnetic stimulation in the acute treatment of major depression: A multisite randomised controlled trial', *Biological Psychiatry*, 62 (11), 1208-16

Pampallona, S., P. Bollini, G. Tibaldi, B. Kupelnick and C. Munizza (2004), 'Combined pharmacotherapy and psychological treatment for depression', *Archives of General Psychiatry*, 61, 714-9

Paquette, V., J. Le'vesque, B. Mensour, J. Leroux, G. Beaudoin, P. Bourgouin and M. Beauregard (2003), 'Change the mind and you change the brain: Effects of cognitive behavioural therapy on the neural correlates of spider phobia', *Neuroimage*, 18, 401-9

Park, A. (2004), 'What makes teens tick', *Time*

Pav, M., H. Kovaru, A. Fiserova, E. Havrdova and V. Lisa (2008), 'Neurobiological aspects of depressive disorder and antidepressant treatment: Role of glia', *Physiological Research*, 57, 151-64

Petersen, T. J. (2006), 'Enhancing the efficacy of antidepressants with psychotherapy', Journal of Psychopharmacology, 20 (3), 19-28

Pezawas, L., A. Meyer-Lindenberg, A. L. Goldman, B. A. Verchinski, G. Chen, B. S. Kolachana, M. F. Egan, V. S. Mattay, A. R. Hariri and D. R. Weinberger (2008), 'Evidence of biologic epistasis between BDNF and SLC6A4 and implications for depression', *Molecular Psychiatry*, 13, 709-16

Pezawas, L., A. Meyer-Lindenberg, E. M. Drabant, B. A. Verchinski, K. E. Munoz, B. S. Kolachana, M. F. Egan, V. S. Mattay, A. R. Hariri and D. R. Weinberger (2005), '5-HTTLPR polymorphism impacts human cingulate-amygdala interactions: A genetic susceptibility mechanism for depression, *Nature Neuroscience*, 8, 828-34

Phelps, E. A. and LeDoux, J. E. (2005), 'Contributions of the amygdala to emotion processing: From animal models to human behaviour', *Neuron*, 48, 175-187

Philips, M. C., W. C. Drevets, S. L. Rauch and R. Lane (2003), 'Neurobiology of emotion in psychiatric disorders', *Biological Psychiatry*, 54, 515-28

Phillips, M. L., W. C. Drevets, S. L. Rauch and R. Lame (2003), 'Neurobiology of emotion perception I: The neural basis of normal emotion perception', *Biological Psychiatry*, 54, 504-14

Phillips, M. L., W. C. Drevets, S. L. Rauch and R. Lame (2003), 'Neurobiology of emotion perception II: Implications for major psychiatric disorders', *Biological Psychiatry*, 54, 515-28

Pilkington, K., G. Kirkwood, H. Rampes, M. Cummings and J. Richardson (2007), 'Acupuncture for anxiety and anxiety disorders-A systematic literature review', *Acupuncture in Medicine*, 25 (1-2), 1-10

Pilkington, K, G. Kirkwood, H. Rampes, P. Fisher and J. Richardson (2006), 'Homeopathy for anxiety and anxiety disorders: A systematic review of the research', *Homeopathy*, 95 (3), 151-62

Pilkington, K., H. Rampes and J. Richardson (2006), 'Complementary medicine for depression', *Expert Review of Neurotherapeutics*, 6 (11), 1741-51

Pilkington, K., A. Boshnakova and J. Richardson (2006), 'St John's wort for depression: Time for a different perspective?', *Complementary Therapies in Medicine*, 14, 268-81

Pilkington, K., G. Kirkwood, H. Rampes, P. Fisher and J. Richardson (2005), 'Homeopathy for depression: A systematic review of the research evidence', *Homeopathy*, 94 (3), 153-63

Pilkington, K., G. Kirkwood, H. Rampes and J. Richarson (2005), 'Yoga for depression: The research evidence', *Journal of Affective Disorders*, 89, 13-24

Pinel, J. P. J. (2003), *Biopsychology*, Boston: Pearson Education

Pjrek, E., D. Winkler, A. Konstantinidis, M. Willeit, N. Praschak-Rieder and S. Kasper (2007), 'Agomelatine in the treatment of seasonal affective disorder', *Psychopharmacology*, 190, 575-9

Plomin, R., J. C. DeFries, G. E. MacClearn and P. McGuffin (2001), *Behavioural Genetics*, New York: Worth

Pomerantz, J. M. (2008), 'Second messenger systems, genes, neurogenesis, and mood disorders', *Psychiatric Times*, 25 (2)

Price, D. D., D. G. Finniss and F. Benedetti (2008), 'A comprehensive review of the placebo effect: Recent advances and current thought', *Annual Review of Psychology*, 59, 565-90

Ptak, C. and A. Petronis (2008), 'Epigenetics and complex disease: From etiology to new therapeutics', *Canadian Annual Review of Pharmacology and Toxicology*, 48, 257-76

Puri, B. K. and H. Boyd (2005), *The Natural Way to Beat Depression*, London: Hodder and Stoughton

Quitkin, F. M., J. G. Rabkin, J. Gerald, J. M. Davis and D. F. Klein (2000), 'Validity of clinical trials of antidepressants', *American Journal of Psychiatry*, 157, 327-37

Quitkin, F. M. and D. F. Klein (2000), 'What conditions are necessary to assess antidepressant efficacy?', *Archives of General Psychiatry*, 57, 323-4

Raison, C. L. (2008), 'Buddhists meet mind scientist in conference on meditation and depression', *Psychiatric Times*, 25 (3)

Rantamaki, T., P. Hendolin, A. Kankaanpaa, J. Mijatovic, P. Piepponen, E. Domenici, M. V. Chao, P. T Mannisto and E. Castren (2007), 'Pharmacologically diverse antidepressants rapidly activate brain-derived neurotrophic factor receptor TrkB and induce phospholipase-C signalling pathways in mouse brain', Neuropsychopharmacology, 32, 2152-62

Rees, A., M. Austin and G. Parker (2005), 'Role of omega-3 fatty acids as a treatment for depression in the perinatal period', *Australian and New Zealand Journal of Psychiatry*, 39 (4), 274-80

Rempel-Clower, N. L. (2007), 'Role of orbitofrontal cortex connections in emotion', *Annals of the New York Academy of Sciences,* 1121 (1), 72-86

Resnick, S. M., M. Lamar and I. Driscoll (2007), 'Vulnerability of the orbitofrontal cortex to age-associated structural and functional brain changes', *Annals of the New York Academy of Sciences,* 1121 (1), 562-75

Ressler, K. J. and H. S. Mayberg (2007), 'Targeting abnormal neural circuits in mood and anxiety disorders: from the laboratory to the clinic', *Nature Neuroscience,* 10, 1116-24

Ressler, K. J. and C. B. Nemeroff (2003), 'Depression', In Rosenberg, R. N., S. B. Prusiner, D. S. DiMauro, R. L. Barchi and E. J. Nestler (2003), *The Molecular and Genetic Basis of Neurologic and Psychiatric Disease,* third edition, Woburn, Massachusetts: Butterworth Heinemann

Reyna V. F. and F. Farley (2006), 'Is the teen brain too rational?', *Scientific American*

Ridderinkhof, K. R., W. P. M. van den Wildenberg, S. J. Segalowitz and C. S. Carter (2004), 'Neurocognitive mechanisms of cognitive control: The role of prefrontal cortex in action selection, response inhibition, performance monitoring, and reward-based learning', *Brain and Cognition,* 56, 129-40

Roffman, J. L., C. D. Marci, D. M. Glick, D. D. Dougherty and S. L. Rauch (2005), 'Neuroimaging and the functional neuroanatomy of psychotherapy', *Psychological Medicine,* 35, 1385-98

Ronnback, L. and E. Hansson (2004), 'On the potential role of glutamate transport in mental fatigue', *Journal of Inflammation,* 1 (22)

Russo-Neustadt, A. A., R. C. Beard, Y. M. Huang and C. W. Cotman (2000), 'Physical activity and antidepressant treatment potentiate the expression of specific brain-derived neurotrophic factor transcripts in the rat hippocampus', *Neuroscience,* 101 (2), 305-12

Sabbagh, L. (2006), 'The teen brain', Scientific American

San, L. and B. Arranz (2008), 'Agomelatine: A novel mechanism of antidepressant action involving the melatonergic and the serotonergic system', *European Psychiatry,* 23, 396-402

Santi, S., S. Cappello, M. Riccio, M. Bergami, G. Aicardi, U. Schenk, M. Matteoli and M. Canossa (2006), 'Hippocampal neurons recycle BDNF for activity-dependent secretion and LTP maintenance', *The EMBO Journal,* 25, 4372-80

Sapolsky, R. (2003), 'Taming stress', *Scientific American*

Saxena, S., A. L. Brody, M. L. Ho, S. Alborzian, K. M. Maidment, N. Zohrabi, M. K. Ho, S. Huang, H. Wu and L. R. Baxter (2002), 'Differential cerebral metabolic changes with paroxetine treatment of obsessive-compulsive disorder vs major depression', *Archives of General Psychiatry,* 59, 250-61

Schlaepfer, T. E., M. X. Cohen, C. Frick, M. Kosel, D. Brodesser, N. Axmacher, A. Y. Joe, M. Kreft, D. Lenartz and V. Sturm (2008), 'Deep brain stimulation to reward circuitry alleviates anhedonia in refractory major depression', *Neuropsychopharmacology,* 33, 368–77

Schwartz, J. M., H. P. Stapp and M. Beauregard (2005), 'Quantum physics in neuroscience and psychology: A neurophysical model of mind–brain interaction', *Philosophical Transactions of the Royal Society,* 360 (1458), 1309-27

Schwartz, J. (2008), *The Four Steps,* from http://www.ocduk.org/2/foursteps.htm

Segal, Z. V., S. Kennedy, M. Gemar, K. Hood, R. Pedersen and T. Buis (2006), 'Cognitive reactivity to sad mood provocation and the prediction of depressive relapse', *Archives of General Psychiatry,* 63, 749-55

Servan-Screiber, D. (2004), *Healing without Freud or Prozac,* London: Rodale

Shang, A., K. L. Huwiler-Muntener, P. Nartey, S. Juni, J. A. Dorig, C. Sterne, D. Pewsner, M. Egger (2005), 'Are the clinical effects of homoeopathy placebo effects? Comparative study of placebo-controlled trials of homoeopathy and allopathy' *The Lancet,* 366, 726-32

Sheline, Y. I., P. W. Wang, M. H. Gado, J. G. Csernansky and M. W. Vannier (1996), 'Hippocampal atrophy in recurrent major depression', *Proclamation of the National Academy of Sciences,* 93, 3908-13

Shelton, R. C. and A. J. Tomarken (2001), 'Can recovery from depression be achieved?', *Psychiatric Services,* 52, 1469-78

Siegle, G. J., F. Ghinassi and M. E. Thase (2007), 'Neurobehavioural therapies in the 21st century: Summary of an emerging field and an extended example of cognitive control training for depression', *Cognitive Therapy and Research,* 31, 235-62

Siegle, G. J., C. S. Carter and M. E. Thase (2006), Use of fMRI to predict recovery from unipolar depression, *American Journal of Psychiatry,* 163, 735-8

Singh, S. and E. Ernst (2008), *Trick or Treatment*, New York: W. W. Norton & Company

Smith, C. A. And P. P. J. Hay (2009), 'Acupuncture for depression', *Cochrane Database of Systematic Reviews*, 1, 1-25

Somerville, L. H., H. Kim, T. Johnstone, A. L. Alexander and P. J. Whalen (2004), 'Human amygdala responses during presentation of happy and neutral faces: Correlations with state anxiety', *Biological Psychiatry*, 55, 897-903

Sotres-Bayon, F., C. K. Cain and J. E. LeDoux (2006), 'Brain mechanisms of fear extinction: Historical perspectives on the contribution of prefrontal cortex', *Biological Psychiatry*, 60, 329-36

Spessot, A. L., K. J. Plessen and B. S. Peterson (2004), 'Neuroimaging of developmental psychopathologies: The importance of self-regulatory and neuroplastic processes in adolescence', *Annals of the New York Academy of Sciences*, 1021 (1), 86-104

Stein, D. J., H. G. Westenberg and M. R. Liebowitz (2002), 'Social anxiety disorder and generalised anxiety disorder: Serotonergic and dopaminergic neurocircuitry', *Journal of Clinical Psychiatry*, 63 (6), 12-9

Stickgold, R. (2002), 'EMDR: A putative neurobiological mechanism of action', *Journal of Clinical Psychology*, 58 (1), 61-75

Straube, T., M. Glauer, S. Dilger, H. Mentzel and W. H. R. Miltner (2006), 'Effects of cognitive-behavioural therapy on brain activation in specific phobia', *Neuroimage*, 29, 125-35

Sussman, N. (2007), 'Functional neuroimaging of anxiety disorders: Focus on the amygdala and insula', *Psychiatry Weekly*, 2 (40)

Szeszko, P. R., B. A. Ardekani, M. Ashtari, A. K. Malhotra, D. G. Robinson, R. M. Bilder and K. O. Lim (2005), 'White matter abnormalities in obsessive-compulsive disorder', *Archives of General Psychiatry*, 62, 782-90

Talan, J. (2006), 'Science probes spirituality', Scientific American

Tamminga C. A., C. B. Nemeroff, R. D. Blakely, L. Brady, C. S. Carter, K. L. Davis, R. Dingledine, J. M. Gorman, D. E. Grigoriadis, D. C. Henderson, R. B. Innis, J. Killen, T. P. Laughren, W. M. McDonald, G. M. Murphy, S. M. Paul, M. V. Rudorfer, E. Sausville, A. F. Schatzberg, E. M. Scolnick and T. Suppes (2002), 'Developing novel treatments for mood disorders: Accelerating discovery', *Biological Psychiatry*, 52, 589-609

Tang, Y., F. Wang, G. Xie, J. Liu, L. Li, L. Su, Y. Liu, X. Hu, Z. He and H. P. Blumberg (2007), 'Reduced ventral anterior cingulate and amygdala volumes in medication-naïve females with major depressive disorder: A voxel-based morphometric magnetic resonance imaging study', *Psychiatry Research: Neuroimaging*, 156, 83-6

Thachil, A. F., R. Mohan and D. Bhugra (2007), 'The evidence base of complementary and alternative therapies in depression', *Journal of Affective Disorders*, 97 (1-3), 23-35

Thase, M. E. (2001), 'Neuroimaging profiles and the differential therapies of depression', *Archives of General Psychiatry*, 58, 651-3

Thomas, A. J., J. T. O'Brien, S. Davis, C. Ballard, R. Barber, R. Kalaria and R. H. Perry (2002), 'Ischemic basis for deep white matter hyperintensities in major depression – a neuropathological study', *Archives of General Psychiatry*, 59, 785-92

Thome, J., F. A. Henn and R. S. Duman (2002), 'Cyclic AMP response element-binding protein and depression', *Expert Review of Neurotherapeutics*, 2 (3), 347-54

Toga, A. W., P. M. Thompson and E. R. Sowell (2006), 'Mapping brain maturation', *Trends in Neurosciences*, 29 (3), 148-59

Ulian, E. M., S. K. Sapperstein, K. S. Christopherson and B. A. Barres (2001), 'Control of synapse number by glia', *Science*, 5504, 657-61

Vaidya, V. A. and R. S. Duman (2001), 'Depression-Emerging insights from neurobiology', *British Medical Bulletin*, 57, 61-79

Vaillant, G. E. (2008), 'Positive emotions, spirituality and the practice of psychiatry', Mens Sana Monographs, 6 (1), 48-62

Van der Watt, G., J. Laugharne and A. Janca (2008), 'Complementary and alternative medicine in the treatment of anxiety and depression', *Current Opinion in Psychiatry*, 21 (1), 37-42

VanRossum, E. F. C., E. B. Binder, M. Majer, J. W. Koper, M. Isling, S. Modell, D. Salyakina, S. W. J. Lamberts and F. Holsboer (2006), 'Polymorphisms of the glucocorticoid receptor gene and major depression', *Biological Psychiatry*, 59, 681-8

Vythilingam, M, C. Heim, J. Newport, A. H. Miller, E. Anderson, R. Bronen, M. Brummer, L. Staib, E. Vermetten, D. S. Charney, C. B. Nemeroff, and J. D. Bremner (2002), 'Childhood trauma associated with smaller hippocampal volume in women with major depression', *American Journal of Psychiatry*, 159, 2072-80

Walsh, M., T. G. Dinan, R. M. Condron, M. Ryan and D. Kenny (2002), 'Depression is associated with an increase in the expression of the platelet adhesion receptor glycoprotein Ib', Life Sciences, 70 (26), 3155-65

Westenberg, H. G., N. A. Fineberg and D. Denys (2007), 'Neurobiology of obsessive-compulsive disorder: Serotonin and beyond', *CNS Spectrum*, 12 (2), 14-27

Wickens, A. (2005), *Foundations of Biopsychology*, Essex: Pearson Education

Willenberg, H. S., S. R. Bornstein, T. Dumser, M. Ehrhart-Bornstein, A. Barocka, G. P. Chrousos and W. A. Scherbaum (1998), 'Morphological changes in adrenals from victims of suicide in relation to altered apoptosis', *Endocrine Research*, 24 (3-4), 963-7

Williams, J. M. G., Y. Alatiq, C. Crane, T. Barnhofer, M. J. V. Fennell, D. S. Duggan, S. Hepburn and G. M. Goodwin (2008), 'Mindfulness-based cognitive therapy (MBCT) in bipolar disorder: Preliminary evaluation of immediate effects on between-episode functioning', *Journal of Affective Disorders*, 107, (1-3), 275-9

Williams, M., J. Teasdale, Z. Segal and J. Kabat-Zinn (2007), *The Mindful Way through Depression*, New York: The Guildford Press

Willson, R. and R. Branch (2006), *Cognitive Behavioural Therapy for Dummies*, Chichester: John Wiley & Sons

Winstanley, C. A. (2007), 'The orbitofrontal cortex, impulsivity, and addiction. Probing orbitofrontal dysfunction at the neural, neurochemical, and molecular level', *Annals of the New York Academy of Sciences*, 1121 (1), 639-55

Wykes, T., M. Brammer, J. Mellers, P. Bray, C. Reeder, C. Williams and J. Corner (2002), 'Effects on the brain of a psychological treatment: Cognitive remediation therapy', *British Journal of Psychiatry*, 181, 144-52

Young, J. (2007), *Complementary Medicine for Dummies*, Chichester: John Wiley & Sons

Yudofsky, S. C. and R. E. Hales (2007), *The American Psychiatric Publishing Textbook of Neuropsychiatry and Behavioral Neurosciences*, Arlington: American Psychiatric Publishing Inc

Zabarenko, L. M. (2004), 'Psychoanalysis, neuroscience, and cognitive psychology', *Psychoanalytic Psychology*, 21 (3), 488-92

Zaretsky, A., Z. Segal and M. Fefergrad (2007), 'New developments in cognitive-behavioural therapy for mood disorders', *Canadian Journal of Psychiatry*, 52, 3-4

Zubenko, G. S., H. B. Huges, D. S. Maher, J. S. Stiffler, W. N. Zibenko and M. L. Marazita (2002), 'Genetic linkage of region containing the Creb1 gene to depressive disorders in women from families with recurrent early onset major depression', *American Journal of Medical Genetics*, 114 (8), 980-7

Zuess, J. (2003), 'An Integrative Approach To Depression: Part 2-Assessment and Treatment', *Complementary Health Practice Review*, 8 (2), 99-115